GLOBAL VALUE CHAINS

D1707052

Global
Value
Chains

Linking Local Producers
from Developing Countries to
International Markets

Edited by
Meine Pieter van Dijk
and
Jacques Trienekens

Amsterdam University Press

 EADI – the European Association of Development Research and Training Institutes – is the leading professional network for development and regional studies in Europe (www.eadi.org).

Cover illustration: © Hollandse Hoogte

Cover design: Mesika Design, Hilversum
Lay-out: V3-Services, Baarn

ISBN   978 90 8964 360 5
e-ISBN   978 90 4851 499 1 (pdf)
e-ISBN   978 90 4851 634 6 (ePub)
NUR   784 / 759

Table of Contents

I   THEORETICAL CONTRIBUTIONS

1   GLOBAL VALUE CHAINS   9
An Overview of the Issues and Concepts
Meine Pieter van Dijk and Jacques Trienekens

2   THE BOTTOM OF THE PYRAMID (BOP) AND THE PRIVATE SECTOR   31
A Value Chain Research Approach
Diederik P. de Boer, Victor L. van der Linden and Ronald S.J. Tuninga

3   VALUE CHAINS IN DEVELOPING COUNTRIES   43
A Framework for Analysis
Jacques H. Trienekens

II   Local Agricultural Value Chains

4   BEER MULTINATIONALS SUPPORTING AFRICA'S DEVELOPMENT?   71
How Partnerships Include Smallholders into Sorghum-beer Supply Chains
Jeroen van Wijk and Herma Kwakkenbos

5   BUSH-TO-ENERGY VALUE CHAINS IN NAMIBIA   89
Institutional Challenges for Pro-poor Rural Development
Michael Brüntrup and Raoul Herrmann

III INTERNATIONAL AGRICULTURAL VALUE CHAINS

6 LOCALISING GLOBAL STANDARDS 119
Illustrative Examples from Kenya's Horticulture Sector
Gloria Otieno and Peter Knorringa

7 USING A PARTNERSHIP TO ACHIEVE SUSTAINABLE DEVELOPMENT OF
THE PALM OIL VALUE CHAIN IN MALAYSIA 137
Meine Pieter van Dijk

IV VALUE CHAINS IN THE INDUSTRIAL AND SERVICES SECTOR

8 GLOBAL COMPETITION IN THE SEMICONDUCTOR INDUSTRY 165
A Comparative Study of Malaysian and Chinese Semiconductor
Value Chains
Paul Goes and Meine Pieter van Dijk

9 BUSINESS-COMMUNITY PARTNERSHIPS 201
The Link for Sustainable Local Development?
Diederik de Boer and Laura Tarimo

V CONCLUSIONS: UPGRADING VALUE CHAINS IN DEVELOPING
COUNTRIES

10 UPGRADING OF VALUE CHAINS IN DEVELOPING COUNTRIES 237
Jacques H. Trienekens and Meine Pieter van Dijk

11 A LEARNING CASE OF A LOCAL VALUE CHAIN 251
The Banana Subsector in Arusha Municipality and Arumeru District:
Producing Banana Beverages
Match Maker Associates Ltd

ABOUT THE AUTHORS 273

INDEX 277

Part I

Theoretical Contributions

I Global Value Chains

An Overview of the Issues and Concepts

Meine Pieter van Dijk and Jacques Trienekens

Introduction

Global value chains are about linking local producers from developing countries to international markets. They link the raw-material producer and the final consumer. Which organizations are involved in this process and how important are they? According to a Chinese consultant quoted in the Chinese journal *China*: "Processing on order will only land a company at the bottom end of the industrial chain". However, "developing a full range of products under a respected brand puts a producer in a different league from traditional manufacturers" (October 2010: 29). This is "trying to climb the value chain" or "progression up the economic value chain". This is also what "upgrading value chains" is all about and in this book seven case studies of developing local and global value chains are presented from that angle. The book provides a combination of theoretical and empirical studies, which may inspire other researchers to develop more case studies in this important field of research, using the theoretical insights presented in the different chapters.[1] We start with two theoretical chapters concerning global value chains, besides this introductory chapter.

In this chapter we discuss the issues concerning the development of global value chains. The case of biofuels will be taken as an example since it is a relatively new value chain and a large number of issues related to value chain development play a role. The case will come back in chapter 5. Then a number of important theoretical concepts concerning value chains are discussed, before giving an overview of the book.

Biofuel chains start in developing countries

Many African countries are setting ambitious production targets for value chains and provide support both at country and regional level for these initiatives. Biofuels are a good example. The conditions for growing biofuels are good in many African countries. Most countries have a good climate, good soils, abundant land (e.g. only 14% of arable land in Zambia is currently under cultivation) and an enormous potential market exists at national and international level. A division of labor is possible between the local/village level (the farm activities), the national level (transport and manufacturing of fuels) and finally the international level, where biofuel has to help countries to meet the high renewable energy targets, for example in Europe and the United States. This is an agricultural value chain and in this book there is a lot of attention for agricultural value chains, for the production of biofuels, but also horticultural products, sorghum to produce beer, bananas to make drinks and the cultivation of palm nuts.

Global biofuel value chains are on the interface of three important phenomena, which play an important role in this book. Firstly, it is an economic activity requiring new business development models (different organizational structures to involve farmers). Secondly, developing a value chain in a certain way can also help to alleviate poverty and thirdly, it can help to deal with sustainability issues. The challenge is to involve poor people in the economic development process of this chain by using the right business development model, while respecting sustainability criteria and remaining competitive. The interrelations between these concerns are depicted in figure 1.

Figure 1 **Interface in a biofuel value chain: Economic development, sustainability and poverty, while remaining competitive**

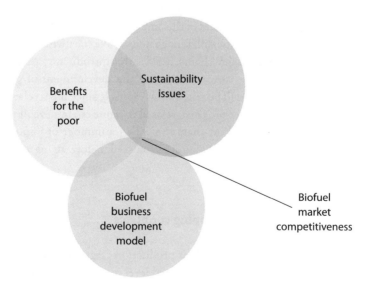

There are a number of issues that come up each time when global value chains like the biofuel chain are discussed, such as decreasing food security when more attention is paid to growing biofuels. Another point of interest is that the dominant trend in biofuels is its commercial cultivation, rather than cultivation by small farmers (Altenburg et al., 2009). This form of cultivation may only be financially sustainable with heavy government subsidies (Keyzer et al., 2009), or if a country could benefit from a scheme for tradable emissions rights.

There is a vast literature on value chains of which the studies on biofuel chains only form a small part. However, this value chain was chosen as an example, since it is an excellent example of the typical challenges developing-country value chains in many sectors of the economy are facing when developing a value chain. It also illustrates an important point emphasized in this book. Besides the vertical relations between the producers and the global markets, also horizontal relations between the (often small) producers and local trading and processing firms (the business models) are important.

Box 1 lists the major issues in this value chain. Many of the issues mentioned in this box will come back in the following chapters when we analyze the development of different global value chains.

Box 1   Major issues related to promoting biofuel value chains

1. Is it possible to assess the effects of producing biofuels on the poor?
2. Can the poor benefit more from developing these value chains?
3. How to involve the poor in value chain development?
4. Which business model is most promising (contract farming, plantations, or outgrowers via cooperatives)?
5. Is international regulation turning against biofuels?
6. Is ecological labeling and fair trade possible for biofuels?
7. Is there a fair sharing of benefits in the biofuel value chain?
8. Are powerful multinational companies driving poor communities from their land by growing biofuels?
9. Are subsidies provided to EU farmers to grow biofuels distorting the international level playing field?
10. Does growing biofuels in developing countries lead to deforestation, and eventually contribute to climate change?
11. What is the current governance structure of the value chain?
12. What are the complementary investments necessary to develop the value chain?
13. To what extent is biofuel production competing with food production?
14. What do trade agreements like the East African Community (EAC) and the Economic Partnership Agreements (EPA) with the EU imply for biofuels in general and sugar in particular?
15. How to save the environment when developing this global value chain?

> 16. What are the factors influencing the sustainability of this value chain?
> 17. What can be done to support a labor-intensive and sustainable development (upgrading) of these activities?
> 18. Which segment of the value chains is in particular profitable?
> 19. How can more benefit from developing this global value chain benefit farmers and processing firms in developing countries?
> 20. Is integration taking place in this value chain?

To allow us to gain insight in the functioning of global value chains it is necessary to know the major concepts used in the analysis. Chapter 2 links the analysis of global value chains to trying to help poor people, while in chapter 3 the concepts are integrated in a theoretical framework, which summarizes what we know already about global value chains.

Ten important concepts concerning global value chains

We will introduce ten concepts considered crucial, starting with the definition and finishing with the big challenge to make value chains more competitive in a global economy. The first five concepts are relatively easy and may be defined and analyzed in a simple way. The second five become more complicated, because several factors play a role and research will have to determine the weight of these factors.

Table 1   Important concepts concerning global value chains

Basic concepts	More analytical questions
1. Definition of global value chains	6 The distribution of value in the global value chain
2. Analysis at the global, national or local level	7 Factors affecting the economic and financial viability of GVCs
3. Vertical and horizontal relations in value chains (cooperation, business models)	8 Constraints to GVC development
4. The influence of production standards	9 Upgrading global value chains and the role of partnerships in upgrading
5. Value chain governance	10 Making value chains more competitive at all levels

1   *The global value chain concept*

Kaplinsky and Morris (2000) provide the following definition of the value chain: "the full range of activities which are required to bring a product or service from conception, through the different phases of production (involving a combination of physical transformation and the input of various producer services), delivery to final consumers, and final disposal after use."

A further distinction is made between simple and extended value chains indicating the complexity in a real world situation. An advantage of the value chain approach is that the effects of upstream and downstream events are taken into account. When we use the global value chain (GVC) concept we emphasize that there may be a huge distance between the local producer of goods or services and its global consumer (Bair, 2005). The big advantage of the GVC concept is that the development of economic activities is put in a context of resources and markets, of individual entrepreneurs and clusters of producers competing in local, regional or international markets (Bair and Gerefi, 2001). The value chain literature focuses on export oriented (agro-) industries, which are usually privately owned and managed and may have a governance structure enforcing compliance with international standards (Humphrey and Schmitz, 2004).

There are big sectoral differences between value chains. A value chain for apples is very differently organized than an iron ore chain. A global automobile chain is difficult to compare with the production of staple foods for the local market. International chains, for example, require market access abroad, which requires good quality products.

Is the value chain concept only relevant in the private sector? We will argue that it can also be used in the public sector and it may add to our understanding of certain activities to analyze the supply of services like water and electricity as a value chain. In the case of water or electricity, which are usually provided by publicly owned utilities, you may find that the raw material (coal or gas) needs to be imported and the management may be delegated to a foreign private firm. The conceptualization of electricity generation and distribution as an international global value chain adds to our understanding of the functioning and dynamics of that chain. Besides the official chain for drinking water and the official network for electricity, there may exist parallel and competing chains of private drinking-water supply (through vendors or by going to the source yourself), or people may use alternative sources of energy, such as small-scale generators. Also for example biofuels, which are a hot topic at the moment, there are many different types of biofuel (chains) and the future for many of these alternative sources of energy is uncertain. They are part of global value chains, but they are facing inter and intra chain competition from similar agricultural products and from other sources of energy (the carbon economy) (Van Dijk, 2010).

2   *The level of analysis: Global, macro, meso or micro*

The level of analysis of value chains can be the global, macro, meso or micro level (Gerefi and Kaplinsky, 2001). In the first case, the whole chain is taken into consideration, while in the last case we focus on the position of the (small-scale) producers in the chain. Macro-level analysis would refer to studying the chain at the national level, while meso usually refers to regional or city-level activities. Figure 2 illustrates how factors influencing the value chain can be global factors, national level factors, regional, cluster or city level factors or internal factors.

Figure 2   Factors affecting the global value chain

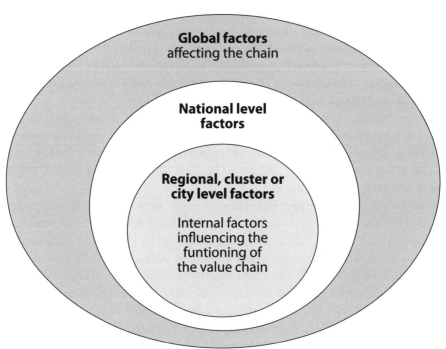

Global factors
affecting the chain

National level factors

Regional, cluster or city level factors

Internal factors influencing the funtioning of the value chain

3   *Vertical and horizontal relations in global value chains*

Most pictures of value chains show a vertical chain. However, local producers work together in all kinds of "business models". We will pay attention to these models and emphasize the importance of producer organizations, clusters and networks. Enterprises in value chains often use different business models, are geographically concentrated in clusters and each cluster has its own level of development and dynamics (Van Dijk and Sverrisson, 2003). Similarly value chains can be emerging, stagnant or dynamic and for each of these stages it is possible to do nothing (to leave the developments to the market), or to develop a value chain upgrading strategy (Guilani et al., 2005). If such a strategy is developed it is important to know which organization could implement the upgrading strategy: An association of entrepreneurs, a local enterprise support institution or local government agencies (Altenburg, 2006). We want to emphasize the interface between clusters and value chain, see figure 3 (Van Dijk, 2006), or between a vertical and a horizontal analysis of related economic activities.

Figure 3   Interface of vertical value chain and horizontal producer cooperation

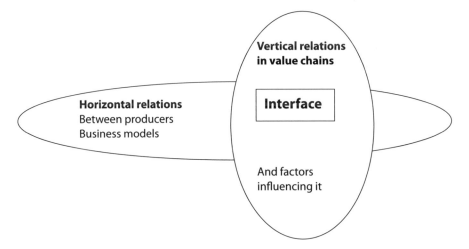

Five research questions that are particularly important concerning the interface between value chains and producer organizations are:

1 What determines the dynamics of these producer organizations or clusters (Guiliani et al., 2005)?
2 What determines the dynamics of the global value chain (Morrison et al., 2008)?
3 How do the two interact (Van Dijk, 2006)?
4 What could be the lead organization for developing and implementing a value chain and a producer organization or cluster upgrading strategy (Humphrey and Schmitz, 2004)?
5 What would be a sustainable value chain upgrading strategy, incorporating elements of social corporate responsibility (Neilson, 2008)?

The competitiveness of value chains depends to an important extent on the development of business models that link small producers to the global value chain. In an increasing number of countries private firms play the role of extension service and marketing organization and farmers accept to pay for their services, or get them for free as part of an outgrowing scheme. Table 2 shows some business models used in Tanzania for jatropha and palm oil, two products that can be used to produce biofuel. Zambia grows jatropha through contract farming, and through plantations in combination with contract farming. We note that many companies try to increase the maximum area they cultivate by planning production from outgrower schemes. Experience with that model has also been gained in Africa with outgrower schemes in the sugar industry.

Table 2   Business models used for jatropha and palm oil in Tanzania

Business model	Crop	Example of an actor
Demo plantation and smallholders	Jatropha	Kakute Ltd, pioneers in jathropa since 1955
Contract farming with smallholders	Jatropha	Prokon Ltd, a German company adapting truck engines
Plantation and smallholders	Palm trees	Felisa from South Africa
Outgrowers via cooperation with farmers network	Jatropha	Safi Anzania Ltd since 2005
Contract farming	Jatropha	Diligent from the Netherlands based in Arusha
Plantation	Jatropha	Bioshape Ltd on an old sisal estate

Source: Adapted from Van Eck et al. (2006) and completed with information from Banda (2009)

Contract farming has been applied in Tanzania for some time, but with different degrees of success. Limited research is available to explain what determines the success or failure of contact farming schemes. It is observed that farmers are sensitive to receiving advice, inputs and regular opportunities to sell. In Tanzania and Zambia the expectations of biofuels were high. Not only could these countries save on imported fuel, but biofuels could also help them to reduce poverty in the rural areas and could promote energy security. Because smallholders have a key position in our research, business models should be developed that link small producers to GVC in a satisfactory way. Box 2 summarizes some value chain research topics and questions.

Box 2   **Value chain research topics and questions**

The scope of the research
- What is the scope of our research, i.e. what value chain stages do we include in the study?
- What type of parties are part of the value chain; does the research concern a local, regional or international value chain, and are MNCs involved?
- Is it a value chain of private or of public parties, or a combination of these?

Level of analysis
- Do we focus on global value chains and global factors of competitiveness?, or
- Are we analyzing the functioning of the value chain on micro (e.g. intercompany relations) or meso (competitiveness between parallel value chains)?
- Do we include the local, urban, regional, national social-cultural-economic environment in the analysis?

Position of value chain in relation to industry clusters
- What are the interfaces between cluster(s) and the value chain?
- Do we analyze vertical relationships in a value chain or between clusters?
- Clusters include multiple value chains, how do we delineate our research?

Standards
- Is production according to standards prescribed by MNCs or Western retailers?
- How do these standards impact on production and distribution processes?
- How do these affect the intercompany exchange relationships in the value chain?

Value chain governance
- How are intercompany relationships in the value chain organized (e.g. contract-based and/or trust-based)?
- What is the impact of government or semi-government regulations on the value chain?
- Is there a role for NGOs or other public parties to establish cooperation of smallholders or other links in the value chain?
- Is the value chain vertically integrated, or cut up in a number of separated segments?

The margins: Who gets what?
- What is the bargaining position of smallholders and other actors in the value chain?
- How can smallholders at the bottom of the pyramid (BOP) increase value addition in their production processes?
- Does the inclusion of smallholders in national or international value chains bring them prosperity or exploitation?

Value chain upgrading and the role of partnerships
- What upgrading options are considered: Product, process, marketing, organizational, etc.?
- Are we focusing on upgrading partnerships between actors of the value chain?, or
- Do we look at multiple public-private partnerships to achieve upgrading?

Business model
- What is/are the business model(s) of the value chain, e.g. contract farming or outgrower schemes?
- What are upgrading opportunities in the business model(s) of the value chain; can the position of smallholders be improved?
- Which internal or external actor(s) have the power to change the business model?

Development constraints
- What are typical barriers for value chain upgrading? (infrastructure, lack of resources, weak enforcement regimes, no market access) and how can these be softened?
- What is the best technology available for the value chain partners?
- What are alternative products or markets for a particular value chain?

Value chain competitiveness
- Are there competing (parallel) value chains aiming at the same markets?
- How do internal and external factors impact on competitiveness between (these) value chains?
- How do internal and external factors impact on competitiveness within value chains?

4   The influence of production standards

Western retailers and multinational companies (MNCs) have defined standards for the production and processing of food and other products. For the food sector there are examples such as British Retail Consortium (BRC), Global-GAP, SQF (Safe Quality Food). The major aims of private production standards are (Trienekens and Zuurbier, 2008):
- to improve the quality of production and enhance consistency of production of suppliers
- to enhance control over production processes of supply chain partners
- to simplify the auditing process through certification for standards requested by multiple customers
- to support consumer and societal demands for safe, high-quality and socially responsible produced products
- to provide concise information to assist with a due diligence defense in case of (food) incidents (Vellema and Boselie, 2003).

These standards are now applied by MNCs and importers all over the world to coordinate supply chain activities and control quality, safety and social responsible process attributes. Retailers and industries increasingly demand for certification of production processes and producer organizations and processing companies in developing countries. From an industry perspective, due to the high costs of certification and further differentiation of standards by (Western) retailers and MNCs in recent years, also private standards tend to strengthen the vertical relationships in food chains. This is one of the major rationales for looking at the emerging competition between (international) food chains instead of just considering competition at the company level. For many developing country producers it is difficult to comply with these standards (Vellema and Boselie, 2003; Giovannucci and Reardon, 2001). Small producers are often excluded from these chains because of high certification costs (for producers) and high monitoring costs (for buyers).

5 Value chain governance

Governance concerns not just the power to control what is happening in a value chain, but also the rules that determine how the game is played. These rules tend to take the form of regulation, the rules of the game. Governance is broader than just the government; it deals with cooperation between all the stakeholders (Altenburg et al., 2009). Who is leading in a certain value chain? Are these chains consumer- or producer-driven? Is it important to distinguish activities of the MNCs, local companies, governmental organizations and NGOs in the value chain? Is the chain vertically integrated, or cut up in different independent segments?

A concept related to governance of the value chain is the level of integration of the chain. For example, traditionally production in the water and sanitation sector has typically been an example of a vertically integrated monopoly. One utility takes care of the drinking water supply from the source to the tap. However, recently we have seen that for many utilities the technological progress, unbundling and competition have led to a separation of different activities along the value chain. For example, in the electricity sector power generation, wholesale distribution and retail distribution can be the responsibility of one, or of different companies.

A GVC may run into market access problems if a receiving country introduces stricter health and environmental conditions. This may limit its exports, or the value chain may be able to overcome these bottlenecks through upgrading. In the same way a local chain may be linked to a GVC and benefit from it, or it may be isolated and operate locally only.

6 The distribution of value in the chain: Who gets what?

An important issue is the distribution of power and value added in the value chain (Pietrobelli and Saliola, 2008). The theory of the lead firm emphasizes that the lead firm has the most power. More Marxist theories would point to exploitation of the small producers in different value chains (Gerefi and Korzeniewicz, eds., 1994).

When we discuss the margins in value chains we try to find an answer to the question: Who gets what? When analyzing value chains this question needs to be asked each time: How are the benefits distributed in the chain? This would require data collection on the margins received by different actors and ideally calculations at the micro level (Van Dijk, 2010).

One of the challenges is to develop products for production or consumption by the Bottom of the Pyramid (BOP, Prahalad, 2005) through unconventional partnering and empowering local producers while stimulating local value creation (see also chapter 2 of this book). This requires a focus on innovation, while keeping an eye open for sustainability. Value chains may lead to poverty reduction in developing countries, by creating employment opportunities and hence income-generating possibilities for the rural poor.

We consider that the global value chain (GVC) and Bottom of the Pyramid (BOP) approaches can be combined and this would in fact increase the positive results of upgrading value chains (Prahalad, 2005 and chapter 2 below). How successful this is depends on the business model, the prices paid and the distribution of the margins in the value chain. Partnerships between foreign investors and local growers are quite common and seem to be a good formula for developing the sector as illustrated in chapter 4, 7 and 9 below. The worries are whether this will also happen in an innovative way and will bring about additional investments, resulting in employment and income for the poor.

7   Factors affecting the economic and financial viability of value chains

The emphasis in Van Dijk (2010) is on the feasibility of different technologies and management models in different African countries. Preliminary research has indicated that much depends on the price of alternative products, including crude oil. Given the link between biofuel and energy prices, and biofuel and food prices, Keyzer et al. (2009) point to the resulting increased volatility of food prices due to all the attention for biofuels. The emphasis in these studies is on calculating the feasibility of different technologies and management models in the countries concerned. They try to answer the question: Which of the possible business models is the most promising (contract farming, commercial plantations, or outgrowers via cooperatives)?

There are often big differences per country. It will, for example, probably be more difficult to have a financially sustainable biofuel sector in landlocked Zambia than in Tanzania, given the location of the country, the high number of large-scale producers involved in Zambia and the policy of providing subsidies by the respective governments. It may be easier to develop the sector in Tanzania, where there exists a tradition of growing jatropha as a separation between fields or between the house and the road, where outgrower schemes are more common and the infrastructure is better developed. In fact in this case the small farmers will absorb the consequences of lower world market prices, which may not be the case in Zambia, where biofuels seem much more of a government driven cultivation scheme. It implies that growing these biofuels is not necessarily pro-poor, but may also make the poor more dependent on fluctuations in the price of different types of energy in the world market.

8   Constraints to value chain development

The development of global value chains may be hindered by certain barriers. In table 3 some of these barriers are listed and the potential negative effects are enumerated. In the following chapters these factors will come back and the effects will be analyzed. Value chain upgrading often implies removing the constraints.

Table 3   Barriers to value chain development

Barriers	Effect
1. Quality standards in developed countries like the EU limit access to these markets	1. Satisfying these requirements makes export more expensive
2. No skilled worker available locally	2. Low level of technology and no innovation in the chain
3. No access to credit and other resources	3. No possibility to finance the necessary investments
4. Too much local regulation or no appropriate governance structure	4. Too much paperwork is necessary, increasing the cost of production
5. Lack of infrastructure	5. High cost of transportation

The cost of production in a global value chain depends on a number of factors, including the organizational structure chosen. Hypotheses concerning the current problems in the case of agricultural value chains that can be formulated:
- Inputs are too expensive, or not available, or of the wrong type
- Extension services are too far away from the farmers, or not adapted to their needs and possibilities
- Small agricultural producers have no access to finance
- There is a lack of intermediary organizations
- These organizations hinder the development of export
- There are no adequate marketing facilities
- Private operators can play a role in providing inputs and extension services and can organize the marketing successfully.

9   *Chain upgrading and the role of partnerships*

Value chain upgrading is important, since we want value chains to contribute to the development of countries and the income of poor households. Value chain upgrading could take place via a partnership between the public and the private sector. This works out differently for global value chains or for local (parallel) chains. In chapter 4 and 7 examples of using partnerships for upgrading value chains will be given.

The role of partnerships in developing value chains is interesting. In such a case the challenge is to find out which factors explain the success of the partnerships. A distinction can be made between internal (or process variables) and external variables (or the impact of the context). Then the question is how the partnership influences the upgrading process of that value chain. There often may be a need for an external agency to organize the farmers at the bottom of the value chain. Different solutions are possible. Not just government or cooperatives, but also private sector and associations can help. In an increasing number of countries private firms play the role of extension service and marketing organizations. Foreign firms have mobilized poorer farmers, for example, in the case of jatropha in Tanzania and Zambia. It is important to stimulate innovation in these value chains and all kinds of projects may be necessary to promote global value chain upgrading.

10   *Competitiveness of value chains*

Global value chains are facing, inter- and intrachain competition, within and between value chains. Porter (1990) introduced competitiveness as a yardstick for the performance of enterprises. The competitiveness measure can be used at the national, the regional, the city, or even at the local cluster, as well as at the enterprise level (Van Dijk, 2006). Here the question of competitiveness will be asked: Is the whole biofuel chain competitive, or only certain stages in the value chain? If competitiveness is defined in an operational way as having a larger than expected market share, one can develop a strategy to see to it that a company (or country) assures to keep at least its current market share constant. The relevant factors are presented in table 4, related to the example of the global biofuel value chain. A distinction is made between largely internal factors, which the government can influence and external factors, which are beyond the control of the national government

Drawing from a number of studies we can conclude that the following *internal factors* determine the competitiveness *within* this global value chain: The policy of the government with respect to this chain, the business model chosen and the cost of production and transportation.

Table 4   Factors influencing the competition within and between value chains

	Internal factors	*External factors*
Within value chains	The policy of the government with respect to this chain	The price of national and international transportation
	The business model chosen (the organizational structure chosen)	The plans of neighboring countries with respect to biofuels
	The cost of production and transportation	International regulations
Between value chains	Policies with respect to different value chains	Liberalization of agricultural imports in Europe
	National regulation	Innovations in seeds & plants or production methods
	The profitability of one type of biofuel chain affects the development of others**	The price of petrol and of competing products, close substitutes of possible replacements*
	The cost of adding reagents to turn biofuels into biodiesel	Technological abilities to mix different biofuels with conventional fuel
	The quality of the product	

* This concerns a large number of prices, ranging from crude oil to the cost of generating a kilowatt of electricity through windmills.
** Cross-elasticity and substitution effects should be determined to obtain a good impression of the importance of these fluctuations.

A number of *internal factors* determine the competitiveness *between* global value chains. In the first place policies with respect to different value chains in different countries and different national regulations. Also the profitability of producing one type of biofuel affects the development of other types of value chains. Finally, the cost of adding reagents to turn biofuels into biodiesel are important and the quality of the final product also plays an important role.

External factors determining the competitiveness *within* a global value chain are the price of national and international transportation and the plans of competitors (e.g. in the case of biofuels for Tanzania and Zambia the behavior of South Africa is very important, since that country tends to lead and to produce these products at a much larger scale). The price of national and international transportation is particularly important for a landlocked country like Zambia. The existing infrastructure is important and transport opportunities for agricultural products need to be improved in many countries. They also determine whether poor people should be involved in modern value chains. Are they also served by the current transport system and does the cost of transportation not undermine the profitability?

An important *external factor between* value chains is liberalization of world markets, for example, in the framework of trade agreements. Innovation is important, but developing countries have little control over innovations concerning the plants or production methods they use, or over the new ways of processing which are often developed in the developed countries. Also the prices of petrol and other biofuels are important. They directly affect the sector. In 2008, when the price of crude oil reached USD 148 per barrel producing any biofuel product was almost financially feasible and prices and investments in the biofuel sector peaked. Six months later crude oil was down to USD 40 per barrel and companies were shelving their alternative energy projects (Royal Dutch Shell, for example). Much depends on the technological abilities to mix different biofuels with conventional fuel: What proportion is possible, what are the characteristics of that particular biofuel mix and what are specific advantages and disadvantages?

An overview of the book

Part I provides the conceptual and theoretical background of the book. This first chapter gave an overview of the issues and major concepts and provided the background to the other chapters. We will now show which issues are addressed in the different chapters. After chapter 1, two more theoretical chapters will deepen our insight into the relations between value chain concepts by presenting the relevant theories. Thereafter, empirical chapters will be presented, before drawing some conclusions about value chain upgrading in chapter 10.

In chapter 2, Diederik de Boer, Ron Tuninga and Victor van der Linden discuss one of the topical approaches in the development literature, the Bottom of the Pyramid (BOP approach; Prahalad, 2005). They show how this approach can be combined with the value chain approach in order to reach consumers and smallholders at the bottom end of the pyramid. Key issues concern on the one hand how upgrading of value chain activities of smallholders can take place and how these smallholders can be enabled to participate in modern domestic or international value chains. A marketing strategy combined with market assessment and assessment of competitors are key issues in this regard. Another key issue, next to the upgrading strategy, is how this integration can be supported by a governance structure that facilitates a just distribution of value added, enables investments and sustainable economic development.

In chapter 3, Jacques Trienekens presents an overview of the literature on value chains and proposes a framework for value chain analysis linking major topics addressed in chapters 1 and 2. Continuing the arguments of the previous chapters this analytical framework selects key elements of the framework from the literature on developing country value chains and from theoretical streams on intercompany relationships. It concludes that value chain analysis includes analysis of value addition in the chain, analysis of the horizontal and vertical network structure and analysis of the value chain governance structure, including distribution of value added. Furthermore, the framework identifies major constraints for value chains: market access restrictions, weak infrastructures and lacking resources, and institutional voids.

After these more theoretical chapters six more empirical chapters follow, of which four chapters deal with agricultural value chains, separated in national and global value chains. The order is from a very simple local value chain to potential regional value chain (sorghum for beer production) to a more mature biofuel chain, which could eventually lead to exports. In the annex (chapter 11) a learning case is presented with tools of value chain analysis in the example of the banana chain, a simple local value chain in Tanzania.

Part II focuses on local and regional value chains. In chapter 4 Jeroen van Wijk and Herman Kwakkenbos report on research concerning beer brewers in Ghana. This chapter addresses the effects and effectiveness of partnerships for sorghum-beer value chain development in Africa from an economic development perspective. A cross-case analysis of five partnerships in four African countries is used to investigate to what extent value chain partnerships have improved the business conditions for smallholders and to what extent these farmers have been able to upgrade their sorghum production.

Chapter 5 deals with value chain development to promote rural development. It is a case study of bush-to-energy in Namibia. Michael Brüntrup and Raoul Herrmann look at the implications of bioenergy value chains in Namibia and the institutions and policies shaping these. Existing and emerging value chains based on the conversion of woody shrubs (bush) into bioenergy (charcoal, pellets, and biogas for electrification) are analyzed in terms of their viability and impacts on food security and social, economic and ecological dimensions of rural development. Furthermore, gaps in the institutional and policy framework are identified and solutions for improvement proposed. The article argues that the analyzed bioenergy value chains have mainly positive consequences if properly managed. In terms of ecological impacts, biodiversity can be increased as well as water and soil conservation improved through eradicating bush encroachment. Socioeconomic impacts in rural areas are mostly positive: higher livestock production, increased water availability for irrigation, increased potential for tourism and employment opportunities for unskilled labor as well as potential energy provision. However, risks remain which are mainly linked to remoteness and nonexistence of local markets creating high dependency of workers on single commercial farmers and weak enforcement of labor regulations. Adjustments in the institutional and policy framework are required in the field of food security, agriculture, labor, land, policy coordination around value chains, and output markets.

Part III deals with international agricultural value chains. In chapter 6 Gloria Otieno and Peter Knorringa argue that there is an increasing concern that so-called global standards, developed explicitly and implicitly along Northern priorities and ways of thinking, fail to incorporate Southern stakeholders' views. Standards are seen as formulated without consideration of the prevailing conditions in developing countries, creating a situation in which producers do not really understand and cannot internalize these standards. They can then become just another Northern tool that Southern producers need to implement in order to ensure (continued) market access, instead of becoming a tool that may offer substantial developmental benefits. This chapter investigates the potential for adapting global standards to national circumstances in horticulture (cut flowers and fresh fruits and vegetables) value chains in Kenya. First an outline of the conceptual framework, explaining the contested role of standards in development processes is presented. Next, the Kenyan horticulture industry is introduced, after which the data are presented on different certification mechanisms. It is argued that one can at least partly avoid a major potential disadvantage of standardization: The exclusion of smaller producers. Finally, two recent attempts at localizing global standards, on involving a mandatory public standard and one voluntary private standard, are presented.

In chapter 7, using partnerships to stimulate sustainable development in the palm oil value chain in Malaysia is discussed. Meine Pieter van Dijk argues that partnerships have become important for economic development and value chain upgrading. The Netherlands, Malaysia and Indonesia agreed to start a partnership in the palm oil value chain in 2002. The aim of the partnership was to identify the bottlenecks in the palm oil value chain and to improve market access for palm oil into the European Union. The partnership is evaluated with respect to its objectives and to what extent it also benefits Malaysia.

A complex collaborative arrangement is analyzed in this chapter. It faced several problems and the Malaysian partners decided to withdraw from the partnership. The complexity and diversity of the partnership challenges such collaborative arrangements. This chapter aims to identify the internal (process) and external (contextual) factors that affected the performance of the partnership. The objective is to learn how to better manage complex partnerships in a global value chain. The study showed that contextual variables such as the history of cooperation between public sector, private sector and civil society as well as internal variables, the imbalances between the resources or power of the stakeholders involved, play a role. The rules governing the partnership and the accountability systems were underdeveloped. This led to nontransparency and hindered trust building between the actors. Flaws in the institutional design challenged shared responsibility and commitment and limited the upgrading of the palm-oil value chain. Van Dijk also formulates some lessons learned.

Then we move to other sectors than agriculture. In part IV, value chains in the industrial and services sector are studied. In chapter 8, Van Dijk and Goes make an effort to study how Malaysia and China create sustainable competitive advantages to attract semiconductor industries. Their efforts are compared, looking at indicators of competitiveness in both countries. Both focus on different types of semiconductor industries. With a higher revealed comparative advantage, Malaysia has a relative competitive advantage and foreign investment inflows to Malaysia remain strong. However, no new semiconductor firm has relocated to this country since the 1990s, while some of its semiconductor firms have relocated to China. China scores better in terms of market and R&D spending, while Malaysia scores better in terms of economic environment and experience in this sector.

In chapter 9, Diederik de Boer and Laura Tarimo report on tourism in Tanzania. This study assesses community-business nature-based tourism partnerships in Northern Tanzania. One of the characteristics of the nature-based tourism industry is the fact that it takes place in rural areas with a lot of wildlife. However, these are often also the areas where the level of development is low, in contrast to the well-developed tourism businesses. From an economic development point of view, the tourism businesses are important as they generate income but also generate nonfinancial and institutional impact in the communities they work in. However, the impact on the economy in communities' remains limited although economic development policies exist on paper.

In part V, the conclusions and an educational case are provided. In chapter 10, the editors review the upgrading strategies in the value chains discussed in the book. First, they define the options for value chain upgrading, distinguishing four different strategies:
- upgrading through an increase of value added
- upgrading by improving market access
- upgrading through better value chain governance structures, and
- upgrading through partnerships.

Subsequently, they determine how each chapter of this book used these upgrading strategies and draw some general conclusions.

The learning case in chapter 11, deals with the banana subsector in Arusha Municipality and Arumeru District, with emphasis on banana beverages. The study is carried out by Match Maker consultants and the work reported in this chapter was conducted in order to develop a real-life case of banana beverage. The case was developed in preparation for the Value Chain Development (VCD) course, which is designed and facilitated by Match Maker Associates Limited (MMA). The banana-beverage case was selected due to its great potential for learning, i.e. the application of the methodologies and tools available. It uses tools like drawing the value chain map and clearly indicates possibilities for improving the functioning of this value chain.

Note

1   This book is the result of a seminar organized by the Sustainable Development Centre (SDC) of the Maastricht School of Management (MSM) together with the Working group Industrial development of the European Association of Training and Development Institutes (EADI). The workshop explored the following issues: Impact of global value chains on local upgrading strategies, the role of governance structures shaping global value chains and the role of buyers in creating, monitoring and enforcing commodity specifications and of international standards in shaping the patterns of chain governance. We also looked at the role of donors, governmental organizations, and civil society in influencing value chains and the importance of partnerships as mechanisms for value chain upgrading.

References

Altenburg, T. (ed., 2006). *Shaping value chains for development.* In: *European Journal of Development Research*, 18 (4), pp. 498-521.

Altenburg, T., H. Dietz, M. Hahl, N. Nikolidakis, C. Rosendahl and K. Seelige (2009). *Biodiesel in India: Value chain organization and policy options for rural development.* Bonn: DIE/GDI.

Altenburg, T. (2006). 'Governance patterns in value chains: Shaping value chains for development'. In: Altenburg, T. (ed., 2006).

Bair, J. (2005). 'Global capitalism and commodity chains: Looking back, going forward'. In: *Competition and Change*, 9 (2), pp. 153-180.

Bair, J. and G. Gerefi (2001). 'Local clusters in global chains: The causes and consequences of export dynamism in Torreon's blue jeans industry'. In: *World Development*, 29 (11), pp. 1885-1903.

Banda, D.L. (2010). *Mango value chains in Tanzania and Kenya.* Draft MPhil thesis. Maaastricht: MSM.

Dijk, M.P. van (2006). 'Different effects of globalization for workers and poor in China and India, Comparing countries, clusters and ICT clusters?' In: *Journal of Economic and Social Geography*, 97 (5), pp. 463-470.

Dijk, M.P. van (2010). Are bio fuels from Tanzania and Zambia competitive without subsidy? Factors determining the competition within and between global value chains. Paper for WICaNeM 2010. Wageningen: WUR.

Dijk, M.P. van and A. Sverrisson (2003). 'Enterprise Clusters and Development, Mechanisms of Transition and Stagnation'. In: *Entrepreneurship and Regional Development*, 15 (3), July-September, pp. 183-207.

Van Eck, R. et al. (2006). *Feasiblity study report: Local biofuel production for use in telecommunication applications in South Eastern Tanzania*. Arusha: Diligentia.

Gerefi, G. and M. Korzeniewicz (eds., 1994). *Commodity chains and global capitalism*. London: Praeger.

Gerefi, G. and R. Kaplynski (2001). 'The value of value chains: Spreading the gains from globalisation'. *IDS Bulletin*, 32 (3), July.

Giovannucci, D. and T. Reardon (2001). 'Understanding grades and standards and how to apply them'. In: Giovannuci, D. (ed.), *A Guide to Developing Agricultural Markets and Agroenterprises*. Washington: World Bank.

Guilani, E., C. Petrobelli and R. Rabellotti (2005). 'Upgrading in global value chains: Lessons from Latin American Clusters'. In: *World Development*, 33 (4), pp. 549-573.

Guiliani, E., R. Rabelotti and M.P. van Dijk (eds., 2005). *Clusters facing competition: The importance of external linkages*. Aldershot: Ashgate.

Hanna, V. and K. Walsh (2008). 'Interfirm cooperation among small manufacturing firms'. In: *International Small Business Journal*, 26 (3), pp. 299-321.

Huber, G.W. and B.E. Dale (2009). 'Grassoline at the pump'. In: *Scientific American*, July, pp. 40-48.

Humphrey, J. and H. Schmitz (2004). Governance and upgrading: Linking industrial cluster and global value chain research. IDS Working Paper 120.

Kalumiana, O. (2009). *How can biofuel companies in Zambia operate in a financially sustainable manner?* Draft MPhil thesis. Maaastricht: MSM.

Kaplynski, R. and M. Morris (2000). A manual for value chain research. www.ids.ac.uk/ids/global.

Keyzer, M., M. D. Merbis and R.L. Voortman (2009). 'The biofuel controversy'. In: De Economist 156 (4), pp 507-527.

Morrison, A., C. Pietrobelli and R. Rabellotti (2008). 'Global value chains and technological capabilities: A framework to study learning and innovation in developing countries'. In: *Oxford Development Studies*, 36 (1), March.

Muller A. (2008). 'Bio fuels'. In: *Development and Cooperation*, 35 (2), p. 53.

Neilson, J. (2008). 'Global private regulation and value chains restructuring in Indonesian smallholder coffee systems'. In: *World Development*, 36 (9), pp. 1607-1622.

OECD (2008). *Biofuel Support Policies: An Economic Assessment*. Paris: OECD.

Pietrobelli, C. and F. Saliola (2008). 'Power relationships along the value chain: Multinational firms, global buyers and performance of local suppliers'. In: *Cambridge Journal of Economics* 32 (6): pp. 947-962.

Porter, M. (1990). *The competitive advantage of nations*. London: MacMillan.

Porter, M. and M. Kramer (2002). 'The competitive advantage of corporate philantrophy'. In: *Harvard Business Review*, December, pp. 27-64.

Prahalad, C.K. (2005). *The fortune at the bottom of the pyramid: Eradicating poverty through profits*. New Jersey: Wharton.

Rabellotti, R., A. Carbabelli and G. Hirsch (2009). 'Italian industrial districts on the move: Where are they going?' In: *European Planning Studies*, 17 (1), pp. 19-41.

Trienekens, J.H., A.J.M. Beulens, J.M. Hagen and S.W.F. Omta (2003). 'Innovation through international supply chain development: A research agenda'. *International Food and Agribusiness Management Review*, 6 (1), pp. 84-98.

Trienekens, J.H. and P.J.P. Zuurbier (2008). 'Quality and safety standards in the food industry: Developments and challenges'. *International Journal for Production Economics*, 113 (1), pp. 107-122.

Vellema, S. and D. Boselie (2003). *Cooperation and competence in global food chains: Perspectives on food quality and safety*. Maastricht: Shaker.

2   The Bottom of the Pyramid (BOP) and the Private Sector

A Value Chain Research Approach

Diederik P. de Boer, Victor L. van der Linden and Ronald S.J. Tuninga

Introduction

The global debate on poverty alleviation is increasingly framed in terms of enabling economic opportunities for the poor, in order to create sustainable economic growth in developing countries (World Resources Institute, 2007). Perhaps the most significant consequence of this shift is the increasing conviction that the private sector should be engaged in the challenge to create economic growth in developing countries. Economic and political developments, in particular, globalization and the increased influence of markets and private investments worldwide, have added to the belief that mobilizing existing private sector financial and intellectual resources is vital in order to achieve sustainable development, reduce poverty and reach ambitious development targets such as the Millennium Development Goals (MDGs)[1] (Dicken, 2003; Wheeler and McKague, 2002).

This conviction, however, is not new, nor is it based on idealism. In the 1994 World Investment Report for example, multinational corporations (MNCs) are described as the main vehicle for the achievement of economic stability and prosperity in developing nations, as they stimulate growth and improve the host countries' international competitiveness (UNCTAD, 1994). A relevant indicator of the importance of the private sector for developing countries is the fact that private sector investment in these countries has been growing for decades. In recent years, Foreign Direct Investment (FDI) by MNCs in developing countries has increased rapidly. For example, it increased from 20 billion USD in 1990 to 240 billion USD in 2000. In the years that followed FDI declined until 2003, but is currently on the rise again. In contrast, Official Development Assistance (ODA) to developing countries today totals about 55 billion USD annually, and has been declining slightly over the last decade. In the mid-1990s, FDI surpassed ODA, and today the sheer scale of foreign direct investment versus ODA has demanded that the role of MNCs in development be taken seriously (Wheeler and McKague, 2002; Dicken, 2003).

The private sector has merited further action in development for a long time. However, a catalyzing moment did not occur until the World Summit on Sustainable Development in Johannesburg in 2002, when emphasis was placed on the role of the private and public sectors as key partners in solving problems on a global scale and improving the standard of living of the world's poor. One of the most noticeable outcomes of the Summit was the focus on multisectoral partnerships as the principle means to pursue sustainable development. Since the Summit, there has been a noticeable increase in multisectoral partnerships among various levels of local and regional governments, UN agencies, small and large companies, academic institutions, NGOs and other civil-society organizations. This includes Public-Private Partnerships (PPPs) and partnerships between civil-society organizations and private sector organizations. Since then, "development" is no longer seen as the exclusive territory of governments, traditional development actors such as the World Bank and the United Nations' development agencies, or civil-society organizations; the private sector is increasingly involved (Wheeler and McKague, 2002; World Bank, 2005; UNDP, 2006).

The Bottom (Base) of the Pyramid (BOP)

With their 2002 seminal article *The Fortune at the Bottom of the Pyramid*, C.K. Prahalad and Stuart L. Hart focused the attention of the business world on the large socioeconomic segment at the bottom of the global economic pyramid, which they argue consists of four billion people worldwide that have an annual per capita income below 1,500 USD at purchasing power parity. A growing body of theory is being created in the wake of their work and an increasing interest in the BoP has been spawned, as evidenced by the creation of research centers, conferences, widespread media attention, BoP initiatives by corporations, and renewed interest from industries such as banking and technology. In the business world, the interest in the BoP can be seen as a logical outcome of the increasing interest and stake of the corporate world in Corporate Social Responsibility (CSR). Several MNCs have even made serving the BoP a strategic priority and are now working on their BoP strategies. Examples range from fast-moving consumer goods firms such as Unilever PLC to consumer electronics firms such as Philips Electronics. In the United States, some early initiatives came from such companies as Procter and Gamble, Du Pont, Hewlett-Packard, SC Johnson, Nike, IBM, Ford, Dow, Coke and Tetrapak (Hart, 2007).

The principal argument of BoP theory – which is aimed at the corporate world in general and at multinational companies (MNCs) in particular – is that the world's poor can be served profitably while at the same time alleviating poverty. The BoP represents a vast, unexploited, multitrillion dollar marketplace, with high demographic and economic growth rates. Whereas Western markets are becoming saturated and unprofitable, this new market shows unprecedented market potential. MNCs have to "identify" and "tap" into these markets. Putting their competencies to work in order to serve the poor will allow these companies to achieve sustainable competitive advantages while improving the developmental paths of many poor people, by facilitating their access to the market place and mainstream economic activity, and addressing their needs. This will lead to increased engagement of the poor in the global economy, increasing their self-esteem and dignity and reducing poverty. In short, BoP theory is about the creation of *win-win situations* (Prahalad and Hart, 2002; Prahalad, 2005; Hart, 2007).

Tapping into BoP markets requires that companies reconfigure their business assumptions, models and practices. New competitive business designs need to be created that involve developing unique products, services or technologies appropriate to BoP needs. BoP theory emphasizes that for most companies this requires reimagining their business. A good way to achieve this is *unconventional partnering*, with Governments, NGOs, or multiple stakeholders to combine the right capabilities and effectively use local knowledge. Another important element of BoP theory is innovation on what Hart (2007) terms *disruptive technology*: The BoP provides a space for experimenting with high technology and environmentally sound products. MNCs aiming to serve the BoP could "leapfrog" to make use of the newest available clean technologies for their products and services aimed at the BoP. When these technologies have been incubated and developed, they can be fed back into companies' existing markets.

Despite its apparent success, however, BoP theory has received its fair share of criticism. Until now, the majority of companies engaging in BoP initiatives have used arms-length strategies to quickly tap into the "new" BoP markets without understanding the needs and aspirations of those living there. As Hart (2007: 197) acknowledges this has created "a growing backlash among academics, civil society and even local partners". Some critics even argue that BoP theory is a veiled attempt at selling products and services to people who can hardly afford it, which will lead to more, instead of less poverty (e.g. Karnani, 2006). Also, critics question the claim that BoP initiatives by MNCs will lead to poverty alleviation. In particular, they doubt whether the "bottom billion" of the BoP can be reached using the strategies outlined in BoP theory (Collier, 2007). These critiques and a further evolution of BoP theory has resulted in what Hart (2007) terms the "next level" of BoP strategies and methodologies, which move away from the unidirectional view espoused in early BoP literature. People at the BoP should be seen as innovators, entrepreneurs, producers, researchers and market creators as well. Hart (2007) emphasizes that "producing in rather than extracting wealth from these communities will be the guiding principle. The objective is indigenous enterprise, co-creating technologies, products and services to meet local needs and building local business from the bottom up" (Hart, 2007: 194).

The relevance of the BOP approach for MNCs remains to be seen. However, it is obvious that many MNCs have been stimulated by Prahalad's BOP approach as the many cases of successful BOP cases in his book on "the fortune at the Bottom of the Pyramid" reveals (Prahalad, 2009).

Role of the private sector at the BOP in development

Participation of the private sector in the sustainable development agenda[2] has been led primarily by MNCs. Increasingly, these companies are embedding concepts such as "sustainability" and "corporate social responsibility" (CSR) in their visions, strategies, business practices and operations. Although the terminology around sustainability and CSR is the source of much debate, there is agreement on the fact that these concepts imply combining economic performance with environmentally and socially sound business practices. Despite the fact that results achieved in the "'social" and "environmental" arenas are difficult to quantify, MNCs trouble themselves to communicate to the public the efforts that are made to improve quality of life in the markets in which they operate, as well as their environmental performance. The emergence of a World Business Council on Sustainable Development[3] symbolizes the increasing commitment of MNCs to sustainability.

The mechanisms behind the private sectors' interest in sustainability are rooted in economic globalization. Perhaps the strongest incentive for MNCs to become more sustainable is public opinion: As a consequence of predominantly negative reporting on their role in globalization, MNCs have become the focal point of anti-globalization sentiments, ranging from skepticism to outright societal distrust. Opportunistic behavior by MNCs – especially in developing countries – has increasingly resulted in public outcries. This watchdog role of civil society vis-à-vis MNCs has been simplified by the increased power and sophistication of the media, ironically also an outgrowth of globalization. At present, the perception of a companies' social and ecological performance has come to act as a societal "license to operate". Those companies that improve their practices and are successful not only in the marketplace but also in the arena of public opinion will have the greatest freedom to conduct their business. Therefore, more and more MNCs are increasing their social and ecological commitment in their "enlightened self-interest" (Spero and Hart, 1997; Dicken, 2003; Leisinger, 2003).

Sustainable business development at the BoP encompasses all business activities that create sustainable economic value for people at the BoP, whether on the consumption or the production side of (international) markets. The private sector – ranging from small entrepreneurs to MNCs – plays an important role as initiator and catalyst of these activities. However, the two other forces in society – the public sector and civil society – are also very relevant for sustainable business development at the BoP. Whereas the public sector is the creator of an enabling environment for business, civil society can act as a business-development partner, connecting people at the BoP with companies and their initiatives, but also acting as a "watchdog" with regard to these initiatives. In this value chain research framework, the complementary nature of the roles of the private and public sectors as well as civil society in sustainable business development are acknowledged. The three forces in society, the private and public sector and civil society, can be seen as three relevant sets of actors in sustainable business development (Van Tulder et al., 2004).

In the case of the private sector these include:
- multinational corporations (MNCs);
- small and medium enterprises (SMEs);
- microenterprises.

In the case of the public sector these include:
- developed country governments;
- developing country governments ;
- development agencies and bilateral institutions.

In the case of civil society these include:
- NGOs (national and international);
- foundations;
- universities.

These sets of actors can be represented in a triangle, as illustrated in Figure 1 below. Actors in the private sector, public sector and civil society increasingly cooperate in multisector partnerships to achieve sustainable business development at the BOP in emerging markets.

Figure 1   The Triangle of the Three Forces for Development in Society

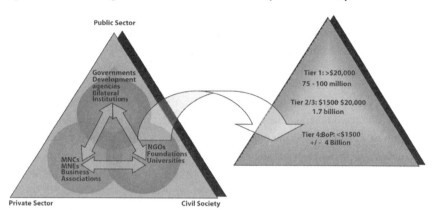

In order to discuss the role of the private sector in sustainable-business develop-ment, it should be taken into account that the private sector is comprised of a very broad range of organizations, ranging from microentrepreneurs through small and medium-sized enterprises (SMEs) to MNCs. In development literature, "the private sector" generally refers to the institution associated with MNCs. The Commission on Private Sector and Development (2004) uses the term "existing private sector" to denote this, as opposed to the local private sector. Clearly, the existing private sector can help address the challenge of enabling the economic opportunities of people at the BoP. It has a role to play in including them in the (global) marketplace and in making markets more efficient, competitive and above all inclusive (WRI, 2007). It can do so both by improving the *consumption* as well as the *production*-related business activities of people at the BoP. The for-mer involves empowering people at the BoP by providing them with services and consumer products, increasing choices and reducing prices, as BoP theory envis-ages. The latter involves developing the local private sector and "unleashing" en-trepreneurship in developing countries. This is an element not explicitly included in BoP theory, but which is included in this approach based on value chains.

The key to the potential contribution of the private sector to *production*-re-lated sustainable business development lies in the role it plays in *business ecosys-tems*, networks of foreign and local companies, in emerging market countries. As the Commission on Private Sector and Development (2004) argues, the ex-isting private sector can develop and strengthen the capabilities of local SMEs and microenterprises through the business ecosystem of which it is a part. More specifically, it can enhance the transfer of skills, technology and quality, enhance positive spillovers from FDI, bring companies into the formal sector, open mar-kets and supply of inputs to smaller firms. Further, it would improve the ability of SMEs and microenterprises to get financing, and increase wages, productivity and standards of local companies. As SMEs and microenterprises are the source of income of the vast majority at the BoP, developing these forms of business is a good way to increase employment and create wealth at the BoP and thus to alleviate poverty (Wheeler and McKague, 2002; Commission on Private Sector and Development, 2004; World Bank, 2005).

An interesting issue is whether the existing private sector necessarily has to be involved in sustainable-business development. Wheeler and McKague (2005), for example, in their article on Sustainable Local Enterprise Networks (SLENs), have argued that emphasis should be placed on the role of smaller indigenous SMEs and their local networks in business ecosystems, as they form the vast majority of businesses around the world and as such contribute greatly to new employment and the maintenance of livelihoods. In this light, Wheeler and McKague (2005) point to a striking omission in the BoP discourse. Given that a local perspective does not necessarily link to international markets, builds on indigenous rather than Western knowledge, and focuses on local value creation, there is potential, they argue, for "self-reliant, sustainable enterprise to emerge in the developing world with or without the involvement of external actors and large domestic firms" (Wheeler and McKague, 2005: 35).

It is in this context important to point at two key elements of BOP partnerships: Level of commitment and mutual benefits (see also Hailey (2000); Van Dijk (2008); Van Tulder and Pfisterer (2008); Van Huijstee et al. (2007)), BOP strategies naturally do face power differences between the local SMEs and the MNCs, as well as a risk of rent appropriation by the MNCs. This can jeopardize the collaboration as the actors feel that there is neither real commitment nor real mutual benefits.

The private sector – both "existing" and "local" – should, thus, be fully considered when researching sustainable-business development at the BoP in emerging market countries. An issue that merits further investigation is the role of MNCs and large domestic businesses: They can contribute to the potential of the local private sector to create sustainable economic value for people at the BoP. As Wheeler and McKague (2005: 40) argue, MNCs should "help create a more bottom-up, networked approach to the role of business and entrepreneurship in developing economies". This involves reconceptualizing their role from that of a pinnacle of the supply chain to that of a player in and a facilitator of a value-creating network.

Wheeler and McKague are in this sense idealistic as MNCs are per definition the pinnacle of the supply chain. However, more attention to a bottom-up involvement is becoming increasingly recognized as an important aspect of the BOP approach by MNCs (Prahalad, 2009).

Value chain research approach

Value chain analysis is an analytical approach that can be used to understand the nature of ties between local firms and global markets, and to analyze links in global trade and production. It provides insights into the way producers – firms, regions or countries – are connected with global markets, which influences their ability to gain from participating in the global economy. Furthermore, it helps to explain the distribution of benefits, particularly income, to actors that are participating in the global economy. This allows identification of policies, which can be implemented to enable producers to increase their share of the gains that globalization can result in (Kaplinsky and Morris, 2002).

One of the main advantages of value chain analysis is that it provides insight into the *mode of insertion* of producers in global value chains. To understand the value of this potential of value chain analysis, it needs to be taken into account that currently, the gains of globalization are not distributed equally. There is a disparity between global economic integration and the extent to which people and countries actually benefit from globalization. An important explanation for this fact is found in the *inappropriate insertion* of firms, regions and countries in global value chains. This is the case when a producer specializes in particular links in the value chain that are subject to intense competition, resulting in a decline in terms of trade. When producers fail to insert themselves in an appropriate way into global markets, this may lead to a "race to the bottom", in which they enter a path of immiserizing growth locking them into ever greater competition and reducing incomes. Kaplinsky and Morris (2002) describe immiserizing growth as a situation where there is increasing economic activity (implying more output and more employment) but falling economic returns. Tropical commodities such as coffee and cotton provide an example of inappropriate insertion. Despite an increase in consumption, most farmers have not benefited from the increasing demand, as this increase has been coupled with an even greater decrease in the price of these commodities. Primarily the level of oversupply in many markets has caused this deterioration in the terms of trade, which, in turn, is a consequence of low barriers to entry (Singer, 2003).

Another advantage of value chain analysis is that it addresses the nature and determinants of competitiveness, and shows that the determinants of income distribution are dynamic. This implies that competitiveness at a single point in time may not provide for sustained economic growth. Value chains allow for a systemic focus and analysis, which is better suited to the dynamic nature of value creation and goes beyond the focus on a single firm or sector in an economy. Rather, by virtue of this analysis, all the links in the chain and all activities in each link are examined, to identify which of these are subject to increasing returns, and which of these are subject to decreasing returns.

By being able to make these distinctions, policymakers can decide which actions to take to facilitate upgrading of links in the value chain to generate better returns. An important example of a policy, which has been formulated as a result of value chain analysis, is forward integration. Its aim is to increase the level of value added in the producing country, for example by processing commodities in the producing country rather than just selling them as inputs. By analyzing economic activity from a value chain perspective, the opportunities in a chain as well as the obstacles to operating sustainable profitable chains become apparent. Obstacles are numerous. The lack of adjusted banking products, the nonexistence of sound (industrial) policies, the absence of organized farmers, high trade tariffs, lack of technology and knowledge of consumer requirements and market demand, etc. are just a few examples. Understanding these opportunities and obstacles in specific chains allows *value chain development*: Identifying where, how and by what actor interventions can or should be made in order to overcome obstacles and increase the value that is created in the chain.

Figure 2   Value chains in different markets

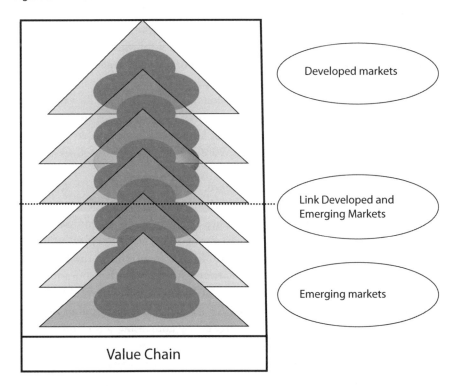

Organizations within the triangle of private sector, public sector and civil society each play a role in value chains, either as a *chain actor* or as an *actor in the context of the chain*. In each value chain, a different combination of actors is involved. By taking a value chain as the unit of analysis, insight can be gained into the opportunities and challenges which the triangle actors face in sustainable-business development at the BoP in emerging markets. The goal of sustainable-business development at the BoP is to create sustainable, closed loop chains, in which all actors benefit from the value that is created in the chain.

Conclusions

Value chains can include different numbers and types of triangle actors and can be found in emerging or developed markets or both. Figure 2 represents these various scenarios, indicated by the semitransparent triangles. To illustrate, the extractive industry sector in South Africa includes the subsector of gold mining. Within the subsector of gold mining an example of a value chain would be the gold value chain in Pretoria, South Africa. This gold chain exemplifies a *global value chain*. The final product of the chain, after various stages of value-adding, is jewelry which is sold in a jewelry shop in London. Another example of a value chain would be the tomato chain in Iringa, Tanzania. In this case, tomatoes are produced and consumed locally, a clear example of a *local* or *regional* value chain.

Value chain analysis as a research approach to BOP theory overcomes some of the weaknesses raised in early discussions of BOP theory. The value chain approach focuses on both the supply and demand side and adds to the analysis of the various links in the business systems. Understanding of the strongest and weakest links in the system may result in a more effective approach to increase economic development in BOP markets.

To date most BOP research has focused on the link of Western MNCs to BOP markets. However, it is clear that in the context of economic development local, or "Southern", private sector companies also play an important role and ultimately will have an essential role since in most economies SMEs play such a role in local employment and economic growth. However, MNCs at the BOP have self-interest and local SME firms do not always gain from the collaboration. But, BOP Partnerships can address the interest of the local private sector. And often these partnerships are strengthened by CSR strategies driven by public opinion. Value chain analysis can facilitate this process by addressing more equally both the interest of the MNC as well as the local private sector actor.

BOP research should, therefore, include a multiperspective approach. Providing insights from public and private sectors and civil society, Western and Southern companies, various intermediaries within the value chain, and a consumer and production perspective, the Value chain research approach to BOP is a comprehensive tool for further BOP theory development and practice.

Notes

1   See http://www.un.org/millenniumgoals/
2   Sustainable development has been defined by the Brundtland Commission as "meeting the needs of the present generation without compromising the ability of future generations to meet their own needs." (UN, 1987)
3   See www.wbcsd.org/

References

Collier, P. (2007). *The bottom billion: Why the poorest countries are failing and what can be done about it.* Oxford: Oxford University Press.

Commission Private Sector and Development (2004). Unleashing entrepreneurship. www.undp.org.mk/datacenter/publications/documents/fullreport.pdf

Dicken, P. (2003). *Global shift: Reshaping the global economic map in the 21st century.* London: Sage Publications Ltd.

Government of Mauritius website (2009). CSR policy guidelines. www.gov.mu.

Hailey, J. (2000). 'NGO partners: The characteristics of effective development partnerships'. In: S. Osborne (ed.) *Theory and Practice in International Perspective*, London: Taylor and Francis, p. 311.

Hart, S.L. (2007). *Capitalism at the crossroads: Aligning business, earth and humanity.* 2nd edition. Upper Saddle River, NJ: Wharton School Publishing.

Kaplinsky, R. (2004). 'Spreading the gains from globalization: What can be learned from value-chain analysis?' *Problems of Economic Transition*, 47 (2), June, pp. 74-115.

Kaplinsky, R. and M. Morris (2002). A handbook for value chain research. Prepared for the IDRC.

Karnani, A. (2006). Fortune at the Bottom of the Pyramid: Mirage. Ross School of Business Working Paper Series No. 1035, July. http://ssrn.com/abstract=914518

Leisinger, K. (2003). 'Opportunities and risks of the United Nations global compact, the Novartis case study'. In: *Journal of Corporate Citizenship*, 1, pp. 113-131.

Prahalad, C.K., and S.L. Hart (2002). 'The fortune at the bottom of the pyramid'. In: *Strategy and Business*, 26, pp.

Prahalad, C.K. (2005, 2009: revised and updated 5th anniversary edition). *The fortune at the bottom of the Pyramid: Eradicating poverty through profits*. Upper Saddle River, NJ: Wharton School Publishing.

Singer, P. (2003). *Stolen fruit: The tropical commodities disaster*. London: Zed Books.

Spero, J.E. and J.A. Hart (1997). *The politics of international economics*, 5th edition. New York: St. Martin's Press.

UNDP (2006) Partnering for development – Making it happen. www.undp.org/partners/business/UNDP-booklet-web.pdf

UN (1987) Global Compact: www.unglobalcompact.org

UNCTAD (1994). *World Investment Report 1994: Transnational Corporations, Employment and the Workplace*. Geneva: UNCTAD.

Van Dijk, M.P. van (2008). Public-private partnerships in basic service delivery: Impact on the poor, examples from the water sector in India. In: *International Journal of Water* 4 (3/4), pp. 149-159.

Van Huijstee, M., M. Francken and P. Leroy (2007). Partnerships for sustainable development: A review of current literature. In: *Environmental Sciences* 4 (2), pp. 75-89.

Van Tulder, R., A. Muller and D. De Boer (2004). 'Partnerships, power and equity in global commodity chains'. Position Paper on cooperation between companies and NGOs in Stimulating Sustainable Development. Utrecht: ECSAD / ICCO.

Van Tulder, R., and S. Pfisterer (2008). *From idea to partnership: Reviewing the effectiveness of development partnerships in Zambia, Columbia and Ghana. Findings from a review of six partnerships from "A Call for Ideas" by DGIS*. DGIS: The Hague.

Wheeler, D. and K. McKague (2005). *Sustainable Local Enterprise Networks*. http://www.yorku.ca/fes/strategies/wheeler.pdf

Wheeler, D. and K. McKague (2002). *The role of business in development*. Paper prepared for the World Bank Annual Conference on Development Economics Towards Pro-Poor Policies, June 24-26, Oslo, Norway.

World Resources Institute (2007). The next 4 billion: Market size and business strategy at the base of the pyramid. www.wri.org/business/pubs_description.cfm?pid=4142

World Bank (2007). *World Bank Development Report 2007: Development and the next generation*. New York: Oxford.

World Bank (2005). *Business action for the MDGs: Private sector involvement as a vital factor in achieving the Millenium Development Goals*. http://siteresources.worldbank.org/CGCSRLP/Resources/business_mdgs.pdf

3   Value Chains in Developing Countries

A Framework for Analysis

Jacques H. Trienekens

Introduction

Chapters 1 and 2 of this book defined key issues for policy and research on developing-country value chains. Globalization and expanding international markets as well as the fast growing middle- and high-income class in many developing countries offer opportunities for developing-country producers to operate in emerging regional, national and international markets. However, important barriers for these producers are the lack of an enabling environment offering institutional and infrastructural support, availability of resources and efficient and effective coordination in value chains. In particular small-scale producers in developing countries are in a disadvantageous position because they have little capital to invest, use traditional techniques, depend on family labor and lack contact with (international) market players. These BoP producers must upgrade to get access to modern markets and improve their position.

Figure 1 depicts two key perspectives on developing-country value chains: the vertical perspective where we focus on the role of multinational companies and companies operating on the national market, and their relation to smallholders (BoP producers), and the horizontal perspective including attention to collaboration between producers in, for example, cooperatives, multi-actor networks where private and public partners interact and (regional) industry clusters.

In the last decades globalization has been characterized by falling barriers on international trade due to the decrease of tariffs and lowering of price support and export subsidies, the emergence of global value chains and increasing concentration and consolidation in various links of these chains. These developments have turned many multinational companies (MNCs) into global players in the sourcing and distribution of products and has at the same time resulted in the emergence of new players in the national markets of many developing countries.

Figure 1   Perspectives on developing-country value chains

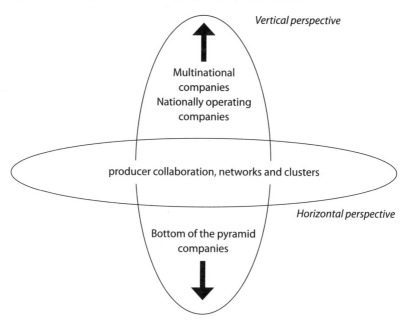

However, unequal power relationships in these chains and trade barriers impact on the distribution of costs and benefits over the chain participants, keeping the high value-adding activities in Western countries. Developing-country producers struggle to strengthen their bargaining position in these chains, by horizontal collaboration between producers, by setting up alliances in sector-wide networks or through the development of regional clusters, in many cases supported by the state, and bringing about new opportunities for various actors and improvements of the competitive position of a region or country.

In this respect, value chains can also be seen as a vehicle by which new forms of production, technologies, logistics, labor processes and organizational relations and networks are introduced. An important example is the car industry, where increasingly fine-meshed production and distribution networks have emerged globally and where developing-countries (DC) suppliers take their share in research and development (R&D) and sophisticated production processes (Ivarsson and Alvstam, 2005). E.g. Fleury and Fleury (2001) show how transfer of technology and standards led to changing structures and upgrading of the plastics industry in Brazil. These examples also show how Western technological standards and systems to guide and control processes and flows of goods and information (such as HACCP – Hazard Analysis of Critical Control Points) are increasingly used by developing-country producers that participate in these value chains as well as in the newly emerging modern domestic value chains. In this respect, in the food sector, supermarkets in many Latin American and Asian countries have initiated total quality management programs for perishables like fresh fish, meat and vegetables. However, an important challenge for the majority of DC producers is still how to enter these value chains and how to upgrade so as to be able to compete in these new markets.

This chapter proposes a framework for DC value chain analysis based on various theoretical streams in the literature, and it will picture the main constraints for DC value chain development from the socioeconomic and institutional business environment. Although the chapter addresses various sectors of the economy the major focus will be on agriculture, as this is for most DCs still the largest sector of economy (highest employment, contribution to GDP, etc.).

The next section describes various perspectives from different theoretical streams on value chains and defines a framework for value chain analysis. Section 3 elaborates on the elements of value chain analysis from the framework. Section 4 will define major developing-country constraints for value chain development. Section 5 concludes.

Theoretical approaches to value chains

During the past decades there has been extensive theory building in the field of value chains (Lazzarini et al., 2001), reflected in many definitions and analytical approaches. Scientific disciplines that add to the development of value chain theory can be grouped into four streams with different perspectives on intercompany relationships:

1   Global value chain analysis, focusing on the position of the lead firm in value chains and power relationships between DC producers and Western markets or MNCs.
2   Supply chain management, studying the management of intercompany operations (flows of products, information and capital) between different links in the chain.
3   New institutional economics, studying the governance/organization of (bilateral) transactions between companies.
4   Social network theory, focusing on vertical and horizontal interrelationships including economic and social interactions in production networks.

In the following section the four approaches are further explained in this order.

Global value chain (GVC) analysis

GVC analysis originates from the commodity chain approach (Gereffi, 1994) and investigates relationships between multinational companies, the "lead firms", and other participants in international value chains. In this theoretical stream power relationships and information asymmetry are key concepts in the analysis of global value chains. Therefore, the focus is on governance and upgrading opportunities in developing-country value chains (Gereffi 1999; Gereffi et al., 2005; Kaplinsky, 2000; Kaplinsky and Morris, 2002; Sturgeon, 2001; Gibbon, 2001; Gibbon et al., 2008).

Kaplinsky (2000) made an important contribution to this theoretical stream by viewing value chains as repositories of rent. According to Kaplinsky (2000), rent arises from unequal access to resources (entry barriers, see Porter, 1990) scarcity of resources and from differential productivity of factors, including knowledge and skills. Economic rent is in principle dynamic in nature.

Nadvi (2004) extends the global value chain view to the poverty perspective by investigating the impact of engagement of local actors in GVCs on employment and income. He finds that employment and income are positively affected by inclusion of companies in global value chains, in particular when MNCs are involved. Although, at the same time, workers in GVCs become increasingly vulnerable to changing employment contracts and casualization of work.

Supply chain management

A literature stream that investigates management of operations in value chains is supply chain management (SCM). Supply chain management emerged in the logistics literature of the 1980s and initially focused on logistics planning and optimization of inventories across the supply chain. Supply chain management is customer oriented, i.e. customer demand is leading in this approach, and aims towards the integration of business planning and balancing supply and demand across the entire supply chain from initial producer to the ultimate customer/consumer (Bowersox and Closs, 1996; Cooper et al., 1997). Information and communication systems are considered the backbone of smoothly running supply chains.

The term value chain, alongside similar approaches like the "filiere" approach (from French origin and the commodity chain concept that originated from the world systems theory by Raikes et al., 2000), was first brought up by Michael Porter (1985) in the 1970s and 1980s, reflecting the value-adding character of business processes within the borders of the company. Both supply-chain and value chain approaches focus on primary processes, i.e. transformation and transaction processes in and across vertically related companies. In developing-country perspective SCM focuses on process and quality improvement and optimization of distribution processes (e.g. in the food sector a lot of research has been devoted to integrated-quality management systems); for example, the study of Francis and Simons (2008) on quality improvement programs in the red-meat chain between Argentina and the United Kingdom (UK).

New institutional economics

A third stream of literature focuses on governance of (bilateral) transactions between companies. New institutional economics (NIE), with branches such as transaction cost economics (TCE) and agency theory, investigates the rationale for governance choices regarding in-company and intercompany organizational relationships. In TCE transactions between companies are the basic unit of analysis (Rindfleisch and Heide, 1997; Williamson, 1985, 1999). Companies select the governance form that minimizes transaction costs, under conditions of bounded rationality and opportunistic behavior of partners. Value chain actors safeguard against risk of opportunism through joint investment, monitoring systems and specific organizational arrangements such as contracts. In agency theory one party (the principal) delegates work to another (the agent), who performs that work (Eisenhardt, 1989). Agency theory defines governance solutions ranging between measurement of output of the supplying party/agent (transferring risk to the agent) and measurement of behavior/processes of the agent (transferring risk to the principal). NIE is increasingly used to determine the best agreement/contract for DC producers in highly uncertain business environments with opportunistic behavior of actors involved and weak (institutional) enforcement regimes (e.g. Ruben et al., 2007).

Network approach

The fourth theoretical stream of relevance for DC value chain research is social network theory. The social network approach views companies as embedded in a complex of horizontal, vertical and business support relationships with other companies and other organizations supporting inputs and services (such as advisory services, credit facilitators and transportation companies). According to network theory, relationships are not only shaped by economic considerations; other concepts like trust, reputation and power also have key impact on the structure and duration of intercompany relationships (Uzzi, 1997). Since the 1990s, social capital theory has become an important branch within the network approach. Network relations may enhance the "social capital" of a company, by making it feasible to get easier access to information, technical know-how and financial support (Coleman, 1990; Burt, 1997) and by encouraging knowledge transfer between network partners (Humphrey and Schmitz, 2002), thereby reducing transaction costs and improving access to markets (e.g. Gulati, 1998). In the last decade a lot of literature has emerged in the field of regional clusters where intracluster vertical and horizontal relationships may support efficiency and effectiveness of business networks (Giuliani et al., 2005). In the context of NIE network theorists argue that trust, reputation and dependencies dampen opportunistic behavior, implying more complex interfirm relationships than NIE would predict (Gereffi et al., 2005; Lu et al., 2008; Ruben et al., 2007).

Based on the theoretical streams previously presented we propose a framework with three main elements of value chain analysis in developing countries:

1 the network structure of the value chain, including the market outlet (local, regional, international) (drawn from SCM and social network theory);
2 the value-added production (drawn from SCM, NIE, value chain theory);
3 the governance and bargaining position of value chain actors, and related distribution of value added (drawn from NIE, value chain theory and social network theory).

These elements can also be used to design (new) value chain business models, characterized by specific choices for network structure, value-added production and governance form. We view value chains as production networks in which business actors exploit competitive resources and operate within an institutional environment. Therefore, we conceptualize a value chain as a network of horizontally and vertically related companies that jointly aim at/work towards providing products or services to a market. Changes in the institutional environment or the competitive base may alter the functioning and performance of value chains. Value chain actors may also be motivated to improve their position in the chain by changing position in the chain, e.g. by getting involved in a different market channel, by enhancing value added by improving quality, lowering costs, improving delivery condition, and by reorganizing the collaboration with value chain partners. Chapter 10 of this book will specifically go into upgrading options and strategies for DC value chains. In the following section the three elements of the framework will be further discussed.

Value chain analysis

Network structure and market channel choices

A network structure has two dimensions: vertical and horizontal. The vertical dimension reflects the flow of products and services from primary producer up to end consumer (i.e. the value chain or supply chain). The horizontal dimension reflects relationships between actors in the same chain link (e.g. between farmers, between processors, etc.).

Lazarrini et al. (2001) developed the concept of the Netchain to show the interrelationships between the horizontal and vertical dimension in value chains, figure 2.

Figure 2   Netchain (Lazzarini et al., 2001)

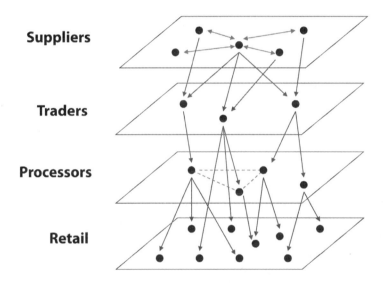

Figure 2 shows vertical relationships between the various value chain links and horizontal relationships between actors in the same link. Vertically relationships may follow all stages in the value chain or may skip value chain links, for example, relationships between traders and retail. Horizontal relationships between actors can also have various shapes, such as farmer cooperatives or price agreements between traders.

The structure of a network (netchain in figure 2) is largely dependent on the market channel(s) that is chosen by various parties. A marketing channel bridges the gap between producers and market and may be defined as a value chain or supply chain forming a "channel" for products and services that are intended for sales in a certain market.

The position of a company in a market channel is dependent on the following key decisions (adapted from Stern et al., 1996):

- Which products or services to deliver to which market? What are require-ments on intrinsic and extrinsic characteristics of product or service (of the product itself respectively of the production process characteristics)?
- Single or multichannel strategy? One company can deliver to more than one market (in terms of market requirements like quality level, delivery conditions, pricing).
- The number of stages in the channel. For example, a producer can deliver di-rectly to customers further down the channel or through intermediary part-ners (such as traders, distributors or processors).

Channel choices are heavily constrained by market-access limitations such as sup-porting infrastructures to reach markets, access to demand and price information and specific demands from these markets such as production according to quality standards. Moreover, the ability of companies to take part in market channels is strongly related to characteristics of these markets, knowledge of the producer of market demands and the technological abilities of the producer. Grunert et al. (2005) find that the more heterogeneous and dynamic the supply of raw material to the value chain, the more market-oriented activities can be expected to take place upstream in the value chain. The other way around, from an end-user mar-ket perspective, they find that the extent of heterogeneity and dynamism on end-user markets is a determinant of the degree of market orientation in the chain.

Market channels vertically structure the value chain/network. The horizon-tal dimension is shaped by purchasing, production and delivery dependencies between parties that are positioned in the same value chain links, such as sourc-ing or marketing cooperatives, or collaborative agreements between small and medium-size processors, such as exchange of packaging materials in case of de-mand fluctuations. It may be clear that market access, market information and exchange of information through the vertical chain, but also control of quality standards, may be strongly stimulated and enabled by horizontal collaboration and information exchange, through communication of knowledge and through joint investments in supporting systems.

A value chain/network structure is in principle dynamic. Globalization for all sectors of economy has led to increasingly fine-meshed sourcing, production and distribution networks around the globe. For example, Gereffi (1999) showed for the apparel industry how the global-sourcing network evolved from links between Asian low labor-cost producers and Western value-added producers, to links be-tween Western brand producers and Asian added-value producers; where Asian manufacturers moved a step forward in production of value added and developed multi-layered global-sourcing networks for themselves, where low-wage assembly could be done in other parts of Asia (see also Bair and Gereffi, 2003, for similar developments in the apparel industry in Mexico, where industry upgraded from mere manufacturing to R&D and design). Also in the food sector, with coffee (Fitter and Kaplinsky, 2001) as a good example, differentiation in the last decades has pushed further specialized distribution and sales networks globally, with increasing market shares of fair trade and specialty coffee to be sold at specialty shops.

Gibbon (2003) shows the important role of international (trade) regulations on shaping international distribution structures, by discussing the example of the impact of the US African Growth and Opportunity Act (AGOA) on the relocation of manufacturing facilities in DCs. AGOA conferred a quota- and duty-free status, from 2000 to 2008, to clothing articles directly imported into the US from beneficiary countries, meeting certain political and economic conditions. This led to an almost immediate move from clothing manufacturing activities from countries like South Africa and Mauritius to Lesotho and Tanzania.

Apart from changing sourcing, production and distribution networks globally, also exchange relationships between partners in these networks become more intense, with increasing exchange of information, knowledge and technology. For example, Pietrobelli and Saliola (2008) describe multifold relationships between Western companies and their DC suppliers where, in particular, MNCs are increasingly getting involved in R&D processes of their suppliers. In many cases these international value chain relationships are more intense than in domestic chains and may lead to higher productivity in these chains. However, a side effect may be the "erosion of local ownership and local technology" (Kaplinsky, 2000), putting new pressure on value-added production opportunities in these countries.

Value added

Value added is created at different stages and by different actors throughout the value chain. Value added may be related to quality, costs, delivery times, delivery flexibility, innovativeness, etc. The size of value added is decided by the willingness of the end customer to pay. Opportunities for a company to add value depend on a number of factors, such as market characteristics (size and diversity of markets) and technological capabilities of the actors. Moreover, market information on product and process requirements is key to be able to produce the right value for the right market.

Value added can be divided into five major categories (Kaplinsky, 2000):
1 trade rents (coming from production scarcities or trade policies);
2 technological rents (related to asymmetric command over technologies);
3 organizational rents (related to management skills);
4 relational rents (related to interfirm networks, clusters and alliances);
5 branding rents (derived from brand name prominence).

According to Kaplinsky (2000) access to high income yielding activities, with high added value, requires participation in global value chains aiming at markets demanding products with high added value. As discussed before, these global value chains are often linked through long-term relationships and supported by FDI. For commodities, however, with low value added the terms of trade with Western countries are in a downwards spiral of decline (Fitter and Kaplinsky, 2001; Kaplinsky and Morris, 2002). This is very well illustrated by a study of Nadvi (2004) on the booming vegetable and fruit sector of several East African countries, that, however, did not lead to an equal increase of production of high value-added products and decrease of poverty: "In Kenya , exports of fresh vegetables rose by over 200% in value terms between 1993 and 1999 [...]. However, over half the population fell below the poverty line in the late 1990s, and rural poverty was particularly acute."

For food production the upstream part of the value chain is not really suited for product differentiation, as in most food chains heterogeneity of raw materials upstream the value chain is not exploited for serving market heterogeneity downstream the chain. Raw materials are first made homogeneous and are differentiated again in processing and distribution stages (e.g. through packaging), because of the high costs of separating and controlling various material flows upstream the chain (Grunert, 2006). In international value chains this upstream part is in many cases located in developing countries, this being another explanation why only little value-added production in these chains takes place in DCs.

However, there also seems to be increasing room for specialization in fair trade and organic products from developing countries, while traditional commodity chains, such as coffee, show more differentiation tendencies. E.g. (Fitter and Kaplinsky, 2001) illustrate that nowadays in Western coffee specialty stores (such as Starbucks) the cost of coffee only represents a very small proportion of the price of a cup of coffee (4% in the case of a cappuccino). The remainder is in the ambiance, the brand, etc. For these kinds of specialty products branding and adding additional value(s) has become a conditional strategy to gain market share (Gereffi, 1999).

At the same time, branding and labeling of specialty products by developing-country producers is constrained by Western (super) markets, due to the private-label policy of many supermarket chains. Dolan and Humphrey (2004) show a raise of private-label penetration of retail in the UK of around 22% in 1980 to around 43% in 2001. Another example is given by Gwyne (2008), who shows that Tesco's private label of Chilean wine (Tesco Finest) covers more than 50% of wine sales in its shops. In general the trend towards increased private-label sales is ongoing in most Western countries, but at the highest speed in the UK.

Value adding in food production focuses in particular on safety and quality of the product. Quality characteristics can be divided into intrinsic characteristics, which can be measured on the product itself, like color, taste, tenderness, and extrinsic characteristics, i.e. process characteristics, such as organic or fair-trade production, which cannot be measured on the product. To safeguard quality and safety of end products, since the 1990s, Western retailers have defined various standards for the production and processing of food, such as the British Retail Consortium (BRC), Global-GAP, Safe Quality Food (SQF). These standards are now applied by supermarkets and importers all over the world to coordinate supply-chain activities and control food quality and safety. Besides generic quality standards that focus on quality and safety of food, we now increasingly find standards that combine intrinsic with extrinsic characteristics, e.g. high quality (and sustainable) "Utz" coffee or the "Rainforest alliance" bananas from Chiquita. While until recently these specific product and processing attributes focused on niche markets in Western countries, they now are swiftly integrated in basic retail and industry standards as indicated above.

For producers to get access to modern retail markets, certification according to these standards is conditional (Jahn et al., 2004). However, because of these standards access to these markets for small and medium-size producers is difficult and in many cases impossible, as was pointed out before (Dolan and Humphrey, 2000). Perez-Aleman and Sandilands (2008) state '... that these well-intended social and environmental norms, or sustainability standards ...' [from a Western consumer point of view], represent significant barriers to entry for these producers (Vellema and Boselie, 2003; Giovannucci and Reardon, 2001). Compliance with standards implies high certification costs (for producers) and high monitoring costs (for buyers). However, in some cases we now see the inclusion of smallholders in modern quality schemes, e.g. through cooperative governance forms or through retail or food industry programs (e.g. tea production in Kenya for Unilever; coffee production for Nescafe in Brazil).

To achieve efficient and competitive production in value chains, management of "seamless" product and information flows are of key importance; which is challenging for DC producers because of lacking or nonfunctioning infrastructures. In the agricultural sector with rapid decay of fresh products, quality of food is strongly dependent on logistical systems connecting the various stages in food chains (Van der Spiegel, 2004). These systems concern exchange of planning data regarding harvesting, storage and transportation, maintenance of the cold chain and use of information and (tele)communication technology such as the internet or cell phones which can strongly improve logistics planning, thereby enhancing the quality of fresh products.

Governance and bargaining position of value chain actors

Firms in value chains are linked in a variety of sourcing and contracting relationships, i.e. forms of governance (see e.g. Williamson, 1985, 1999; Gereffi et al,
2001). We distinguish two perspectives in the concept of governance of DC value
chains:

1 The transaction (cost) perspective that focuses on governance of transactions
   in vertical bilateral relationships between firms (Williamson, 1985, 1999; Rindfleisch and Heide, 1997).
2 The global value chain perspective of Gereffi, Kaplinsky and others, where
   power relationships, the position of the "lead firm" and consequences the distribution of value added are subject of study (Gibbon et al., 2008). Gereffi
   (1994, p. 97) defines governance as "authority and power relationships that
   determine how financial, material and human resources are allocated and flow
   within a chain".

In the transaction (cost) perspective transactions between firms are governed
under conditions of bounded rationality and opportunism of actors involved.
Transaction characteristics are largely explanatory for governance structures in
a value chain. According to Williamson (1995, 1999) joint investments, the ability
to measure the agent's performance and uncertainty are deciding factors for the
costs of transactions. If transaction costs are low, actors will favor market governance. If they are high they favor contracting or integration, thereby lowering these
costs. Governance forms range from (spot) market relationship, though hybrid
governance forms (e.g. contracts), to vertical integration or hierarchy (meaning
bringing the activities of various companies together within one legal entity).

In this respect developing-country business relationships are subject to many
uncertainties caused by poor physical infrastructures (storage facilities, roads, telecommunication, etc.), weak institutional infrastructures (government support,
sanction systems, etc.), unbalanced trade relationships (dependencies, opportunistic buyer behavior) and unfavorable social and political conditions, leading to
uncertainties and risks for DC producers. Transactions are enabled and need to
be supported by information exchange about characteristics of the product/ser-
vice and delivery conditions. However, information exchange between companies
in developing countries is in many cases hampered by information asymmetries
between chain partners, lacking communication infrastructures, and diffuse market channel structures. This makes monitoring of transactions difficult (David
and Han, 2004; Grover and Malhotra, 2003). In the context of the food sector
the introduction of quality and certification schemes goes hand in hand with

increased monitoring and control by, in most cases, Western buyers and more integrated governance in the value chain, such as long-term contracts, thereby reducing the uncertainties stipulated above. In this regard use of standards implies reduction of coordination costs, but it may also reduce innovation capabilities that could lead to new value added, as innovation and standardization seem to be opposite forces in value chain development (Dolan and Humphrey, 2006).

In general, business relationships in international and modern domestic value chains with high investments, uncertain supply markets and weak monitoring and enforcement regimes are safeguarded through more integrated governance forms such as long-term contracts, joint ventures or vertical integration. Control over international value chains does not necessarily mean ownership over production activities throughout the value chain. As discussed earlier coordination and control are in many cases facilitated by standardization and advanced monitoring and communication systems (Trienekens et al., 2009; Gereffi et al., 2005).

From the global value chain perspective Gereffi et al. (2005) developed a categorization based on three factors explaining the structure and organization of these chains (Gereffi et al., 2005):

1   the complexity of information and knowledge transfer required to sustain a particular transaction, particularly with respect to product and process specifications;
2   the extent to which this information and knowledge can be codified and, therefore, transmitted efficiently and without transaction-specific investment between the parties to the transaction;
3   the capabilities of actual and potential suppliers in relation to the requirements of the transaction.

They arrive at a categorization in five governance types: market, modular, relational, captive and hierarchy, which reflect differences between the position of the lead firm and specific power/dependency relationships in the chain. This typology is intrinsically dynamic in the sense that governance types can develop from one type into another, from market type in the direction of hierarchy but also from hierarchy type in the direction of market depending on changing market demands and supply structures:

–   Information complexity changes as lead firms seek to obtain more complex outputs and services from their supply base.
–   Within industries there is a continuous tension between codification and innovation.
–   Supplier competences change overtime.

Suppliers roughly rank from commodity suppliers, delivering products through arms-length market relationships to turnkey suppliers, who deliver customer-specific products produced with advanced capabilities (see also, Gereffi et al., 2005; Sturgeon, 2001). Moving from turnkey to commodity-supplier information asymmetry and power balance is in most cases in favor of the Western value chain partner. In that respect increasing capabilities of suppliers and subsequent decommoditization (Fitter and Kaplinsky, 2001) of the value chain can lead to more balanced power and bargaining relationships in these chains.

Roles of value chain partners may change over time. For example, Dolan and Humphrey (2006) describe the development in the UK fresh vegetables and fruit market where importers are given the role of category managers by the large retail chains, with tasks such as organizing the supply chain, integrating the management of the (whole) chain, developing the category and information exchange on prices, costs and margins. The rise of global value chain "managers" or coordinators (also, for example, 4th party logistics providers, Hsiao et al., 2009) lead to a specific form of relational rent accruing from governorship itself, as already defined by Kaplinsky (2000). In this regard Gereffi et al. (2005) speak of "mundane" transaction costs – the costs involved in coordinating activities along the chain. These mundane transaction costs rise when value chains are producing nonstandard products, products with integral product architectures, and products whose output is time sensitive (Baldwin and Clark, 2000). Agricultural value chains are very time sensitive, meaning that highly developed coordination capabilities are needed in these chains, such as in the Dutch flower chain where flowers from countries from all over the world have to be distributed through the auction halls in The Netherlands to customers all over Europe and the rest of the world in a very limited time frame (Vollebregt et al., 2010). The auction organization (a growers' cooperative in The Netherlands) is the global value chain coordinator in this respect.

Distribution of value added

Distribution of value added over various actors is strongly related to the governance form of the chain and depends on the power and bargaining position of actors, information asymmetry between chain stages and also the production technology used. Although inclusion in global value chains often brings a larger share of value added to DC producers (Nadvi, 2004), prices in Western markets do not automatically translate into prices for DC suppliers. As Fitter and Kaplinsky (2001) showed, increasing differentiation of coffee prices at the retail or specialty shop outlets does not translate in increasing variance in prices paid at the farm gate (see also Bacon, 2005). Differences in market power and dependency relationships have a clear impact on the (choice of) governance regime in trade relationships. A powerful party can dictate governance mechanisms (e.g. Schmitz, 1999). In this respect, small-scale producers depend in many cases on downstream parties in the chain, such as intermediaries, transporters or export-ers, for input supplies and credits on the one hand and market access on the other.

In communities with strong social structures trust and number and intensity of relationships play an important role in collaborative agreements between horizontal parties and subsequent increase of bargaining power. Therefore, the embeddedness of small-scale producers in a network of social relationships can provide them with the social capital to strengthen their position in the value chain (Gulati, 1997; Coleman, 1990). Trust may play an important role in both horizontal and vertical relationships. Trust is dependent on the duration of a relationship, consistency of exchanges be-tween parties and (economic and social) reputation. Reputation may even play a role at the country level, as Roy and Thorat (2008) point out in their study of the Indian cooperative Mahagrapes:"... Indian horticultural producers are largely perceived [by international buyers] to be inept at meeting standards, negotiating and initiating marketing contracts in developed country markets ...", which makes it difficult for all Indian producers to get access to international markets. In many value chains trust and reputation replace more integrated governance mechanisms as a safeguard against opportunistic behavior and to keep transaction costs low.

The next section will go into typical developing-country value chain develop-ment constraints that must be taken into account in value chain analysis or in the design of value chain business models.

Constraints for DC value chain development

The main aim of a value chain is to produce value-added products or services for a market, by transforming resources and through the use of infrastructures, both within the opportunities and constraints of its institutional environment. There-fore, constraints for value chain development are in our view related to market access (local, regional, international) and market orientation (e.g. Grunert et al., 2005), available resources and physical infrastructures (Porter, 1990: factor con-ditions) and institutions (regulative, cognitive and normative: Scott, 1995).

Market access and market orientation

Quality demands, internationalization and market differentiation have led to the emergence of distinct food subsystems with specific quality and safety require-ments, leaning on different market channels, e.g. local, national and international market (see Figure 3).

Figure 3   Economic subsystems in developing countries (Ruben et al., 2007)

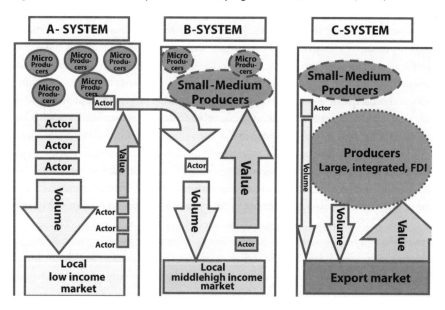

Figure 3 illustrates the key distinctions between three subsystems. The A-system can be characterized as the local low-income chain. Producers are usually small with traditional production systems. These chains aim at local market outlets with staple products. Because of many intermediary parties (traders), A-system chains are relatively long, implying limited availability of (end) market information, distribution of value added over a large number of actors, and longer transportation distances (both in distance and time). A-systems in developing countries deliver a high share of agricultural production volume, but generate relatively little value. The B-system can be characterized as the local middle- to high-income chain. They aim at the emerging supermarket sector in many developing countries. Most of the volume in these chains is delivered by small/ medium-size producers, organized in cooperatives and/or linked in subcontracting arrangements. Microproducers deliver inputs on demand to balance demand and supply in this system (buffer function). Although the production volume produced by B-systems is smaller than that of A-systems, the value generated is larger. B-systems increasingly produce according to national and sometimes international retail quality and safety standards. Finally, the C-system can be characterized as the export chain. It is completely focused on export, although low-quality or rejected products are sold at the national, in many cases retail, market. The trend is towards increasing economies of scale and foreign direct investments. Export chains tend to become more integrated and shorter. Although volumes are small compared to local markets, the value added is relatively high.

These subsystems largely function independently, although one system may use input from another system to balance demand and supply, see e.g. the flow between the A- and B-system in the figure. The coexistence of such weakly connected subsystems poses important challenges to the development of harmonized quality and safety standards in developing countries (Ruben et al., 2007).

Market access is dependent on technological capabilities of producers, available infrastructures, bargaining power and market knowledge and orientation. Market orientation and market knowledge are conditional to market access. In this subsection we focus on market orientation and market knowledge. Grunert et al. (2005) define market orientation of a value chain as "chain members' generation of intelligence pertaining to current and future end-user needs, dissemination of this intelligence across chain members and chain wide responsiveness to it." The more heterogeneous the end market, the more market-oriented activities are expected to take place by upstream parties in the chain. This implies, in particular for noncommoditized products with high added value, that market orientation should be present at multiple parties in the chain. Therefore, to be able to participate in high value-adding value chains, various parties in the chain up to the primary producer should have knowledge of and be willing to comply to demands in the value chain's end market (Grunert et al., 2005).

Resources and (physical) infrastructures

According to Porter (1990), factor conditions relate to the nation's endowment with resources such as physical and human knowledge, technology and infrastructure. These factors enable or constrain value chain upgrading. For DCs typical constraints faced by companies include lack of specialized skills and difficult access to technology, inputs, market, information, credit and external services. (Giuliano et al., 2005)

First, low levels of available physical resources, such as input materials for production, and other input supplies, such as energy and water, constrain value chain upgrading. E.g. high energy costs in many Eastern African countries limit growth possibilities for companies and value chains. Second, the geographic position of a company or value chain may impact on its competitive position, e.g. because of large distance to high-value markets (such as countries and regions in Central Africa). Third, availability of educated labor and the availability of knowledge (production, distribution, marketing) is an important condition for innovative behavior of value chain actors. A fourth category is the level and availability of technology that can be used for production and distribution activities in the value chain.

Besides availability of resources, the presence of an adequate distribution and communication infrastructure is a basic condition for value chain development and upgrading. Weak infrastructures hamper efficient flows of products to markets and the exchange of market information upstream value chains.

Institutions

Institutions impact organizational life. In our definition of institutions we follow Scott (1995) who makes a distinction between regulative, normative and cognitive institutions. Regulative institutions encompass legislation and government regulations and policies that companies can use and/or have to comply with. Normative institutions are embedded in business practices, business policies and ethical standards. Cognitive institutions reflect the way people interpret and make sense of the world around them on the basis of rules and schemata. Hence, diverse cultural belief systems, values and identities inform people (in different roles as consumers, producers, policymakers, citizens, etc.).

Developing countries are often characterized by institutional voids, defined as "situations where institutional arrangements that support markets are absent, weak or fail to accomplish the role expected from them" (Marti and Mair, 2008). Hence, government legislation, regulations and policies can constrain value chain upgrading, amongst others by setting trade barriers for production materials and production technology, by limiting the flow of information, national as well as international, by unfavorable tax policies and denying infrastructural investments to value chains. Furthermore, business practices and characteristics of business relationships can limit value adding and profit orientation in valued chains. For example, interpersonal and intercompany relationships may enhance the social capital of a company, yet may also imply relational constraints that limit a free flow of goods and information (Lu et al., 2008). Moreover, cognitive institutions may prevent innovations in products or processes and can limit a free flow of information and knowledge, mobility of labor, and relationships between communities.

A facilitating government that supports innovation and upgrading is often considered conditional for development (e.g. Murphy, 2007). Moreover, standards, norms, regulations set by Western retailers and industries and supported and enforced by local governments and NGOs shape the institutional environment of DC producers (Perez-Aleman and Sandilands, 2008; Riisgaard, 2009; Muradian and Pelupessy, 2005; Dolan and Humphrey, 2000).

Two value chain analysis cases

This section pictures two DC value chain cases reflecting on the major elements of our framework and of value chain business environment constraints.

Case 1   **Enhancing value-added production in the Nile Perch value chain (adapted from Kambewa, 2007)**

Kambewa (2007) focusses on the challenges facing small-scale fishermen at Lake Victoria in meeting downstream quality demand and to cope with pressure from declining fish stocks of Nile Perch. The study shows that lack of proper knowledge about fish quality is an important factor to be addressed in order to improve quality and *value-added production*. Lack of proper knowledge is reflected by poor handling such as throwing, beating and stepping on fish. The study also shows flaws in the *enabling infrastructure* and that lack of cooling and storage facilities essential to keep fish fresh, the type of fishing gears, and the time it takes before the fish is processed are potential factors that may contribute to quality deterioration. Upgrading of processes is therefore conditional for getting *access to markets*, implying that investment in quality management facilities such as ice or cold storage facilities in the landing sites or investments in larger boats that can carry ice are needed. This may require even more *infrastructural* investments, such as electricity, which is currently not available in the beaches studied. Poor handling practices could also be minimized through educating the fishermen and middlemen on the effect of poor fish handling on quality. To provide the necessary infrastructure, financial resources and training there is an important role for *institutions*, such as the local government and NGOs.

The results also show that degradation of the fisheries is largely blamed on the lack of sufficient *resources* like the use of bad fishing gears, which is attributed to high prices for the good gears and ineffective and biased enforcement (against fishermen) by relevant authorities. This implies that public *institutions* should improve their effectiveness in enforcing sustainable fishing practices. But sustainable practices, i.e. use of good gears could be enhanced by a combination of both enforcement and affordability of the gears. Moreover, fishermen that implement sustainable practices should be rewarded through better prices or through better access to recommended fishing gears, access to storage facilities, access to more profitable markets, i.e. processing factories that may pay them better prices.

The results also show that the fishermen's position in the *channel/supply network* is compromised by lack of price information and interlocked fish/credit markets. Information asymmetries especially concerning prices lead to abrupt price changes and conflicts between fishermen and middlemen, requiring new governance solutions. There is need therefore to create market-information systems and institutions through which price information could be communicated to the fishermen rather than the fish buyers, e.g. by sending daily text messages with current prices to subscribed fishermen. This might be a fish marketing institution that could coordinate information flow to fishermen. For example, use of mobile phones by fishermen to access market information is being used in Asia (see The Economist, 2001 a&b, 2005). However, this can only work if alternative *governance* mechanisms are designed, i.e. if fishermen were free to decide where to sell fish based on the market prices and other factors, such as transactions costs, rather than when they are tied up to particular middlemen from whom they obtain fishing gear.

The above case shows the vivid interaction between social-economic business environment (market access, infrastructures and resources, institutions) and elements of the value chain: value-added production, network structure and governance forms. It also shows that in many cases an integrated approach is most suited to achieve in-depth understanding of the mechanisms and development of DC value chains.

**Case 2   Channel differentiation in the mango value chain in Costa Rica
               (adapted from Zuniga and Ruben, 2007)**

Mango *channel* and *market-outlet* selection is a strategic decision of producers, who have to decide on their market portfolio mix in terms of maximizing their (family) welfare and guaranteeing their strategic market position. Since price differences between local and export markets are not substantial, other market delivery conditions related to guaranteed and stable *market access* and potential cost advantages tend to be of higher importance. While deliveries to the export market might be attractive if producers can benefit from reduced transport and transaction costs, they also incur higher input costs, have to face higher rejection rates and must pay fees for their EurepGap certification, in order to increase *value added* in the production process. This implies that all production activities should be registered and that producers lose their independency, since they should accept in situ inspections. Given these requirements, many producers preferred different *governance* arrangements and moved to the local market because they were unable to meet the certification requirements.

The mango supply-chain *network structure* clearly shows a distinction between chains aiming at local market outlets and chains aiming at the export market. It is important to notice that for the export market the vertical integration process is already advanced: producers deliver on demand of the buyer and therefore face higher rejection rates, but in compensation they get *access* to stable market outlets, receive input and (subsidized) credit and benefit from lower transport and delivery costs. For the local market, the producers' experience and their historical knowledge and *social (network) relationships* with the market are of key importance. In addition, the flexibility to sell to a large number of different clients, the cash payments and the reduced possibilities of holdup may make this a preferred market outlet. Sales to intermediaries that live close to the producer and visit the producer often to see whether rejected mango can be bought provide an important secondary market outlet. Since local markets are less strict with respect to quality (but nevertheless control for color and maturity) intermediaries purchase *higher-value* mangoes that are riper than those delivered to the export market. However, intermediaries buying mango usually pay one week later (after having sold the produce) and therefore they build on an established relationship with the producer, while for local sales spot-market transactions are the rule, showing clearly the distinct *governance forms* for both channels. Given the variability in prices (at local and export markets) and the additional differences in production conditions (input and credit costs) and supply conditions (rejection rate), *market-outlet choice* is a complex decision involving both welfare objectives and risk and transaction costs considerations. Even while producers delivering to the local market at the *Feria* might sometimes perceive higher prices, they also face higher costs for delivering their mangoes to this outlet, and they need specific skills and knowledge to guarantee successful operations. Building such a reputation and trust requires particular experience that asks for a long-term engagement and *governance*. Otherwise, direct cash payments at the retail and wholesale market tend to reduce risks. The operations of local intermediaries are somewhat closer to the producer and enable deliveries of rejected produce to an alternative market outlet. Compared to exporters, intermediaries face major financial constraints for direct payments, and usually take advantage of opportunisms in their pricing policy.

Given the risk involved in mango production, exporters will contract with producers instead of engaging in production themselves. Export contracts are mainly arranged with medium-scale and larger mango plantations that use up-to-date procedures and cultivate modern varieties, while located close to the processing plants. In the export chain, producers are the least informed about market conditions and opportunities, and are basically preoccupied with the upgrading of primary production. Traders and intermediaries are the best informed agent in the chain, since through their logistic operations they link the production and marketing part of the chain. (Zuniga and Ruben, 2007)

This second case is more focused on the relationship between channel choice and value added on the one hand and (social) relationships in the supply network and governance of vertical relationships on the other hand. Though less attention is given to typical business environment aspects, the case clearly demonstrates the distinct features of the two channels.

Conclusions

In this chapter, we introduced value chain analysis in terms of its theoretical background and its application to value chains in developing countries. Although studies on VCs have provided valuable insights into their operations, our understanding of how value chains develop toward improved performance is limited. Most value chain studies to date focus on market relations and pay little attention to the competitive and institutional environment in which chain actors operate. Yet this environment may both enable and constrain value chain upgrading processes. Our framework for studying value chains in developing countries depicts value chains as networks in which organizational actors exploit competitive resources and operate within an institutional environment. Changes in the institutional environment or the competitive base may alter the functioning and performance of value chains. For a balanced analysis of value chains we proposed three key elements: network structure, of horizontal and (vertical) market-channel relationships, value added, as related to the key competitive aim of any business chain, and governance, covering organizational arrangements between value chain actors. These elements should always be studied embedded in the value chain's business environment where we focus on markets, resources and infrastructures and institutions. Value chain actors may be motivated to improve their position in the chain by changing their production of value added, their relationships (governance) with other actors in the value chain and by choosing different market channels for their products. In chapter 10 typical upgrading options and strategies for DC value chains will be discussed.

References

Bacon, C. (2005). 'Confronting the coffee crisis: Can fair trade, organic, and specialty coffees reduce small-scale farmer vulnerability in northern Nicaragua?' In: *World Development* 33 (3), pp. 497-511.

Bair, J. and G. Gereffi (2003). 'Upgrading, uneven development, and jobs in the North American apparel industry'. In: *Global Networks* 3, pp. 143-69.

Baldwin, C.Y. and K.B. Clark (2000). *Design Rules, Volume 1: The Power of Modularity*. Cambridge MA: MIT Press.

Bowersox, D.J. and D.J. Closs (1996), *Logistical Management: The integrated supply chain process*. New York: Macmillan.

Burt, R. S. (1997). 'The contingent calue of social capital'. In: *Administrative Science Quarterly* 42, pp. 339-365.

Coleman, J.S. (1990). *Foundations of social theory*. Cambridge, MA: Harvard University Press.

Cooper, M.C., D.M. Lambert and J.D. Pagh (1997). 'Supply Chain Management: More than a new name for logistics'. In: *International Journal of Logistics Management* 8 (1), pp. 1-14.

Eisenhardt, K.M. (1989). 'Agency Theory: An assessment and review'. In: *Academy of Management Review* 14 (1), pp. 57-74.

David, R.J. and S.-H. Han (2004). 'A systematic assessment of the empirical support for transaction cost economics. In: *Strategic Management Journal* 25 (1), pp. 39-58.

Dolan, C. and J. Humphrey (2000). 'Governance and trade in fresh vegetables: The impact of UK supermarkets on the African horticulture industry'. In: *Journal of Development Studies* 37 (2): pp. 147-176.

Dolan, C., J. Humphrey (2004). 'Changing governance patterns in the trade in fresh vegetables between Africa and the United Kingdom'. In: *Environment and planning* 36, pp. 491-509.

Fitter, R. and R. Kaplinsky (2001). 'Who gains from product rents as the coffee market becomes more differentiated? A value chain analysis'. In: *IDS Bulletin* 32 (3), pp. 69-82.

Fleury, A. and M.T. Fleury (2001). 'Alternatives for industrial upgrading in global value chains: The case of the plastics industry in Brazil'. In: *Ids Bulletin-Institute of Development Studies* 32 (3): pp. 116-126.

Francis, M. and D. Simons (2008). 'Value chain analysis in the UK beef foodservice sector'. In: *Supply Chain Management – an International Journal* 13 (1), pp. 83-91.

Gereffi, G. (1994). 'The organization of buyer-driven global commodity chains: How US retailers shape overseas production networks'. In: G. Gereffi and M. Korzeniewicz (eds.) *Commodity chains and global capitalism*. London: Greenwood Press.

Gereffi, G. (1999). 'International trade and industrial upgrading in the apparel commodity chain'. In: *Journal of international economics* 48, pp. 37-70.

Gereffi, G., J. Humphrey, T. Sturgeon (2005). 'The governance of global value chains'. In: *Review of international political economy* 12 (1), pp.78-104.

Gibbon, P. (2001). 'Upgrading primary production: A global commodity chain approach'. In: *World Development* 29 (2), pp. 345-363.

Gibbon, P. (2003). 'The African growth and opportunity act and the global commodity chain for clothing'. In: *World development* 31 (11), pp. 1809-1827.

Gibbon, P., J. Bair, and S. Ponte (2008). 'Governing global value chains: An introduction'. In: *Economy and Society* 37 (3), pp. 315-338.

Giovanucci, D. and T. Reardon (2001). 'Understanding grades and standards and how to apply them'. In: D. Giovannuci (ed.), *A guide to developing agricultural markets and ago-enterprises*. Washington: The World Bank.

Giuliani, E., C. Pietrobelli, and R. Rabellotti (2005). 'Upgrading in global value chains: Lessons from Latin American Clusters'. In: *World Development* 33 (4), pp. 549-574.

Grover, V. and M.K. Malhotra (2003). 'Transaction cost framework in operations and supply chain management research: Theory and measurement'. In: *Journal of Operations Management* 21 (4), pp. 457-473.

Grunert, K., L. Fruensgaard Jeppesen, K. Risom Jespersenand A. Sonne (2005). 'Market orientation of value chains: A conceptual framework based on four case studies from the food industry'. In: *European Journal of Marketing* 39 (5/6), pp. 429-455.

Grunert, K. G. (2006). 'How changes in consumer behaviour and retailing affect competence requirements for food producers and processors'. In: *Economía Agraria y Recursos Naturales* 6 (11), pp. 3-22.

Gulati, R. (1998). 'Alliances and Networks'. In: *Strategic Management Journal* 19, pp. 293-317.

Gwyne, R.N. (2008). 'UK retail concentration, Chilean wine producers and value chains'. In: *The Geographical Journal* 174 (2), pp. 97-108l.

Hsiao H.I., R.G.M. Kemp, J.G.A.J. van der Vorst and S.W.F. (Onno) Omta (2009). 'Make-or-buy decisions and levels of logistics outsourcing: An empirical analysis in the food manufacturing industry'. In: *Journal on Chain and network Science* 9 (2), pp. 105-118.

Humphrey, J. and H. Schmitz (2002). 'How does insertion in global value chains affect upgrading in industrial clusters?' In: *Regional Studies* 36, pp. 1017-1027.

Humphrey, J. (2006). 'Policy implications of trends in agribusiness value chains'. In: *The European journal of development research* 18 (4), pp. 572-592.

Ivarsson, I. and C. G. Alvstam (2005). 'Technology transfer from TNCs to local suppliers in developing countries: A study of AB Volvo's truck and bus plants in Brazil, China, India, and Mexico'. In: *World Development* 33 (8), pp. 1325-1344.

Jahn, G., M. Schramm and A. Spiller (2004). 'The trade-off between generality and effectiveness in certification systems: A conceptual framework'. In: H.J. Bremmers, S.W.F. Omta, J.H. Trienekens and E.F.M. Wubben (eds.), *Dynamics in Chains and Networks. Proceedings of the sixth international conference on chain and network management in agribusiness and food industry*. Wageningen: Wageningen Academic Publishers, pp. 335-343.

Kambewa, E.V. (2007). *Contracting for sustainability, An analysis of the Lake Victoria-EU Nile perch chain*. Wageningen: Wageningen Academic Publishers, p. 176.

Kaplinsky, R. (2000). 'Globalisation and unequalisation: What can be learned from value chain analysis'. In: *Journal of Development Studies* 73 (2), pp.117-146.

Kaplinsky, R. and M. Morris (2002). 'The globalization of product markets and immiserizing growth: Lessons from the South African furniture ndustry'. In: *World Development* 30 (7), pp. 1159-1177.

Lazzarini, S.L., F.R. Chaddad and M.L. Cook (2001). 'Integrating Supply Chain and Network'. Journal on Chain and Network Science, 1 (1), pp. 7-22.

Lu, H., J.H. Trienekens, S.W.F. Omta and S. Feng (2008). 'The value of guanxi for small vegetable farmers in China'. In: *British Food Journal* 110 (4/5), pp. 412-429.

Martí, I. and J. Mair (2008). 'Bringing change into the lives of the poor: Entrepreneurship outside traditional boundaries'. In: T. Lawrence, R. Suddaby and B. Leca (eds.), *Institutional Work*. Cambridge: Cambridge University Press.

Muradian, R. and W. Pelupessy (2005). 'Governing the coffee chain: The role of voluntary regulatory Systems'. In: *World Development* 33 (12), pp. 2029-2044.

Murphy, J.T. (2007). 'The challenge of upgrading in African industries: Socio-spatial factors and the urban environment in Mwanza, Tanzania'. In: *World Development* 35 (10), pp. 1754-1778.

Nadvi., K. (2004). 'Globalization and poverty: How can global value chain research inform the policy debate?' In: *IDS Bulletin* 35 (1), pp. 20-30.

Perez-Aleman, P. and M. Sandilands (2008). 'Building value at the top and the bottom of the global supply chain: MNC-NGO partnerships'. In: *California Management Review* 51 (1), pp. 24-48.

Pietrobelli, C. and F. Saliola (2008). 'Power relationships along the value chain: Multinational firms, global buyers and performance of local suppliers'. In: *Cambridge Journal of Economics* 32, pp. 947-962.

Porter, M.E. (1985). *Competitive Advantage*. New York: Free Press.

Porter, M.E. (1990). *The competitive advantage of nations*, New York: Free Press

Raikes, P., M. Friis Jensen, and S. Ponte (2000). 'Global commodity chain analysis and the French Filiere approach: Comparison and critique'. In: *Economy and Society* 29 (3), pp. 319-417.

Rindfleisch A. and J.B. Heide (1997). 'Transaction cost analysis: Past, present, and future applications'. In: *Journal of Marketing* 61, pp. 30-54.

Riisgaard, L. (2009). 'Global value chains, labor organization and private social standards: Lessons from East African cut flower industries'. In: *World Development* 37 (2), pp. 326-340.

Roy, D. and A. Thorat (2008). 'Succes in high value horticultural export markets for small farmers: The case of mahagrapes in India'. In: *World Development* 6 (10), pp. 1874-1890.

Ruben R., M. van Boekel, A. van Tilburg and J. Trienekens (eds., 2007). *Governance for Quality in Tropical Food Chains*. Wageningen: Wageningen Academic Publishers, p. 309.

Schmitz, H. (1999). 'Global competition and local cooperation: Success and failure in the Sinos Valley, Brazil'. In: *World Development* 27 (9), pp. 1627-1650.

Scott, W.R. (1995). *Institutions and organizations*. London: Sage.

Spiegel van der, M. (2004). *Measuring effectiveness of food quality management*. Wageningen: Ponsen & Looijen.

Stern, L.W., A.I. El-Ansary and A.T. Coughlan (1996). *Marketing channels*, 5th ed. London: Prentice Hall International.

Sturgeon, T.J. (2001). How do we define value chains and production networks?, IDS Bulletin, 32 (3), pp. 9-18.

Trienekens J., B. Petersen, N. Wognum and D. Brinkmann (2009). *European Pork Chains: Consumer-oriented production and distribution*. Wageningen: Wageningen Academic Publishers, pp. 288.

Uzzi, B. (1997). 'Social structure and competition in interfirm networks: The paradox of embeddedness'. In: *Administrative Science Quarterly* 42, pp. 35-67.

Vellema, S. and D. Boselie (2003). *Cooperation and competence in global food chains: Perspectives on food quality and safety*. Maastricht: Shaker Publishing.

Vollebrecht, H.M., F.P. Scheer, J.G.A.J. van der Vorst and K.G.L. Pauls-Worm (2010). 'Florilog regie: Logistics orchestration in the pot plant supply chain network'. In: J. Trienekens et al. *Towards effective food chains*. Wageningen: Wageningen Academic Publishers, pp. 47-63.

Williamson, O.E. (1985). *The economic institutions of capitalism: Firms, markets, relational contracting*. New York: Free Press.

Williamson O.E. (1999). 'Strategy research: Governance and competence perspectives'. In: *Strategic Management Journal* 20, pp. 1087-1108.

Zuniga-Arias, G. and R. Ruben (2007). 'Determinants of market outlet choice for mango producers in Costa Rica'. In: R. Ruben, M. van Boekel, A. van Tilburg and J. Trienekens (eds.), *Governance for quality in tropical food chains*. Wageningen: Wageningen Academic Publishers, pp. 49-68.

Part II

Local Agricultural Value Chains

4 Beer multinationals Supporting Africa's Development?

How Partnerships Include Smallholders into Sorghum-beer Supply Chains

Jeroen van Wijk and Herma Kwakkenbos1

Introduction

Restrictions on the import of barley malt by the Nigerian government in the 1980s have facilitated an import substitution strategy that is now widely adopted by the African brewing industry. Barley malt is a key resource for beer brewing. Due to the Nigerian import ban, it was discovered that locally produced sorghum could serve as an adequate substitute for barley (Ogun, 1995). At present, all major brewers on the African continent partially substitute imported barley by sorghum and other locally produced crops, because they are cheaper and do not entail currency losses (Lapper, 2010; Wiggens, 2008). The African informal market of artisanal beers, wines and other drinks made from local ingredients, such as sorghum, is estimated to be four times bigger than the formal sector, and has a value of about USD 3 billion. Heineken, Guinness and SABMiller now compete with this African home-brew market (Capell, 2009).

The shift to local resources serves as an incentive for the development of local supply chains that could stimulate agricultural production in Africa. However, such chains are not easily created. In Sub-Saharan Africa, the sorghum grain (*Sorghum bicolor*) is grown in unpredictable "rain-fed" agriculture contexts, while farmers cannot afford the use of additional inputs. With 300 kg/ha the productivity of African sorghum farming is far below yields in other regions of the world that may reach 9,000 kg/ha (ICRISAT, 2008). In 2001, Guinness Ghana tried to set up a sorghum supply chain in Northern Ghana, but failed completely. The company had facilitated farmers in acquiring fertilizer, agrochemicals, as well as certified seeds of a new sorghum variety, *Kapaala*, but had to reject most of the grain one year later because of low quality (Kudadjie, 2006). The harsh climate and limitations in the institutional business environment hindered the African farmers to integrate into a modern value chain.

Considering the challenges of setting up robust sorghum supply chains for industrial brewing, multinational brewers have sought collaboration with NGOs and government agencies. In several African countries, partnerships have been established to advance the institutional changes required for the production of high-quality sorghum.

Partnerships can be defined as voluntary, collaborative arrangements between actors from the different societal domains – the state, market, and civil society –, which have an institutionalized, yet nonhierarchical structure and strive for a sustainability goal (Glasbergen et al., 2007). Such collaborative arrangements between private and public actors are increasingly popular to overcome market or government failures, because partners can pool their resources, knowledge and capabilities (Kolk et al., 2008), and because they can offer partners advantages in terms of increased flexibility, productivity, cost reduction and innovations (Jenkins, 2007). Private companies can also gain local market knowledge in emerging economies. Cooperation with governments and civil society organizations abroad partially offset the risks that are inherent to operating in new developing-country markets (Muller and van Tulder, 2006).

Partnerships can promote pro-poor economic development when they address institutional barriers that hinder the inclusion of smallholders into (global) supply or value chains. The aim is a win-win scenario: The partnerships serve firms in establishing a cost-reducing and robust supply chain while they offer farmers a new market opportunity embedded in an improved business environment that may result in additional income generation. However, some authors have pointed out that success of this strategy is all but guaranteed. Development partnerships may be a mechanism for "institutional capture", whereby corporate interests come to dominate or heavily influence the decision-making process of public-private institutions (Utting, 2000). They may also distract attention away from asset development which is just as important as income growth when fighting poverty (Boyle and Boguslaw, 2007). The discussion of whether or not value chain partnerships are benefiting both farms and firms is still ongoing because empirical evidence on this issue is lacking (Rein et al., 2005).

The aim of this chapter is to address this knowledge gap by exploring ways to assess partnership interventions intended to include smallholders in commercial value chains. The focus is on the partnership's ability to induce changes in the institutional environment. We analyze five partnerships for the development of sorghum-based beer value chains in four African countries: Sierra Leone, Ghana, Uganda and Zambia. The cross-case analysis tackles two questions: a) To what extent have the partnerships succeeded in making the institutional business environment of value chains more conducive to smallholders; and b) To what extent have smallholders actually benefited from those changes, judged from the actual upgrading in sorghum production?

The chapter is structured as follows. The first section offers a brief overview of institutional challenges to small-scale farming. The methodology section describes the five case studies and the ways data was collected and analyzed. The third section provides the analysis and is followed by a discussion of the most significant findings.

Partnerships addressing barriers to value chain development

Agriculture is Africa's most important sector that can address poverty and food security, but its fragmented nature hinders further development. Most farmers in Africa are smallholders who face huge barriers to enter national and global markets. Yet, access to these markets is considered critical to growth in developing countries (OECD, 2006; World Bank, 2008). The most important institutional challenges to smallholder inclusion in commercial value chains concern the formal rules, interorganizational arrangements, and informal customs that prevent farmers from having access to knowledge and technology, credit, markets, and farmer-based organizations.

Access to knowledge and technology

Farmers must acquire knowledge, and adopt quality standards that lead firms in the chains require. They need to invest in structural and procedural initiatives that win buyers' trust and make them feel confident about the quality and safety assurance mechanisms for their produce (Henson and Jaffee, 2006; Garcia Martinez and Poole, 2004). Quality-standard certification improves the reputation of farmers and that may eventually help them retain a higher share of the chain income (Muradian and Pelupessy, 2005). Since the quality of rural education in developing countries is relatively low there is a need for farmer support and training in good agricultural practices (World Bank, 2008).

Access to credit

Lack of affordable credit is a major constraint for many smallholders to improve their process and product quality (Altenburg, 2007; Kaplinsky and Morris, 2001). Financial institutions are reluctant in providing credit to small-scale farmers because agriculture is vulnerable to unpredictable climatic circumstances and because farmers lack collateral. Broader access to financial services would expand their opportunities for technology adoption and resource allocation (World Bank, 2008).

Market predictability

Farmers are exposed to highly volatile markets, which hinders investments in the agricultural sector. A more stable business climate for suppliers through buyer commitment and price stability would motivate farmers to invest in production capacity and quality improvement (Gibbon and Ponte, 2005).

Farmers' organization

Smallholders need to be organized in larger organizations to meet a buyer's requirements in terms of volumes, quality and consistency of supply. Farmer alliances facilitate risk sharing and the pooling of resources. They enable collective learning in farm management and offer farmers the opportunity to operate as a group actor that can develop a countervailing power vis-à-vis other chain actors (KIT et al., 2006).

The institutional obstacles that deter farmers from investing also hinder private enterprises that follow a strategy of local sourcing and establishing backward linkages with agricultural producers in the region. For that reason some private companies join forces with development organizations in what can be coined "value chain partnerships" to develop a commercial supply chain (Fortanier, 2006). In this collaborative arrangement, partners particularly address the chain's institutional environment, i.e. the formal and informal rules that regulate the behavior of value chain stakeholders. For example, partnerships may promote shifts in farming customs, support banks in finding new ways of lending to farmers, encourage contract compliance among both farmers and buyers, and help farmers in organizing themselves. The changes induced in attitude and newly built trust create opportunities for an improvement of linkages between supply chain actors, and between chain actors and facilitators.

Value chain development requires continuous attention to technical and social innovations at farmers' level. This "upgrading" refers to the ability of a farm to acquire new technologies or management techniques in order to increase its competiveness and resilience, and eventually improve its power position in the value chain (Bair, 2005; Giuliani et al., 2005). Commonly four different forms of upgrading can be distinguished (Humphrey and Schmitz, 2004):

1 *Process upgrading* – Improving efficiency in the transformation of inputs into outputs by reorganizing the production process or by introducing innovations.
2 *Product upgrading* – Moving into more qualitatively improved product lines, resulting in the addition of a new trait to the product.

3 *Functional upgrading* – Acquiring new functions in the chain (such as design, marketing, branding) to increase overall skill content of activities.
4 *Interchain upgrading* – Using the knowledge acquired in particular chain functions to move horizontally into more than one, or alternative chains.

Upgrading is conditional to smallholders' participation in value chains. Only by investing in social and technological innovations can smallholders enter, maintain or improve their position in value chains. Value chain partnerships are expected to facilitate upgrading opportunities for smallholders. In this way they promote sustainable improvement in the livelihoods of rural populations.

Methodology

For our cross-case analysis we selected five sorghum-beer value chain development partnerships in Africa, which comprised a brewing company – the chain's lead firm – and a nongovernmental organization (NGO). The five cases cover four countries: Sierra Leone, Ghana, Uganda and Zambia and include three beer multinationals: Heineken, Guinness, SABMiller, and their local subsidiaries. Together, these firms currently control nearly 75 percent of the African beer market. SABMiller (UK) has a 43 percent share, Heineken (Netherlands) 19 percent, and the British drinks group Diageo (owner of the Guinness brand) 12 percent (Capell, 2009).

All partnerships were analyzed in respect of a) the changes they brought about in the institutional value chain environment, referred to as "conditions for upgrading", and of b) changes in the actual upgrading at farmer's level, which are used as measure of the effect of the institutional changes. Data on the partnership effects was collected from relevant documents and in stakeholder interviews. In the period September 2008-July 2009, 41 persons were interviewed covering 37 of the most important stakeholder organizations that were involved in any of the five cases. The total sample of interviewees represents farmers' organizations (9), breweries (8), local and international nongovernmental organizations (9), R&D centers (7), private grain-trading companies (4), finance institutions (2), a government organization, and an academic advisor. Nearly half of these interviews took place face to face in Ghana, while the remainder was done electronically or by telephone.

Box 1   Sorghum beer partnerships in Africa: 5 cases

Three of the five cases form part of the *West African Sorghum Chain Development* (WASCD) project that includes the Irish brewer *Guinness* (part of the British beverages group *Diageo*), the Dutch brewer *Heineken*, the *UN Common Fund for Commodities* (CFC), *EUCORD* (an NGO and an affiliate of the American *Winrock International*), and the American *NGO TechnoServe*. The project intends to create new income opportunities for smallholders in Ghana and Sierra Leone, and supports the local breweries of Guinness and Heineken in substituting more expensive, imported barley malt by locally produced sorghum. The five-year WASCD project has a budget amounting to in total USD 2.8 million provided by CFC (60%) and the two private sector partners (40%), i.e. Guinness and Heineken.

1 Guinness-TechnoServe partnership in Ghana (2006-2011)
The partnership under the WASCD has *Guinness Ghana Breweries Ltd* and the NGO *TechnoServe* as main partners. The latter supports farmers in Ghana's Upper West, as well as the nucleus farmers who act as grain trading intermediaries between the farmers and the brewer. The Ghanaian government participates through its *Capital Venture Trust Fund* that is related to the *SINAPI ABA Trust*, and which provides credit to farmers. The partnership was established after an attempt to establish a sorghum supply chain in Northern Ghana by Guinness had failed (Kudadjie, 2006). It is based on an agreement in which the brewery agreed to buy sorghum produced under the partnership for a period of five years at a price that could vary within a certain price band.

2 Guinness-ACDEP partnership in Ghana (2006-2011)
This partnership includes the *Association of Church Development Projects* (ACDEP), a local NGO that supports farmers, and the *Savanna Farmers Marketing Company* (SFMC), a private trading company and spin-off from ACDEP. SFMC serves as commercial intermediary between farmers and Guinness Ghana. The Dutch development organization *ICCO* is sponsoring. The *Guinness*-ACDEP partnership was initiated in 2002 to serve smallholders in Ghana's Upper East, and could expand after the establishment of the WASCD project.

3 Heineken partnership in Sierra Leone (2006-2011)
In Sierra Leone the WASCD project resulted in a partnership including the *Sierra Leone Brewery Ltd* (largely owned by *Heineken*) and *Vancil Consultancy Services*, a local NGO that supports farmers and acts as grain-trading intermediary between farmers and the brewer. Other partners are *Finance Salone*, a local nonprofit credit provider that operates with a grant from the *Rabobank Foundation* provided via EUCORD, the *Sierra Leone Agricultural Research Institute*, and the *Rokupr Agricultural Research Center*.

4 Eagle Lager partnership in Uganda (2000-)
Eagle Lager is the brand name of sorghum-based beer sold in Uganda. The Eagle Lager partnership in Uganda started in 2003 after *SABMiller*'s Ugandan subsidiary *Nile Breweries* had unsuccessfully tried to develop a local sorghum supply chain. The partnership includes *Afro Kai*, an indigenous commodity trading company, which was contracted to coordinate the *Epuripur* sorghum supply chain, the Ugandan government, and the *Serere Animal and Agricultural Institute* (SAARI). The local NGO *Enterprise Uganda* is taking care of farmer training.

> **5 Eagle Lager partnership in Zambia (2005-)**
> Because of its success in Uganda, the Eagle Lager model was also implemented in Zambia in 2005. Partners are *Zambian Breweries* (owned by *SABMiller*) and the Zambian government. The brewery contracted *CHC Commodities*, a local grain trader, for supply-chain coordination. *CARE International*, a development-aid NGO, was attracted for supply-chain facilitation and to support Zambian farmers producing a crop that meets the standards set by the brewery.

The analysis followed a qualitative and interpretative approach. The interviewees' perception of partnership effectiveness, i.e. whether the partnerships had effectively induced changes in the (conditions of) upgrading at the farm, was summarized in one of three possible scores: "none" (-), a "modest positive change" (+ / -), or a "considerable positive change" (+). The average scores per item were later used to generate overall perceptions by stakeholders per case. The issues on which stakeholders differed in their opinions are explained in the analysis. Box 1 provides the overview of the five partnership cases.

Establishing commercial sorghum value chains

Table 1 shows that all partnerships have managed to create a local value chain for sorghum. The largest volumes have been produced under the Ugandan Eagle Lager partnership where over 70 percent of the brewer's demand was met in 2009. This is partially related to the favorable growing conditions in Uganda (Balya, 2006).

Table 1   Sorghum supply for commercial brewing under five African partnerships, key characteristics

Guinness-TechnoServe (Ghana) 2009 [1]	Guinness- ACDEP (Ghana) 2008 [1]	Heineken (Sierra Leone) 2009 [1]	Eagle lager (Uganda) 2009 [1]	Eagle Lager (Zambia) 2010 [2]
Production				
Total volume supplied (MT kgs)				
2,500	58	150-180	4,700	300
Total potential demand buyer (MT kgs)				
10,000 [2]	10,000	200	6,500	N/A
Farmers				
# of farmers involved (2009)				
>5000	6800	2500	8000	4500
% of smallholders (<5 acres)				
85	100	75	90	>90

1) *Source:* Interviews with various stakeholders and internal NGO documents
2) Mutumweno (2010)

In contrast, farmers producing under the two Guinness partnerships in northern Ghana have to cope with erratic rains and poor soil conditions. They have supplied less than a quarter of total industrial demand for sorghum. Since the breweries expect the partial shift from imported barley to locally produced sorghum to continue in all four countries in the future, the market for commercial sorghum is likely to remain and perhaps even to grow.

The five partnerships have also been successful in establishing the backward linkage between breweries and smallholders. Sizeable numbers of farmers have been included in the chains, the far majority being smallholders. The actual numbers are likely higher when unregistered outgrowers and farm laborers are included. The Zambian supply chain started with commercial large-scale producers but in less than four years smallholders have become the prime sorghum suppliers.

Conditions for upgrading

All partnerships have addressed the main institutional challenges for local sorghum farmers. Table 2 presents the findings in the four main areas, which are explained below.

Access to knowledge and technology

The sorghum-beer partnerships have promoted the adoption of specific sorghum varieties that are suitable for industrial beer processing. Generally there are two kinds of varieties. Red and brown varieties contain tannins that cause a bitter taste and cloudiness in lager beer. White and yellow varieties contain significantly less tannins and are the only ones accepted by the breweries. In all cases national research institutes have been working on varietal improvement in order to offer farmers higher-yielding varieties. Nevertheless, everywhere farmers resort to local varieties that were already in use. In Ghana, one NGO pointed out that the new Guinness chain had made the national research institute more focused on varietal characteristics that farmers need for their market. The agricultural stations were said to have become more business minded too. The extension workers were perceived to be more aware of production costs which they now try to reduce, and of the importance of quality, including documentation and traceability.

All partnerships (except Sierra Leone) encourage farmers to change their custom of using a part of their crop as seed for the next crop cycle, which reduces costs and ensures seed availability. Instead, farmers are encouraged to buy fresh, certified seeds for every crop cycle. Nile Breweries in Uganda does not even allow the farmers to retain their seed. There was consensus among the research institutes, grain traders, and breweries that certified seeds are genetically more homogeneous; they yield bigger and neater grains, and their germination and oil content are better. The main impediment to the spread of certified seeds in the three West African cases is their limited availability. Since sorghum is an open-pollinating crop farmers can easily reuse grains as seed for the next crop cycle, a practice that reduces farmers' costs, but also the incentive to invest for seed producers.

Another significant shift brought about by the partnerships is the investment in farmer training. Every partnership includes an NGO to complement existing governmental extension services in the training of sorghum farmers in farm management, quality issues, financial matters and farmer organization. In the Ghanaian Guinness-TechnoServe partnership, nucleus farmers play a significant role in training. Only in Uganda, the brewery is also active in farmer training.

The Guinness-TechnoServe partnership emphasizes the role of advanced technology in the sorghum production, while this is considered to be less relevant in other partnerships. In Zambia, sorghum farmers have often opted for "conservation agriculture", which requires a minimum of equipment. This reportedly results in better crop yields, improved soil fertility, better rainwater harvesting, nitrogen fixation and fewer weed problems (Mutumweno, 2010).

Access to affordable credit

Partnerships have two options for improving farmers' access to affordable credit. The first involves credit that is made available from within the chain, by the grain trader or the brewery. All partnerships have managed to improve access to credit in this way. In both Ghanaian Guinness chains, sorghum farmers can apply for a credit from the agricultural development bank that can tap from a government fund. The loan is made available through either the grain trader or nucleus farmers. In the Ugandan and Zambian cases, changes in the credit opportunities were deemed not necessary, because sorghum is considered to be a low-cost product and inputs are being subsidized. However, the breweries in both countries offer seed as in-kind loan to farmers, while Zambian Breweries also pays in advance. In all cases, the interest rates for (in-kind) loans tend to be lower than commercial rates.

The second option involves financial sources external to the chain, notably commercial banks. Success in this area was only reported by the two Guinness partnerships that benefited from the WASCD project. Some rural banks have become more willing to lend to farmers, because the five-year market prospect provided by this project enhanced the credibility of sorghum farmers. In the Guinness-ACDEP case, around 60 percent of the farmers sourced credit from banks. The Heineken partnership in Sierra Leone involves a local microcredit provider (Finance Salone) that uses a grant from a foreign microfinance institution to make loans available to sorghum farmers. In the two Eagle Lager partnerships the breweries have recently opened up negotiations with banks. In all cases the banks are only interested in group lending.

Market opportunities

All five partnerships address the unpredictability of the market. The brewing companies involved agreed to negotiate a guaranteed annual price in the preplanting period. In Ghana and Sierra Leone the negotiations are basically between respectively Guinness Ghana and Heineken, the NGOs, and advisors. The involvement of farmers in price negotiations is negligible. The NGOs develop a crop budget based on latest input prices, which serves as a guideline in the negotiations. The nucleus farmers in Sierra Leone and Ghana and the grain trader SFMC in the ACDEP-Guinness chain follow the price set in this meeting. Because sorghum can also be sold on local food markets, side selling is discouraged by setting the price slightly above the local market price. In Uganda and Zambia the partnerships are, according to a brewery representative, based on "hard-nosed business principles", which means that the breweries pay the market price only. The brewery says it tries to reduce price volatility though.

In respect of purchase commitments, all breweries enter into annual purchase agreements with the private commodity trader or the nucleus farmers. In the three West African cases, the annual agreements are part of a longer-term commitment by Guinness and Heineken for a period of five years.

Farmer organization

The partnerships have achieved farmer integration in the sorghum supply chains in two distinct ways. The Heineken and Guinness-TechnoServe partnerships have organized smallholders through the nucleus farmer-outgrower model under facilitation of the NGOs. The farmers' organizations follow a hierarchical model: the registered smallholders work under the management and control of commercial farmers. The model ensures a clear structure and ownership and eases monitoring. The nucleus farmers are supposed to become the key suppliers to the brewery when they take over the chain coordination after the NGO has left in 2011. The Ugandan Eagle Lager partnership develops a similar model. Because of risks of quality and supply disruption, the partnership intends to have 70 percent of production supplied by farmers organized and under the management of medium and large-scale commercial farmers by 2014.

A more horizontal organization for smallholder integration in the sorghum chains has been achieved in the two other partnerships. In Zambia, all small-holders are organized in sixteen FBOs, primarily cooperatives, which take care of collection and monitoring, and serve as intermediary between the farmers and traders. All farmers linked to FBOs are considered to be contract farmers. The Ghanaian Guinness-ACDEP partnership stresses the importance of horizontal farmer organizations even more. The NGO attributes the absence of economies of scale and the weak bargaining power of farmers to a lack of organization. It disapproves of the nuclear farmer model that is being followed by the second Ghanaian partnership and explicitly promotes democratic farmer organizations through the training of group formation.

Table 2   Partnership effects: Stakeholder perceptions of changes in the conditions for upgrading

	G-T Gha	G-A Gha	Hein SL	EL Ug	EL Za
Access to knowledge and technology					
Availability of new, improved sorghum varieties					
Farmers promoted to use fresh, certified seed	-	+/-	-	-	+/-
Fertilizer and agrochemicals made available	+	+/-	+	+	+
Training in crop management and postharvest	+	-	-	-	-
treatment	+	+/-	+	+	+
Access to affordable credit					
Banks more willing to lend					
Lead firm or special chain-related funds more	+/-	+	+	-	-
willing to lend	+	+	-	-	-
Market opportunities					
Multiple-year market prospect	+	+	+	-	-
Annual purchasing commitments	+	+	+	+	+
Annual preplanting price guarantees	+	+	+	+	+
Farmer organization					
Cooperative farmer-based organizations	-	+	-	-	+
Nucleus farm-outgrower organization	+	-	+	+	-

Upgrading at the farm

A relevant indicator for the degree of changes in the institutional environment is whether upgrading at the farmers' level has indeed taken place. Table 3 shows the effectiveness of the partnerships in this respect. The explanation of the perceived changes in upgrading follows below.

Process upgrading

Yields per acre have reportedly doubled in Guinness-TechnoServe and Ugandan Eagle Lager cases, and "improved" in the Heineken and Zambian Eagle Lager cases, although they remained among the lowest in the world. The Ugandan Eagle Lager partnership was so successful in 2006 that farmers produced an excess supply. Partners now face the challenge of combining a higher productivity with containing the overall growth in sorghum supply, which is done through the distribution of seeds. Only in the Guinness-ACDEP case no productivity increase was reported. The NGO is reluctant to focus narrowly on yields, because it would encourage farmers to take investment risks in unpredictable markets and an unstable natural environment. According to the NGO, farm viability and sustainability require a focus beyond yield (van Wijk et al., 2009).

Better farm management, lower crop losses and improved postharvest treatment were among the reasons for higher productivity. The Guinness-TechnoServe partnership also invested in technology, including tractors, threshers and fertilizer that were acquired by nucleus farmers. In all partnerships the interviewees said that the use of certified seeds had substantially increased. On the other hand, production costs increases were reported especially in the three West African cases. Higher oil prices have significantly raised prices of fertilizer, plowing and transportation.

Product upgrading

The sorghum that is supplied to the brewers must have qualities that make it suitable for industrial beer processing and needs to be tested by the brewery before seeds of the variety can be distributed. Although national and international research institutes were said to work on varietal improvement, none of the partnerships has resulted in new sorghum varieties that make it easier for farmers to meet the quality standard of the breweries. One newly developed variety, *Kapaala*, had been introduced in northern Ghana by Guinness in 2002, but it proved to be not suitable to the environment (Kudadjie, 2006). Instead, farmers resorted to a well known and suitable local variety, *Dorado*, as did farmers in the other partnerships. Ugandan farmers have shifted to *Epuripur*, a variety that was bred in the 1990s, before the partnership was established. Apart from varietal improvements, all interviewees point out that there is more attention to quality aspects along the chain, resulting in lower rejection rates.

Functional upgrading

The relatively short length of the sorghum-beer value chain implies that there are few new value-added opportunities. Most possibilities can be found in sorghum collection, bulk storage, cleaning, weighing, bagging, quality checking and transportation. These functions are generally taken care of by the grain trader (Uganda), an NGO that is assigned by the grain trader (Ghana-ACDEP), the nucleus farmers (Sierra Leone en Ghana-TechnoServe), or the farmer cooperatives (Zambia). Most interviewees point out that these are the actors that can move the sorghum business a scale up and improve efficiency in the chain. The same actors have also been able in most partnerships to provide new services to (groups of) smallholders, such as access to credit, access to improved and/or certified seeds, fertilizers, tractors and threshing services.

From this point of view, the partnerships did result in functional upgrading by the better-equipped chain actors. However, with the exception of sorghum collection, the outgrowers or other smallholders lack the logistic capacity for these activities. For them, the partnerships have achieved little in terms of functional upgrading.

Interchain upgrading

In a narrow context, interchain upgrading comprises of opportunities to sell sorghum in alternative chains, but there are very few of such chains. The partnerships have managed to develop an interesting new commercial supply chain for sorghum as an alternative to local food markets, which in itself is an example of interchain upgrading. Only in Ghana a competing firm – Accra Breweries – reportedly considers using sorghum for beer, which would open up an alternative chain for commercial sorghum.

In a broad context, interchain upgrading refers to farm-level diversification which is vital to farmers operating in largely unpredictable markets and natural environments. The risk of farmers being included in commercial supply chains is that monocropping is encouraged by the buyer for efficiency and quality purposes. Only under the Guinness-ACDEP partnership in Ghana are farmers actively supported to grow other cash crops next to commercial sorghum. In other partnerships, stakeholders consider farmers smart enough to spread their risks themselves.

Table 3　Partnership effects: Stakeholder perceptions of upgrading at the farm

	G-T Gha	G-A Gha	Hein SL	EL Ug	EL Za
Process upgrading					
Productivity increase	+	-	+	+	+
– Increased use of certified seeds	+	+	+	+	+
– Better farm management	+	+	+	+	+
– Investment in technology	+	-	-	-	-
Product upgrading					
Shift to varieties accepted by the brewery	+	+	+	+	+
Enhanced attention to quality aspects	+	+	+	+	+
*Functional upgrading**					
Collecting, storing, cleaning, checking, bagging and transporting sorghum	-	-	-	-	-
Interchain upgrading					
Diversification actively encouraged by partnership	-	+	-	-	-

* Refers to farm level only; some functional upgrading opportunities for traders and nucleus farmers have increased

Conclusion and discussion

The sorghum market for commercial beer production in the four African countries constitutes a unique opportunity for agricultural development. Breweries have embarked on a longer-term strategy to substitute imported barley by local, cheaper substitutes, and these new supply chains are not affected by international trade barriers or demanding foreign quality standards. However, these chains could not develop without partnerships that were necessary to initiate a number of important institutional changes. In all cases stakeholders agreed that the partnerships have played an important role in stabilizing the market through the promotion of contract farming and in organizing farmers into more efficient production units. Some knowledge and technology has been transferred through farm-management training, and the three West African partnerships advanced arrangements that offer farmers better credit opportunities. The institutional changes are to some extent reflected in adjustments in farm customs: More use of certified seed, better farm management, and, overall, more attention to quality aspects.

The cross-case analysis also showed a number of interesting differences among the partnerships. First, only the Ghanaian Guinness-ACDEP partnership addresses the potential problem of value chain partnerships becoming too focused on a single crop. Such a narrow focus is reflected in the improvements at farm level that were observed: In all cases these are limited to productivity and quality, and hardly extend to interchain upgrading. The latter form of farm improvement is not the prime interest of the breweries, but could significantly support the resilience of farmers who have to rotate their crops and spread their risks. The Guinness-ACDEP partnership supports farmers in producing a set of cash crops rather than just one.

Second, the Eagle Lager partnerships work with private grain traders as intermediary between farmers and brewery, and appear to have a more commercial foundation compared to the three West African partnerships where NGOs play a key role as grain intermediary. This is presumably related to the more developed business environment in Uganda and Zambia. In the West African regions, grain traders had to be founded first before a "chain" could actually develop, and NGOs temporarily fill the void. The West African partnerships therefore depend more on donor funding than the Eagle Lager cases. Nevertheless, in all chains NGOs are required to complement existing governmental extension services in farm and management training.

A third major difference was found in the way the partnerships organize farmers. Three partnerships follow hierarchical models to integrate smallholders into the chain mainly by using nucleus farmers, whereas two partnerships intentionally support more horizontal, farmer-based organizations. The Guinness-ACDEP partnership is fully committed to establishing democratic farm organizations that work on the up-scaling of production and empowerment of farmers. The partners are reluctant to follow the nucleus farm model, because it would introduce new hierarchies and opportunities for exploitation by the nucleus farmer. However, in terms of volumes produced, the second Ghanaian Guinness partnership performs far better.

Finally, a question can be posed in respect of the durability of the institutional changes induced by partnerships. It is not yet clear how the differences among the partnerships influence longer-term effects of the interventions. Additional research is required to examine the effects under the various partnership strategy modalities: single/multiple crop focus, the nature of the grain traders, and the manner smallholders are included in cash crop chains.

Another aspect concerns the role of governments. In the five African partnerships, governments are only remotely involved and play a limited role through their research and extension services, tax policies to encourage smallholder inclusion (Zambia), or credit opportunities (Ghana). This raises the issue of value chain partnerships potentially replacing rather than complementing governments in providing the appropriate institutional infrastructure needed for sustainable supply or value chains. Yet, it is the government that is required to make institutional changes durable and have them adopted in other chains and other sectors in the country.

Note

1   The authors wish to acknowledge the Dutch development organization ICCO for financing and facilitating the field study of one of the two Ghanaian cases that is included in this study, and to thank Pim Quaedackers for his help in editing this chapter.

References

Altenburg, T. (2007). *Donor approaches to supporting pro-poor value chains.* Report prepared for the Donor Committee for Enterprise Development Working Group on Linkages and Value Chains. German Development Institute, July 2006 (rev. 9 January 2007).

Bair, J. (2005). 'Global capitalism and commodity chains: Looking back, going forward'. In: *Competition and Change* 9 (2), pp. 153-180.

Balya, C. (2006). Supporting smallholder farmers to grow in Uganda: The story of Eagle Lager. *Afro Kai Ltd.* Website Donor Committee for Enterprise Development. www.value-chains.org/dyn/bds/docs/574/Balya.pdf.

Boyle, M. and J. Boguslaw (2007). 'Business, poverty and corporate citizenship: Naming the issues and framing the solutions'. In: *Journal of Corporate Citizenship* 26, pp. 1-20.

Capell, K. (2009). 'SABMiller's plan for cheaper African beer'. In: *Business Week* 8 April.

EUCORD, 2005. *West African Sorghum Value Chain Development Project (Sierra Leone and Ghana).* Project Proposal Common Fund for Commodities and EUCORD.

Fortanier, F. (2006). *Partnerships, power and equity in global commodity chains: Multinational enterprises, commodity chain partnerships and host country development goals.* Utrecht: ECSAD/ICCO.

Garcia Martinez, M. and N. Poole (2004). 'The development of private fresh produce safety standards: Implications for developing Mediterranean exporting countries'. In: *Food Policy* 29, pp. 229-255.

Gibbon, P. and S. Ponte (2005). *Trading down: Africa, value chains, and the global economy.* Philadelphia: Temple University Press.

Giuliani, E., C. Pietrobelli and R. Rabellotti (2005). 'Upgrading in global value chains: Lessons from Latin American clusters'. In: *World Development* 33 (4), pp. 549-573.

Glasbergen, P., F. Biermann and A.P.J. Mol, (eds.) (2007). *Partnerships, governance and sustainable development: Reflections on theory and practice.* Cheltenham: Edward Elgar.

Henson, S. and S. Jaffee (2006). 'Food safety standards and trade: Enhancing competitiveness and avoiding exclusion of developing countries'. In: *The European Journal of Development Research* 18 (4), pp. 593-621.

Humphrey, J. and H. Schmitz (2004). 'Chain governance and upgrading: Taking stock'. In: H. Schmitz (ed.). *Local enterprises in the global economy: Issues of governance and upgrading*. Cheltenham: Edward Elgar, pp. 349-381.

ICRISAT (2008). *Sorghum production practices. Learning module: The Virtual Academy for the Semi-Arid Tropics*. Website International Crops Research Institute for the Semi-Arid Tropics (ICRISAT), accessed 25 October 2008: www.icrisat.org/vasat/learning_resources/crops/sorghum/sorghum_insectpest/html/m1l1/resources/2267.html

Inspiris Limited (2006). *Bottling Success. The case of Eagle Lager in Uganda and Zambia*. Lusaka: Inspiris Limited.

Jenkins, B. (2007). *Expanding economic opportunity: The role of large firms*. Corporate Social Responsibility Initiative Report No.1, Kennedy School of Government, Harvard University.

Kaplinsky, R. M. and Morris (2001). *A handbook for value chain analysis*. A report prepared for IDRC, pp. 1-113.

KIT, Faida MaLi and IIRR (2006). *Chain empowerment: Supporting African farmers to develop markets*. Amsterdam: Royal Tropical Institute (KIT); Arusha: Faida Market Link; Nairobi: International Institute of Rural Reconstruction.

Kolk, A., R. van Tulder E. and Kostwinder (2008). 'Business and Partnerships For Development'. In: *European Management Journal* 26, pp. 262-273.

Kudadjie, C.Y. (2006). *Integrating science with farmer knowledge: Sorghum diversity management in north-east Ghana*. Ph.D. Thesis, University of Wageningen, the Netherlands.

Lapper, R. (2010). 'Cheaper African beer to brew more consumers'. In: *Financial Times* January 5.

Muller, A. and R. van Tulder (2006). *Partnerships, power and equity in global commodity chains: A 'rough guide' to partnerships for development*. Utrecht: EC-SAD/ICCO.

Muradian, R. and W. Pelupessy (2005). 'Governing the coffee chain: The role of voluntary regulatory systems'. In: *World Development* 33 (12), pp. 2029-2044.

Mutumweno, N. (2010). 'The Eagle flies in Zambia'. In: *Farming Matters* June, pp. 1820.

OECD (2006). *Promoting Pro-Poor Growth – Agriculture* [online]. Available from: www.oecd.org/dac/poverty.

Ogun, O. (1995). 'Country study Nigeria: Brewing'. In: S.E. Wangwe (ed.). *Exporting Africa: Technology, trade and industrialization in Sub-Saharan Africa*.

New York/London: INTECH Institute for New Technologies: UNU press Tokyo and Routledge London, pp. 246-295.

Porter, G. and K. Phillips-Howard (1997). 'Comparing contracts: An evaluation of contract farming schemes in Africa'. In: *World Development* 25 (2), pp. 227-238.

Rein, M., L. Stott, K. Yambayamba, S. Hardman and S. Reid (2005). 'Working together: A critical analysis of cross-sector partnerships in southern Africa'. Paper No. 4, The University of Cambridge Programme for Industry.

Utting, P. (2000). 'Business Responsibility for Sustainable Development'. Occasional Paper No. 2, United Nations Research Institute for Sustainable Development, Geneva.

Van Wijk, J., V. van der Linden and D. de Boer (2009). *Developing effective partnerships for development in global value chains. Lessons from sorghum and mango value chains in Ghana, Burkina Faso and Mali.* Expert Centre for Sustainable Business and Development Cooperation, The Netherlands.

Wiggins, J. (2008). 'Africa's new thirst for a local brew'. In: *Financial Times* January 10.

World Bank (2008). *Agriculture for Development.* World Development Report 2008. Washington: The World Bank.

5 Bush-to-energy Value Chains in Namibia

Institutional Challenges for Pro-poor Rural Development

Michael Brüntrup and Raoul Herrmann

Introduction

Modern bioenergy production has received a lot of attention in recent years.[1] There are different reasons for that. On the one hand, modern bioenergy is believed to play an important role in the transformation of existing fossil-fuel energy systems to reduce global greenhouse gas (GHG) emissions (see WBGU, 2008). Modern energy is further seen as a requirement for social and economic development (World Bank, 2009a). On the other hand, recent strong criticism of bioenergy production, particularly larger-scale liquid biofuels, concerning potential negative environmental and social impacts has shown that bioenergy also brings along substantial challenges (see Cotula et al., 2008).

From a development-policy point of view, the concern that modern bioenergy production competes with food production and hampers food security is a particularly critical issue. Two levels of competition can be distinguished: At the global level via world food markets and prices, and at the local level where investments to produce bioenergy feedstock may compete with local food production. Whereas at the global level biofuel programs of industrial countries (USA, European Union) are in the center of the debate, for the local level Sub-Saharan Africa (SSA) has been in the focus for three reasons: a) food insecurity is particularly widespread and subsistence food production and local markets are the main source of food security, b) most recent foreign investments in land and biofuels in developing countries have targeted the region, and c) the need for a transformation towards modern energy use is the strongest in the region, since a majority of the population still relies on traditional, unsustainable and unhealthy fuel wood for most energy uses, notably cooking and heating (see World Bank, 2009a).

This chapter addresses these concerns about bioenergy for rural development in SSA by investigating several bush-to-energy value chains in Namibia. The purpose of the chapter is threefold: First, it tries to understand the various factors affecting the viability of modern bioenergy production. Second, it seeks to identify potential impacts on rural development and food security. Third, it intends to derive policy options to influence the value chains' competitiveness as well as its environmental sustainability and social inclusiveness.

In Namibia, bioenergy production and use are considered to have a high potential. Government and private sector actors are struggling to find the right means to bring this potential into use. One of the most promising bioenergy feedstock resources is the conversion of woody shrubs (invasive bush) into bioenergy. The bush that is considered for these technologies are native bush species that encroach dry pastures in livestock production systems in Namibia and throughout the southern African savannas (see de Klerk, 2004). In Namibia alone, such bush covers an area of approximately 26 million ha (ibid.).

There are three main bioenergy value chains in Namibia that use bush as basic feedstock: a) charcoal, b) woodfuel briquettes, and c) woodgas (for electricity generation). The first two are marketed both locally and internationally, while the third feeds energy locally into the grid and is therefore a national value chain, although in principle electricity could be transported across the border. Only the charcoal value chain is already commercially viable and widespread. The others are at an experimental stage: woodfuel briquettes are produced but not (yet) at commercially viable scale (CCF, 2009); a pilot woodgas facility was to be established in autumn 2009 (DRFN, 2009). Most information in this chapter, particularly concerning the feedstock production stage, is therefore based on charcoal production. But the other value chains have provided valuable insights concerning the repercussions of various factors, notably of output market structures and policies on the viability and impact of (bush-to-)energy value chains. In addition, they show how slight changes in the technology, in the exact kind of products and by-products or the characteristics and interests of key value chain actors change the entire chain, the key challenges and the needs for regulating policies and institutions.

The rest of the chapter is structured as follows: First, we present a conceptual framework to understand the characteristics of bush-to-energy value chains and their relations to rural development. Second, we describe the methodology used during the field study. We then discuss the value chain context, i.e. the state of rural development, food security and bioenergy in Namibia, followed by an assessment of the bush-to-energy value chains regarding viability and (potential) development impacts. Based on these findings, we identify and analyze key policy and institutional challenges for Namibia and present major recommendations.

Value chain analysis, rural development and food security

Production and trade are today often characterized by coordinated mechanisms other than anonymous spot markets. To understand the roles of different actors in such more or less integrated markets, their interactions and the implications for overall performance, value creation and distribution, different concepts have been developed such as the filière approach, the Global Value Chain (GVC), and Global Commodity Chain (GCC) analysis (see, for example, Altenburg, 2007).

A value chain is commonly understood as "the full range of activities which are required to bring a product or service from conception, through the different phases of production [...], delivery to final consumers" (Kaplinsky and Morris, 2001). A key concept in GVC analysis has been that of governance (Gereffi et al., 2005), which is based on the notion that certain powerful actors, often lead firms, exert strong influence in determining participation and defining and enforcing standards of exchange throughout the value chain (Kaplinsky and Morris, 2001; Altenburg, 2006). Kaplinsky and Morris (2001) distinguish additionally between internal and external rule setting, which means that in some chains government or nongovernment institutions exert strong influence by determining the market rules (ibid.), for example, governments setting market standards (Kaplinsky, 2001). While GVC literature has focused largely on internationally traded goods and the role of global lead firms, value chains serving domestic markets are becoming increasingly important in developing countries due to higher quality demand of the growing middle classes. From a development-policy perspective it is important to understand how to influence value chains in a way that they are competitive and at the same time socially inclusive and environmentally sustainable.

In the case of bush-to-energy value chains in Namibia, we find a mix of national and international marketing outlets. While international markets are characterized by higher standards, domestic markets are going in the same direction since Namibia is a middle-income country and bush-to-energy value chains often target the relatively large middle class. In addition, the mix of marketing outlets and the possible switch between different marketing channels creates incentives for primary producers to adhere to the standards of the more demanding international channels. These channels fetch a price premium but are not always available for the entire volume of production.

Value chains are embedded in a broader regulatory and socioeconomic environment. Concerning bioenergy value chains, particularly the primary feedstock production takes place in rural areas. There, it can be intimately linked with food production (see above) but also with other aspects of food security and rural development such as labor markets, income generation, nature conservation, water, wildlife, tourism or rural energy supply. All these areas have some aspects of public goods which require coordination, are of high relevance for development and are, thus, subject to relatively strong government interventions and regulations. In a developing-country context, it is particularly important to look not only at formal institutions, mostly framed in policies and mandates of government institutions, but also at their application on the ground and at relations with informal institutions (Williamson, 2000). External factors strongly affecting a value chain's viability and the distributional effects can for instance be local traditional institutions, land ownership rules, or policies and institutions regulating energy, agriculture, environment and natural resource use. The interactions are likely to be different for different societal actors and different environmental dimensions, which requires considering complex value chain trade-offs (Altenburg, 2006).

There is a lack of studies that integrate a value chain perspective with analyzing wider socioeconomic and environmental implications for rural regions (see Bolwig et al., 2010), in spite of the importance of value chain development for poverty reduction in developing countries. Introducing modern value chains carries the promise to promote rural pro-poor development by promoting competitive labor-intensive activities (World Bank, 2007). Poverty is still largely a rural phenomenon throughout Sub-Saharan Africa, with the vast majority depending on agriculture as a main livelihood source.

Figure 1 summarizes the overall approach of integrating a value chain perspective and performance analysis with a wider approach to investigate development impacts, embedded into a network of outside institutions, policies and actors.

Figure 1   Policies and institutions influencing viability and development effects of domestic value chains

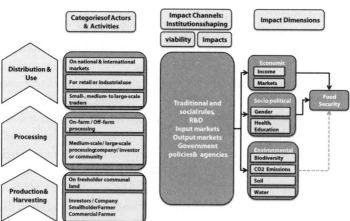

Source: Own design

The most important concern with regard to bioenergy value chains is certainly food security (see above). Food security is a key policy objective for most of Sub-Saharan African countries (including Namibia), and in many countries the key stumbling block for governments to engage more proactively in bioenergy production. There have been strong concerns on the negative effects of bioenergy policies and investments on food security, particularly after the 2008 food price crisis, for which increasing biofuel-crop production has been partly made responsible (e.g. Mitchell, 2008). There is also a wide agreement, however, that food security is a very complex, multi-dimensional challenge, commonly defined as a situation when "all people, at all times, have physical, social and economic access to sufficient amounts of safe and nutritious food that meets their dietary needs and food preferences for an active and healthy life" (FAO, 2009).

Four key food-security dimensions have been identified: Availability, access, stability and utilization (ibid.). Hence, the relation between bioenergy production and food security is not monocausal, but comprises of different, partly contradicting effects (e.g. reducing food production and increasing prices versus improving incomes, government transfers through taxing enhancing the food access).

Methodology

The analysis relies on qualitative data collected during a three-month field research between February and May 2009 in the capital of Namibia and various rural regions in the central-north and northern part of the country. Initial selection of interviewees followed the value chain structure, i.e. actors at different levels along the chains: Small- and large-scale farmers, livestock and bush harvesters/charcoal producers, processors, traders and electricity distributors. Workers were interviewed at various steps of the value chains, particularly at the feedstock production level. Not participating local farmers were interviewed as they were assumed to be the most important group of people affected indirectly. Whenever possible, stakeholder representatives such as heads of local farmer's organizations, traditional chiefs and professional associations were consulted. In addition, policy organizations and other institutions that influence the value chain were interviewed: Ministries for agriculture, environment, energy, forestry and rural extension services, administrative decentralized units, etc. Also researchers and NGOs working in these areas were interviewed.

In total, about 130 semi-structured interviews for the bush-to-energy and an additional research on Jatropha investments were conducted. Several group discussions were conducted with smallholder farmers and charcoal/agricultural workers. In a final workshop, preliminary results were presented to and discussed with about 50 stakeholders in a day-long workshop in Windhoek.

The information from interviews was cross-checked with other interviews and secondary literature (government documents, NGO papers and research papers). The information presented in this chapter is derived from these interviews, if not indicated differently. The names of actors and organizations were removed to ensure confidentiality. A computer program for qualitative data analysis, called atlas.ti (www.atlasti.com), was used for coding interviews, to derive causal relationships and identify further research questions.

Development challenges and bioenergy context in Namibia

Due to steady income growth over the last years, Namibia is now an upper-middle-income country (World Bank, 2009). However, the country still faces substantial development problems and suffers particularly from extremely high unequal income distributions, with a Gini coefficient of 0.6 (see World Bank, 2009b; Rosendahl 2010). The unequal distribution manifests itself especially in a stark divide between the north and the south and the rural and urban areas. While overall unemployment is already high at 36.7 percent, unemployment in rural areas reaches 44.7 percent but is "only" 29 percent in urban areas (NPC, 2008). Accordingly, "only" 17 percent of the urban population is considered poor, compared to 49 percent in rural areas (Schmidt, 2009).

The Government of the Republic of Namibia (GRN) formulates in its Vision 2030 the ambitious national objective of becoming a highly urbanized knowledge society by 2030 (NPC, 2004). However, the majority of Namibians continue to live in rural areas with subsistence-oriented agriculture being the largest source of income and employment, supporting directly or indirectly 70 percent of the population (Mendelsohn, 2006). The agricultural base is considered to be too weak to offer a sustainable basis for long-term prosperity (Namibia has the driest climate in southern Africa with an average of 270 mm rainfall, increasing from south to north from about 100 to 700 mm). Yet, urban development, tourism and mining, major pillars of Namibia's development, do not (yet) provide sufficient jobs, or require skills, which only few rural poor have. Improving rural incomes is therefore indispensable for reducing poverty, at least in the short and medium term.

A key feature of agricultural development in Namibia with important repercussions for value chains is the dual land tenure system. Access to land is divided into "commercial" farmland with freehold tenure south of the former "red line" or veterinary fence (44 percent of the country, see Figure 2), "communal" areas without freehold property north of the line (41 percent), and state land scattered across the country (15 percent) (Odendaal, 2006; SEEN 2008).[2]

Figure 2   Location of Namibia's main bioenergy feedstocks

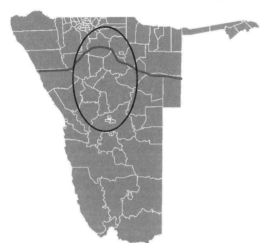

──── Former red line, divides commercial & communal lands

◯ Area with potentials for bush-to energy production

Source: Own design

South of the red line, Namibia has a well-developed, capital-intensive and export-oriented commercial farming sector. Some staple crops (basically maize) as well as horticultural products are produced, often with additional irrigation. However, most of the land is used for extensive livestock and, increasingly, for game rearing and private farm tourism.

In contrast, although half of Namibia's population lives in the communal areas north of the veterinary fence with higher (but still relatively low) rainfalls, the region only contributes 24 percent to the national agricultural production (Mendelsohn, 2006; SEEN 2008). The communal farming sector in the north is dominated by agropastoral subsistence farmers with average cropping plots of 1-4 ha (Mendelsohn, 2006). There is little use of more advanced technology and inputs (fertilizers, irrigation, tractors) and large parts of fields are left fallow because of declining fertility after some years of production (ibid.; Mendelsohn and Obeid,

2007). In the extreme north, rainfall is sufficient for staple food production (mahangu or pearl millet, maize and sorghum), mainly produced for subsistence purposes (Odendaal, 2006). Still, a majority of rural households in communal areas does not meet their basic food needs from subsistence farming, but relies on food purchases for a considerable time of the year (NPC, 2006). Agriculture is not the only and often even not the dominant source of income of rural households (in Kavango for only 42 percent), but also includes wages and salaries, pensions, remittances and nonfarming activities (ibid.).

Namibia imports 50 percent of its domestically consumed food, while temporary food import restrictions (for maize, some vegetables and recently for millet) assure the viability of domestic commercial food production (Mendelsohn, 2006). Although food markets were mentioned to be well developed, reliable and with relatively low price variability, there is food supply stress during sporadic periods of inundation in some northern areas which is tackled by emergency government food supply. Thus, due to domestic production and food imports, food availability does not appear to be a major problem at the national level and the rural north for most of the year. A more pronounced problem is the access to food, which many households in the rural areas lack given their low incomes. A particular situation exists in the commercial farm areas, where markets are underdeveloped due to an extremely low population density and workers have to rely on their employers for accessing food markets.

The underperforming agricultural sector in the north and lack of employment alternatives exacerbate rural poverty and food insecurity (UNDP, 2004; Mendelsohn, 2006; NPC 2008).[3] Many rural poor are therefore migrating to urban and other rural areas, several ten thousands of them to work as laborers on commercial farms south of the veterinary fence (Angula and Sherbourne 2003; Karamata 2006). According to a study by Karamata (2006), less than 40 percent of farmworkers are registered as members of the social security scheme, most lack knowledge of the existence of labor unions, while only half of all farm owners have implemented the official minimum wage regulation.

A major impediment for economic development in the communal areas is the lack of modern energy sources. The Ministry of Mines and Energy (MME) therefore strives to provide all households with access to affordable and appropriate energy supplies, partly through sustainable use of natural resources (Joubert et al., 2009). Attracting investors is seen as one way of reaching this goal. The rural population is so far only little served by the national electricity grid. Only 15 percent of rural population is connected, against 70 percent of the urban population (von Oertzen, 2008). In 2000, a Rural Electrification Master Plan was completed and revised in 2005, which identifies the need for continued development of on-grid and off-grid infrastructure (Interim Bioenergy Committee, 2006).

Debushing for producing energy is a major opportunity closely linked to these energy and agricultural challenges. Severe bush encroachment is referred to as "the invasion and/or thickening of aggressive undesired woody species resulting in an imbalance of the grass-bush ratio, a decrease in biodiversity, and a decrease in carrying capacity" (de Klerk, 2004). Bush encroachment has severely limited the grazing potential for cattle and sheep in the affected areas (affecting almost 50 percent of the commercial ranching areas and an estimated six million ha of communal land) and reduced the carrying capacity from one large stock unit (LSU) per ten ha to one LSU per 20 or 30 ha. 65,000 households in communal areas and 6,283 commercial farmers and their employees are directly affected and the overall economic loss is estimated at more than NAD 700 million per year or about 1 percent of agricultural GDP (ibid.; Hager et al., 2008; SADC, 2006).[4] About 35,000 wage laborers working on commercial livestock farms are affected by bush encroachment (Hager et al., 2008). Reducing bush encroachment is said to positively impact on underground water tables by reducing evapotranspiration of trees (ibid.), which in a drought-prone country like Namibia is important for agriculture and livestock keeping as well as drinking water. Bush encroachment further affects biodiversity negatively and reduces productive land available for redistribution.

The GRN has set the goal of reducing the areas encroached to 22.1 million ha (NPC, 2008; Hager et al., 2008). For various reasons further described below, debushing is not taking place at the intended pace. Under these circumstances, an important motivation for promoting bush-to-energy technologies is to create additional incomes as incentives for farmers to debush, while further contributing to solving the energy problems in Namibia.[5] In an assessment undertaken by the Technical Research Center of Finland, Leinonen (2007) calculates a bush-to-energy potential of 40.8 TWh (Terra Watt hours) per year, which by far exceeds Namibia's total energy need (12.6 TWh in 1999).

Bioenergy value chains in Namibia

A central role in bush-to-energy value chains is played by the farmers involved in harvesting bush and sometimes in the processing as well. It is important to understand that these activities in Namibia are generally pursued by farmers within a multiple goal setting, the general goal usually being to thin out bush-infested areas and not completely remove it (JPC, 2008). Farmers seek at least two out of the following three goals in parallel: Clearing land for creating or increasing livestock carrying capacity, selling the energy, and improving the ecological conditions of the land. Each purpose entails different species and sizes of bushes and trees to cut or leave on the field, different optimal bush densities, different postclearance treatments and, thus, different activities, remuneration schedules and supervision tasks. In general, the following situations can be distinguished:

- Farmers usually opt for not clearing the land completely; they want to have an optimum number of trees for shade and some bushes for fodder (in complementation to grass) and are therefore interested in cutting bushes (rather than trees). In order to achieve permanent effects, care has to be taken to remove most bushes permanently.

- Environmental entrepreneurs (briquette technology is developed by an environmental NGO aiming at recovering the habitat of cheetahs) are also interested in a stable postharvest ecosystem and therefore eradicate bush roots. For more ecological effects of bush harvesting see below.

- Non-farmer commercial entrepreneurs (presently only commercial charcoal producers) who do not own the land and do not have a long-term interest in the land production are not interested in the ecological improvements and grazing capacity of the land they clear, but in the maximum biomass harvest. Sustainability of debushing is therefore not their concern − they are mainly interested in cutting larger trees, which produce a maximum of charcoal with a minimum of effort.

- In contrast, if biomass is to be harvested permanently (for instance for a fixed electricity plant) a commercial entrepreneur will see to it that regrowth of woody vegetation is optimal and will not uproot bushes.

As this closer consideration of basic feedstock producers/harvesters shows, the exact purpose of the bush-to-energy activity in this multigoal setting strongly determines which kind of vegetation is mainly targeted, and whether permanent debushing is aimed at or to the contrary, bush regrowth is opted for. This choice strongly affects production costs and the risk of environmental degradation (and thus necessary environmental regulation and supervision) linked to the bush-to-energy value chains decisively: Bush may be harvested selectively or across all species, may be permanently eradicated or not, and be eradicated by herbicides or uprooted. Herbicides can be applied manually, which is still relatively labor intensive, or alternatively through aerial application which, however, is not a real sustainable option.[6] Without use of herbicides, uprooting bushes is an extremely labor-intensive operation. Charcoal production from invader bush, for instance, needs 4.5 times more labor than when simply clearing land (de Klerk, 2004).

On the other hand, the different goals of debushing mean that the benefits are also multifaceted: In addition to the sale of the energy carrier and/or the energy, it is improved livestock, better wildlife, more ecological stability and, potentially, tourism, and more water availability. These benefits are often assumed to be stronger than the energy.

All bush-to-energy value chains start from the same bush-harvesting considerations, but differ in further processing and marketing (see Figure 3) as examined in the following.

Figure 3   Bush-to-energy value chains in Namibia

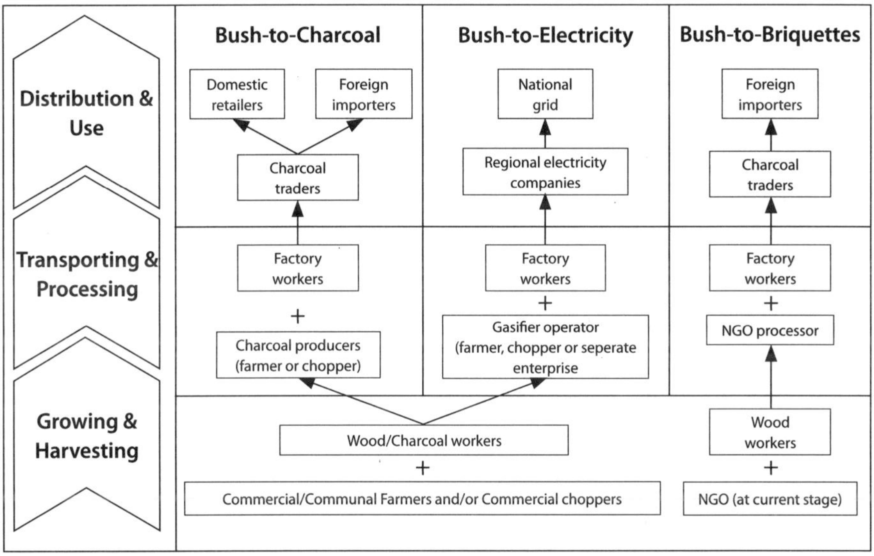

	Bush-to-Charcoal	Bush-to-Electricity	Bush-to-Briquettes
Distribution & Use	Domestic retailers / Foreign importers — Charcoal traders	National grid — Regional electricity companies	Foreign importers — Charcoal traders
Transporting & Processing	Factory workers + Charcoal producers (farmer or chopper)	Factory workers + Gasifier operator (farmer, chopper or seperate enterprise	Factory workers + NGO processor
Growing & Harvesting	Wood/Charcoal workers + Commercial/Communal Farmers and/or Commercial choppers		Wood workers + NGO (at current stage)

Source: Own design

a   The charcoal value chain

As mentioned, only the charcoal value chain is already fully operational and has proven its economic viability under present conditions. In the prevailing charcoal business, farmers or specialized charcoal producers employ teams of mainly male wood- or charcoal workers who manually chop and burn trees and bushes to charcoal in mobile kilns. Small farms employ five to ten woodworkers, while larger charcoal producers use additional land from neighboring farms (mostly against a fee) to employ up to several hundreds of charcoal workers. Some communal farmers are also engaged in charcoal production, either as an income-diversification strategy or as a main source of income. Charcoal is then sold to processors, mainly for export (Europe and South Africa) but also for the domestic market. The market is dominated by one major processor, buying about a quarter of the total production. Many charcoal producers use the Forest Stewardship Council (FSC) standards for most of their production to secure oversees markets. This is not always necessary – for instance, the South African market, where charcoal is mostly used industrially in silicon production, does not require FSC and at times pays very competitive prices. However, as these markets are not stable, maintaining diversified marketing channels is a prudential praxis for which additional certification costs are accepted.

Major market barriers particularly on export markets are the economies of scale. As is often the case in the charcoal industry, small communal farmers have to sell to bigger producers, which adds to transport and transaction costs and reduces profitability. Second, international quality, social and environmental standards seem to hamper market access, not only through official regulations, but also private standards, notably the FSC standards in European charcoal markets. The small producers are extremely difficult to monitor, not only for the forestry administration but also for private standard companies due to logistical reasons (see above), as well as the informality particularly of smaller charcoal producers. Often they do not have a permanent contract or marketing relation with traders. Including small communal charcoal producers in these markets is therefore a major challenge.

Labor and transport costs are main cost components, as well as supervision of charcoal workers. Wages are basically determined through an agreement between the Namibian Charcoal Producers Association and labor unions, which guarantees the laborers 40 percent of the selling price (around NAD 350-400 per ton). Not all producers are bound to this agreement, particularly not smaller informal ones. In addition, recruitment costs and expenditures for housing, water and sanitation in the bush camps have to be borne. Personal working tools are typically handed out as credits and deducted from the remuneration in the first months. Since this practice reduces wages particularly in the early months and because of harsh working conditions (see below), drop out of workers is very high, which increases the recruitment costs. Supervision of workers on the farms is an important nonwage cost, not only for the quality of work (correct uprooting, respect of environmental laws) but also due to problems linked to the presence of many people, mainly young men, in the bush: Commercial farmers often prefer not to employ too many strangers on their land as they fear insecurity and illegal actions, such as poaching, fires and theft.

Transport costs are composed of loading charcoal from the production site to on-farm feeder roads, to the farm or to larger collection points from where they are transported to the processor. Transport costs are strongly determined by location and infrastructure, the latter is much better in Namibian rural areas than in many parts of the continent. In addition, loading and unloading and other handling costs have to be calculated. Further down the value chain, after sorting and packaging, the transport to the south is carried out by trucks that come back empty from the north, so are relatively cheap to hire. Cell phones have eased the searching and communication between sellers and buyers and increasingly allow a direct sale at the road side, without going through a processor – however, this also reduces the vertical integration and, thus, supervision of production conditions.

b   Wood chips and woodgas value chains
New bush-to-energy value chains differ only slightly in debushing activities from charcoal, which can, however, constitute important costs differences. While for charcoal producers smaller bushes and branches are less attractive, for wood chips and woodgas producers this may be different, depending on total product, quality and energy yield. For instance, chippers may not accept larger trunks of wood, the tar content of certain species may be a problem for gasification, or larger combined harvesters (not yet operating in Namibia) may require flat land, relatively uniform vegetation and tree-free rows. Again, it is in combination with other goals that the labor efforts and costs are determined – whether bushes are uprooted, whether this can be done manually or using herbicides, how many trees are to be left on the field, etc. Information on these differentiated labor costs is not yet available.

Large differences between bush-to-energy value chains exist in processing and marketing the final products. Whereas charcoal has the advantage of reducing the weight of the energy carrier at the production site, in the other two cases more bulky products have to be transported. In the case of woodgas, transportation is only possible over a shorter distance to the gasifier, which has to be linked to a (local) electricity network. In the case of woodfuel briquettes only volume is reduced, not weight. However, a low value for weight ratio is the advantage of charcoal, at the expense of energy loss. Modern transport, substitution for barbecue charcoal or wood, and a higher (ethical) value of the briquettes (see below) need to compensate for this disadvantage. Commercial experiences are still few, but it is clear that transport costs can be prohibitive for these new products. This limits the size of a factory or gasifier and therefore handicaps potentials to exert economies of scale.

Factors affecting the value chains' performance

Technology
For charcoal production, adapted technology has been developed, taking into account the level of skills available and specific local conditions. These are easily replicable; the major problem is management of the labor-intensive process, including social conditions. For the other two innovative processes, electricity and woodchip briquettes, the technology is not yet fully developed. They are not high tech and are imported from elsewhere in the world (though not from Africa) but have to be adapted to the local conditions.

Markets and prices of products and by-products

For charcoal, the prices are determined by supply and demand. Namibian charcoal is high though not best quality due to heterogeneity of the trees used. Prices have been remunerative in the last years. European certified markets fetch price premiums, but need larger pieces of charcoal and are only accepted with eco (FSC) certification. In recent years, the South African market (see above) was also competitive, and it is less demanding in terms of size, quality and certification. In addition, charcoal is sold on the local market, where it competes with wood. Often, all markets are served in parallel, with grading done at the level of traders. Over the last years, a ton was sold for NAD 800-1,100 internationally, compared to domestic prices of NAD 850.

The demand and prices for the innovative products electricity and woodchip briquettes are yet not clearly established: Briquettes are marketed under a special NGO conservation label, allowing high prices which may not be achievable for "ordinary" successors. Electricity can be fed into the national grid which, however, is limited to some corridors. This feed-in possibility has been institutionally opened by reorganizing the electricity market, organizationally separating the import and main distribution from retailing, and by allowing (or enforcing the acceptance of) feeding in locally produced electricity. However, prices up to now have not been subsidized, so that local electricity has to compete with low-priced electricity from South Africa. This imported electricity is currently subsidized and not cost-covering, but future prices are expected to increase massively as South Africa now has a homegrown supply problem. South Africa has already started to guarantee higher feed-in prices for electricity from renewable sources; for Namibia this is debated.

In bush-to-energy value chains, additional revenue is generated through the marketing of by-products. Meat is the most important by-product (or main product, according to the main motivation of debushing). The value is partially determined by the amount of cattle and/or financial resources and credit available to buy and raise more animals. Farmers with limited credit access have less utility from the cleared land since existing herds can only slowly be stocked up. This is particularly relevant for the newly established black farmers under the land-redistribution schemes, who often start as first-time farmers with limited financial resources and no appropriate social networks to park other farmers' herds on their (improved) lands.

An additional source of income for some bioenergy value chains might be the sale of carbon certificates, for instance via the Clean Development Mechanism (CDM) or voluntary carbon markets for substituting fossil fuels through renewable ones (e.g. coal through charcoal, electricity produced from coal or oil through renewably produced). Before this source of income can be tapped, important hurdles have to be overcome. Although Namibia was one of the first countries in SSA to establish a national authority for certifying CDM projects, a precondition for having access to the carbon market, hardly any projects are yet accredited. The carbon market potentials are not well known or understood and existing schemes are not well adapted to the special situations in Namibia. Especially for bush it is not certain whether carbon credits can be acquired since debushing destroys a carbon sink, though it is not considered as a natural forest but degraded, desertified land.

Labor

The major challenge for bush-to-energy value chains are future developments of the labor-market regulation. Unions recently demanded a remuneration of NAD 700 per ton of charcoal for workers, thus only slightly higher than the sales price which would make production unprofitable.

An even more fundamental risk seen by commercial farmers is the position of the Ministry of Labor (MoL) towards self-contracting. The MoL requires that woodworkers need to be treated as farmworkers under the Labor Act No. 11 of 2007 (GRN, 2007). The act provides for enhanced protection and rights of employees, which concern, among others, social security regulations, the prohibition of labor hire companies[7], food shops, accommodation (provision of adequate accommodation if the worker lives on farmer's land, also for dependants), minimum remuneration, working hours, leave, termination of employment and health and safety. Bush-to-energy producers insist on more flexible contract choices to take into account the differences between farm and bush-harvesting work and business models, for instance that bush workers are rarely permanent and do not live in fixed settlements. This also includes the demand to pay by output (not fixed salaries) which would provide more incentives to employ woodworkers given the difficulties of labor supervision. Farmers criticized that political negotiators and farmworker unions do not have sufficient knowledge of the charcoal-business realities.

In addition, for a small scale communal farmer and small debushing enterprise it will be even more difficult to abide by labor legislation than it would be for a large commercial farmer or an investor. Informal labor often results from the economic need to by-pass strict labor regulations (not excluding the fact that this also happens arbitrarily). As is often the case in rural labor arrangements between small farmers, informal employment is a coping strategy for both the employer and the employee. In Namibia's communal areas, family or community members are often employed on a casual basis to help with agricultural work (weeding, plowing) on small and medium-size farms. It is most likely that these employers would not have the financial and administrative capacity to comply with labor regulations.

Land rights

Land is an extremely sensitive issue in Namibia, not the least due to the Apartheid legacy, which current land reform efforts try to address (e.g. Mendelsohn, 2008; LAC, 2005; Fuller, 2006; Werner, 2003). Land tenure issues impact on a bioenergy project's viability in different ways: Insecure land rights prevent investors from taking longer-term investment decisions, inhibit access to credit, and also challenge good environmental practice.

In commercial areas, existing commercial farmers are uncertain about which farms might be expropriated by the MoL. The reason is that areas earmarked for resettlement are not clearly defined due to recurrent political debate as to how to accelerate land redistribution. This uncertainty reduces farm prices and incentives for freehold farmers to invest in their land.

On the other hand, newly resettled farmers lack access to capital or experience to correctly use the credits offered to many of them through the government loan schemes. Previous, more generous credit schemes to resettlement farmers did not yield good results, and jeopardized the viability of the governmental agricultural-development finance arm, Agribank. This led to increased conditionality and made conditions for new credits more restrictive. In consequence, fewer farmers in communal and commercial areas are willing or able to allocate resources for clearing their land in a sustainable way. The lack of debushing threaten the success of the land reform as a whole as it leaves less farmland available for redistribution, requires more land to be redistributed per family to have viable farm sizes, and reduces profitability per area of land.

As long as permits are handed out smoothly and corruption does not take place, environmental regulation is not a handicap for bush-to-energy value chains. Whether this is always true is doubtful, however (see below). In communal areas, farmers additionally face the "problem of the commons" (Hardin, 1967). Most farmers graze their cattle on land they have no exclusive rights to and from the use of which they cannot exclude others by putting up fences. Thus, communal farmers not only lack capital for investment in debushing or fencing, but can neither be sure to benefit from their efforts fully and have few incentives to manage the areas in a sustainable manner. On the other hand, bush harvesters such as charcoal enterprises get their concessions from traditional chiefs and communities but have no incentive to stick to good environmental practices, which reduces the quality of the pastures and thus the willingness to provide concessions.

Environment

Since debushing is environmentally friendly in theory, environmental regulations do not restrict it but only try to avoid negative effects of excessive clearing. The law restricts total bush clearing and requires certain species to be protected, which is basically in line with farmers' interests, though not necessarily with those of private enterprises (see above). In addition, Namibia's Forestry Act requires a permit for debushing land when exceeding 15 ha. Thus, as long as permits are handed out smoothly and corruption does not take place, environmental regulation is not a handicap for bush-to-energy value chains, except that it can reduce the profitability of charcoal production.

Table 1 summarizes the factors affecting the viability of bush-to-energy value chains in Namibia.

Table 1   Main challenges for bush-to-energy value chain viability

Dimensions	*Main challenges for different value chains*		
	Bush-to-charcoal	Bush-to-pellets	Bush-to-woodgas
Output Markets	Instability of prices Problem of economies of scale (esp. when serving stable niche markets like FSC) (Market barriers)		Feed-in tariff regulation unclear
Labor	Woodworkers are in a gray area. No clear regulations exist Negotiations between government, farmers and unions are stalled Objections of farmers to employ strangers on their land		
Land	Insecurity about land reform process "Problem of the commons" in communal areas		
Capital	Indebtedness and cash-flow problems of commercial farmers Access to credit in communal areas		
Other Options	Application of herbicides is faster (but more expensive and not sustainable) Development of land prices		
Knowledge and Skills	Insufficient knowledge transfer for communal and black emerging farmers Lack of management skills		Insufficient knowledge and skills for operating power plant

Factors affecting the value chains' development impacts

Income and poverty

As bush-to-energy value chains are labor intensive under current technologies, it is expected that the additional income for woodworkers contributes to poverty alleviation (e.g. Hager et al., 2009). On average, according to commercial farmers, a worker can produce between two and four tons of charcoal per month, which results in an earning of NAD 700-1400 per month, clearly above minimum salaries. Earnings by woodworkers might also affect poverty in the sending regions through remittances. Karamata (2006) found, for example, that farmworkers sent 22 percent of their wages home. Group interviews with woodworkers, though not representative, have confirmed this pattern. However, performance varies considerably among workers. For this and other reasons (e.g. working conditions), many beginners drop out early. Small-scale communal farmers might directly earn income from selling bush or charcoal.

Regaining rangeland for livestock production could secure employment and income of farmworkers and lead to more employment in processing and distribution. This would arguably be the most important indirect poverty effect of bush-to-energy value chains outside the chain.

Risks for wood- and farmworkers arise from wage insecurities, side conditions and high dependency on the employing farmer as sole provider of cash income, food and other goods. Informal and mostly seasonal arrangements do not provide workers with continuous cash income.

More mechanized bush-harvesting techniques are discussed, which would increase demand for skilled labor, enhance labor productivity, payments and working conditions, but would reduce demand for unskilled labor. The consequences for the extremely poor could be severe as they lack income alternatives. The main impediment for the implementation of these techniques seems to be lack of skilled manpower.

Food security

The additional income rural households would gain through working in the bush-to-energy value chain could enhance food security given the high expenditure shares of households for food items (NPC, 2006; Karamata, 2006). Under the extreme conditions of woodworker (very remote sites), food security is also determined by in-kind payments to which farmers are obliged under the Labor Act. However, workers often become indebted from borrowing at farmers' shops. Prices were said to be higher than at markets due to transport costs – profit-making objectives of the farmers and a strong dependency situation may add to that.

Other social and economic effects

Higher incomes might lead to other positive socioeconomic effects in terms of spending on health and education, while the harsh working conditions without proper use of protective clothing and little control by the labor inspectorates expose workers to health risks. Formal labor arrangements would provide workers with benefits from Namibia's social security system. While debushing and charcoal production likely create more male than female jobs, this is not necessarily the case for processing jobs.

In the case of woodgas production, local cheap electricity would be an important indirect effect. Rural electrification is a key element of rural development with a wide variety of benefits (SADC, 2006; UNDP/GEF/MME, 2007; World Bank, 2009a).

Environment
In contrast to the negative environmental effects attached to large-scale crop investments for liquid biofuels, well-managed debushing creates substantial positive environmental impacts (see above). Debushing permits issued by the Department of Forestry (DoF) only regulate protection of endangered species while more extensive sustainable harvesting is only ensured in FSC production. In any case, effective control of regulation may not always be warranted, even though in Namibia the rule of the law is certainly better implemented than in most other SSA countries. Thus, there is a certain risk for the environment from lack of implementation of regulations and standards. Effects on GHG emissions are yet unclear: Harvesting invader bush immediately releases carbon but reduces emissions if replacing fossil fuel use elsewhere.

Figure 4 summarizes the major effects of bush-to-energy on rural development and food security. It is worth noting that these very different effects are not quantified, some are indeed very difficult to quantify.

Figure 4   Summary of effects of bush-to-energy value chains on rural development and food security

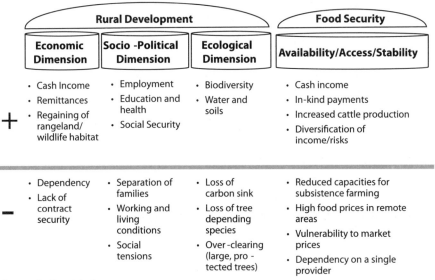

Source: Authors' design

Policy analysis and conclusions

The previous section has identified several positive effects of bush-to-energy value chains for enhancing rural development, without hampering food security and environmental sustainability in Namibia, even suggesting that this will be enhanced, too. However, some risks concerning labor and living conditions of woodworkers in remote debushing camps and risks of excessive vegetation clearing were also identified. Environmental risks are particularly real for communal areas.

Economic viability of the value chain is a key precondition for bioenergy production to contribute to domestic development policies. Viability is currently only proven for the case of charcoal value chains, while viability of woodchip (particularly at large-scale) and woodgas production is not yet guaranteed. But even expansion of charcoal production faces several obstacles as discussed above (land insecurity, labor legislation, social challenges, etc.).

Reconciling these different objectives concerning profitability on the one hand and social inclusiveness and sustainable rural development on the other, is particularly difficult for the case of bush-based value chains that need to integrate several policy areas. Various actors and institutions are involved in the governance of the value chains and in shaping the framework conditions. Figure 5 lists all the policies, from general frameworks to sector policies that provide the overall context to the government and nongovernment stakeholders in the bush-to-energy value chains. The sheer number of policies and actors makes it clear that policy coordination is a complicated task. It partially explains why these value chains have difficulties to emerge in African countries where it already is problematic to implement individual sector policies, let alone intersectoral ones. In addition, the analysis of risks and impacts has shown that the interests and targets of stakeholders are often not identical, sometimes conflicting.

At the level of value chain actors, there is no clear champion who would be expected to push for (policy or other) support. Many farmers are less eager in restoring land fertility and carrying capacity by the looming land reform. Charcoal producers have a small association, but they are more concerned with managing their businesses, not enhancing policies, the exception being appropriate labor rules which is a rather defensive struggle. New value chains are at an experimental stage and have not yet created large commercial interests. In contrast, the electricity market faces resistance from large monopoly suppliers, and the briquette market is championed by an environmental NGO which is not the kind of actor who could push for policy coordination needed beyond the environmental sphere. The many different uses of bush, without any being

Figure 5   Policies and stakeholders influencing bush-to-energy value chains in Namibia

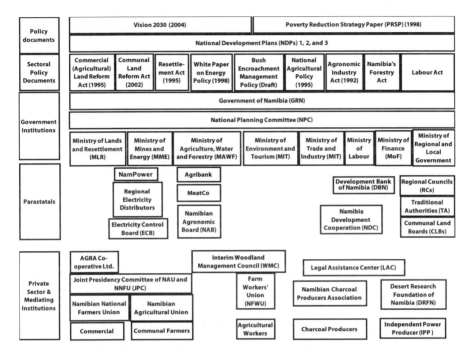

Source: Own design

very remunerative in itself (but only in conjunction with livestock and environmental benefits) makes joint initiatives of all actors for specific political claims unlikely.

At the policy and government level, concerns of the environmental ministry to preserve the natural habitat usually conflict at least partially with interests of the ministries responsible for agricultural and industrial development and in this case also energy development. A problem concerning bush-to-energy production is that no institution in Namibia yet governs the bio-energy sector. Many Ministries need to play an active role, though it is not completely clear who takes the lead and has the final say in this field. An interim Woodland Management Council was established as a mediating body but merely functions as an advisory council and has been inactive for most of its time. Taking charge of debushing control would ideally be within its mandate.

Since no mediator exists to facilitate communication between different stakeholders and to overcome conflicts of interest, procedures at policy level are slow or stuck. Most likely due to the above "power vacuum", no bioenergy policy exists in Namibia which would attribute an important place to the bush-to-energy production. Though provisions for renewable energy development are made in Nampower's (the parastatal utility company) internal strategy papers, in MME's Rural Electrification Masterplan 2000/2005 and in the Energy Policy White Paper (1998), no national policy exists, only a commitment. To enhance overall policy coordination, development of a National Renewable Energy Policy as well as a lead ministry would be useful, guiding and feeling responsible for implementing the policy.

Apart from the general need for coordination between different institutions and organizations in an intersectoral policy field such as bioenergy, coherent policies, i.e. food security, rural development, agricultural development, land, labor, environment and energy, and their implementation are indispensable for the emergence of a larger bush-to-energy subsector. Some specific issues are indicated below.

Labor policies are central to the viability as well as the poverty and food-security impact of bush-to-energy value chains. They should take due account of the particularities of the rural economies (seasonality, piecework wage, remoteness, internal and transboundary migration) and carefully balance employment opportunities, job qualities and production costs. Communication channels should be improved between the actors, particularly with regards to the informal bush workers in order to make their concerns heard when formulating labor policies. The Woodland Management Council should therefore be strengthened, as well as other actors such as woodworker unions, and the labor law adapted to the realities of the bush sub-sector. A strategic plan for long-term employment goals in the bioenergy sector could include providing skills for workers to access possible "new" and higher qualified jobs.

Concerning land-tenure issues, the disadvantages (lack of access to credit, lack of control/management of the commonages) and advantages (safety net for the poor, continuation of traditional leadership) of communal land rights for the rural poor need to be openly discussed and communal land laws eventually further developed. This is clearly easier in Namibia than in other SSA countries. Tenure security for existing and resettlement farmers should be enhanced to attract investments. Possible other linkages between bush-to-energy and land policy should be highlighted and, if feasible, combined in strategies (e.g. debushing and land distribution or credit and technical support).

Independent research on environmental issues of bioenergy value chains such as carbon capture, water and biodiversity must be enhanced. This knowledge has to be systematically spread as a decision support for political decision makers, the public, farmers and investors. Integrated land and water use planning must take due account of environmental impacts. Forestry and environmental authorities must be strengthened to implement and enforce regulations as well as to provide permits and authorization.

Some bioenergy forms may need special attention in terms of output markets, for instance in the form of feed-in tariffs for electricity. However, it is clear that a developing country should be very restrictive with subsidies and instead prefer support to investment, for instance through support to research coordination and to Public-Private Partnerships, support to standard setting for bioenergy products, contact facilitation or legal and contract assistance. If subsidies are given, they should be smart, for instance declining over time, differentiating according to scale of operation, or including contributions from the use of nonrenewable energy.

Notes

1   As defined in this paper, bioenergy is the final product derived from biomass whereas biofuel is the energy carrier. Adopting the FAO definition, biofuel also includes biogas and solid materials (such as fuelwood, charcoal or wood pellets) (FAO 2008). It should be mentioned that biomass in general contributes 77% to the total renewable energy use worldwide, mostly in its traditional forms, notably firewood. Biomass provides 22% of the energy consumption in developing countries, and up to 90% in some poor countries of SSA (Fritsche et al., 2009).

2   The dualism of communal and commercial land tenure dates back to the first land policy for the territory implemented by the German Colonial Authority in 1892 through fencing off white-owned, commercial lands in the cattle pest-free southern zone from the pest-burdened black-owned communal lands north of it. For a long time, this line also demarcated the area of free settlement for black people.

3   An alternative land-use activity in Namibia is tourism, the third largest foreign exchange earner of the country. Enhancing rural incomes from tourism and enabling communities to benefit from natural resources in a sustainable manner have been major governmental motives for creating conservancies (common wildlife protection areas) and community forests (Mendelsohn 2006).

4   EUR 1 was between NAD 10 and NAD 12 in 2009.

5   The electricity market is regulated by the Electricity Control Board (ECB). The government-owned generation and transmission utility NamPower provides electricity and manages the network at a national level. Regional Electricity Distributors (RED) buy electricity from Nampower and distribute it to the final consumers.

6   With aerial debushing by herbicides, an exact control of bush density and respect of environmental regulations for protected species and trees is not possible. Often, dead bush is left rotting in the field – setting it on fire after drying bears important risks for bush fires. Thus, it is not really a sound alternative, but it is practiced and even supported by government – a sign that the pressure to act against bush encroaching is strong.

7   Section 128 of the Labor Act (prohibition of labor hire companies) was legally challenged during the field survey by commercial farmers with a Supreme Court decision still pending.

Bibliography

Altenburg, T. (2006). 'Governance patterns in value chains and their development impact'. In: *The European Journal of Development Research* 18 (4), pp.
498-521.

Altenburg, T. (2007). *Donor approaches to supporting pro-poor value chains*. Report prepared for the Donor Committee for Enterprise Development Working Group on Linkages and Value Chains.

Angula, M. and R. Sherbourne (2003). *Agricultural employment in Namibia: Not
the engine of wage employment growth*. IPPR Briefing Paper No. 16.

Bolwig, S., S. Ponte, A. du Toit, L. Riisgaard and L. Halberg (2010). 'Integrating
poverty and environmental concerns into value-chain analysis: A conceptual
framework'. In: *Development Policy Review* 28 (2), pp. 173-194.

CCF (Cheetah Conservation Fund) (2009). *Bushblok fuel logs help the cheetah's
cause*. Available from: www.cheetah.org/?nd=ccf_bush_projec> (Accessed 11
May 2011).

Corbin, J., and A. Strauss (1990). 'Grounded theory research: Procedures, canons,
and evaluative criteria'. In: *Qualitative Sociology* 13, pp. 3-21.

Cotula, L., N. Dyer, and S. Vermeulen (2008). *Fuelling exclusion? The biofuels
boom and poor people's access to land*. London: IIED.

Da Silva, C. A. and H. M. de Souza Filho (2007). *Guidelines for rapid appraisals
of agrifood chain performance in developing countries, agricultural management,
marketing and finance*, occasional paper 20. Rome: FAO.

De Klerk, J.N. (2004). *Bush encroachment. Report on Phase 1 of the bush encroachment research, monitoring and management project, Ministry of Environment and
Tourism*. Available from: www.met.gov.na/programmes/napcod/encroach-
ment.htm.

DRFN (Desert Research Foundation of Namibia) (2009). *CBEND-Bush to Electricity – Combating bush encroachment for Namibia's development*. Available
from: www.drfn.org.na/htm/energy_desk/energy_cbend_bush_to_electric-
ity.htm (Accessed on 1 March 2010).

Eaton, D. and M. Meijerink (2007). *Markets, institutional change and the new
agenda for agriculture, Markets, Chains and Sustainable Development*, Strategy
& Policy Paper, No. 4. Wageningen: Stichting DLO.

FAO (Food and Agriculture Organisation) (2008). *The state of food and agriculture 2008*. Rome: FAO.

FAO (2009). *Declaration of the world summit on food security*, Rome, 16-18 November 2009. Rome: FAO.

Fritsche, U.R., B. Kampmann and G. Bergsma (2009). *Better use of biomass for
energy, position paper of IEA REDT and IEA Bioenergy*. Available from: www.

iea-retd.org/files/IEA_RETD_BIOENERGY_position_paper091215.pdf (Accessed on 11 May 2011).

Fuller, B. (2006). *Improving tenure security for the rural poor: Namibia – a country case study.* Rome: FAO.

Gereffi, G., J. Humphrey and T. Sturgeon (2005). 'The governance of global value chains'. In: *Review of International Political Economy* 12 (1), pp. 78-104.

GRN (Government of the Republic of Namibia) (2007). *Labor Act No. 11 of 2007.* Windhoek: GRN.

Hager, C., R. Schultz and D. von Oertzen (2008). *Turning Namibian invader bush into electricity: The CBEND Project. 12th Congress of the Agricultural Scientific Society of Namibia, Neudamm, Namibia, 3-4 July 2007.* Windhoek: DRFN.

Hardin, G. (1968). 'The tragedy of the commons'. In: *Science* 162 (3859), pp. 1243-1248.

Joint Presidency Committee (2008). *Rangeland management.* Windhoek: JPC.

Joubert, D., I. Zimmermann and P. Graz (2009). A decision support system for bush encroachment by Acacia Mellifera in the Highland Savanna, Report, Windhoek: Polytec of Namibia.

Kaplinsky, R. (2001). *Spreading the Gains from Globalisation: What Can be Learned from Value Chain Analysis?*, Working Paper 110. Brighton: IDS.

Kaplinsky, R. and M. Morris (2001). *A handbook for* value chain research. IDRC. Available from www.globalvaluechains.org/docs/VchNov01.pdf (Accessed on 1 March 2010).

Karamata, C. (2006). *Farm workers in Namibia: Living and working conditions.* Windhoek: Labour Resource and Research Institute (LaRRI).

LAC (Legal Assistance Centre) (2005). *Customary laws on inheritance in Namibia: Issues and questions for consideration in developing new legislation.* Windhoek: LAC.

Leinonen, A. (2007). *Woodchips production technology and costs for fuel in Namibia.* Available from: www.vtt.fi/publications/index.jsp (Accessed on 11 May 2011).

Mendelsohn, J. (2006). *Farming systems in Namibia.* Windhoek: NNFU (Namibia National Farmers Union).

Mendelsohn, J. (2008). *Customary and legislative aspects of land registration and manage-ment on communal land in Namibia.* Windhoek: Ministry of Lands and Resettlement / Rural Poverty Reduction Programme.

Mendelsohn, J. and S. Obeid (2007). *Kavango biofuel project environmental impact assessment: Specialist component report on socio-economic impacts.* Windhoek: RAISON for Colin Christian and Associates.

Mitchell (2008) *A note on rising food prices.* Policy Research Working Paper 4682. The World Bank.

NPC (National Planning Commission) (2004). *Vision 2030: Policy framework for long-term national development.* Windhoek: NPC.

NPC (2006). *2003/2004 National household income and expenditure survey (NHIES).* Windhoek: NPC.

NPC (2008). *Third National Development Plan (NDP3) 2007/2008-2011/2012 Vol. I.* Windhoek: NPC.

Odendaal, W. (2006). *The SADC land and agrarian reform initiative. The case of Namibia,* Namibia Economic Policy Research Unit (NEPRU) working paper No. 111. Windhoek: NEPRU.

Rosendahl, C. (2010). *Industrial Policy in Namibia.* DIE Discussion Paper 5/2010. Bonn.

SADC (Southern African Development Community) (2006). 'Invader bush for energy generation'. In: *SADC Today* 9 (2), p. 10.

Schmidt, M. (2009). *Poverty and inequality in Namibia: An overview,* briefing paper. Windhoek: Institute for Public Policy Research (IPPR).

SEEN (Supporting Environmental Education in Namibia) (2008). 'Namibia's land issue', SEEN environmental learning information sheet No. 5.

UNDP (United Nations Development Programme) (2004). *Common country assessment Namibia.* Government of Namibia and United Nations System in Namibia.

UNDP/GEF/MME (United Nations Development Programme / Global Environment Facility / Ministry of Mines and Energy) (2007). *Off-grid energisation master plan for Namibia.* Windhoek: UNDP/GEF/MME Barrier Removal to Namibian Renewable Energy Programme (NAMREP).

Von Oertzen, D. (2008) *Namibian national issues report on the key sector of energy with a focus on mitigation.* For: UNDP Environment & Energy Group. Available from www.undp.org/climatechange/docs/Namibia/Namibian%20 national%20issues%20report%20on%20key%20sector%20of%20energy.pdf (Accessed on 11 May 2011).

Vosti, S.A. and T. Reardon (1997). *Sustainability, growth, and poverty alleviation: a policy and agroecological perspective.* Baltimore: Johns Hopkins University Press.

WBGU (Wissenschaftlicher Beirat der Bundesregierung für Globale Umweltveränderungen) (2008). *Welt im Wandel: Zukunftsfähige Bioenergie und nachhaltige Landnutzung.* Berlin: WBGU.

Werner, W. (2003). *Synopsis: Land reform in Namibia.* Windhoek: GTZ.

Williamson, O. (2000). 'The new institutional economics: Taking stock, looking Ahead'. In: *Journal of Economic Literature* 38, pp. 595-613.

World Bank (2007). *Agriculture for development – World Development Report 2008.* Washington: World Bank.

World Bank (2009a). *Africa energy poverty. G8 energy ministers meeting 2009, May 24-25*. Rome. Washington: World Bank.

World Bank (2009b). *Namibia country brief*. Available from: http://web.worldbank.org (Accessed on 12 May 2011).

Part III

International Agricultural Value Chains

6 Localizing Global Standards

Illustrative Examples from Kenya's Horticulture Sector

Gloria Otieno and Peter Knorringa

Introduction

Farmers in developing countries increasingly need to comply with a bewildering array of standards and codes of conduct in order to be able to export. These standards encompass a wide range of quality, health, environmental and ethical concerns, implemented either as mandatory public standards or as voluntary private standards. Standards diverge in terms of compliance requirements and certification practices, and especially private voluntary standards frequently change over time. Until recently, standard setting and certification were primarily seen as technocratic processes to ensure more quality-conscious and sustainable production processes. However, standard setting and certification processes are also an important governance mechanism in the sourcing strategies of lead firms. There is an increasing concern that so-called global standards, developed explicitly and implicitly along Northern priorities and ways of thinking, fail to incorporate Southern stakeholders' views (Tallontire, 2007; Blowfield and Dolan, 2008; Riisgard, 2008). Standards are seen as formulated without consideration of the prevailing conditions in developing countries, creating a situation in which producers do not really understand and cannot internalize these standards. Standards can then become just another Northern tool that Southern producers need to implement in order to ensure (continued) market access, instead of becoming a tool that may offer substantial developmental benefits.

This chapter investigates the potential for adapting global standards to national circumstances in horticulture (cut flowers and fresh fruits and vegetables) value chains in Kenya. First, Section 2 will outline our conceptual framework, explaining the contested role of standards in development processes. Next, Section 3 introduces the Kenyan horticulture industry, after which Section 4 presents data on how different certification mechanisms can at least partly avoid a major potential disadvantage of standardization: the exclusion of smaller producers.

Section 5 presents two recent attempts at localizing global standards, on involving a mandatory public standard and one voluntary private standard. The final section presents our conclusions.

Global standards and localized development

This section briefly outlines our conceptual framework. Within development studies, two opposite perspectives exist on the developmental relevance of standards. The first focuses on the exclusionary effects of standards, stressing that many developing countries simply lack the administrative, technical and scientific capacities to comply with emerging requirements, presenting potentially insurmountable barriers to trade in the short or medium term. Moreover, given the significant fixed up-front costs of initial certification, especially smaller independent indigenous firms will be excluded from the more attractive higher end international markets in which a variety of certifications increasingly become a sine qua non.

An alternative view emphasizes the potential opportunities provided by the mainstreaming of standards and the likelihood that certain developing countries can utilize such opportunities to their competitive advantage. From this perspective, many of the emerging public and private standards are viewed as a necessary bridge between increasingly demanding consumer requirements and the participation of distant (and international) suppliers. Many of these standards therefore provide a common language within the supply chain and promote the confidence for consumers in product safety and quality.

Moving beyond this dichotomy, and accepting that standards will be an increasingly important phenomena in international trade, this chapter aims to look at ways in which one might enhance the potential opportunities offered through standardization, while lessening its potential drawbacks. We posit that it makes sense from a developmental perspective to strengthen the localization[1] and harmonization of standards and of certification procedures at the national, local, and sectoral level. The argument behind localization is that it reduces the costs of compliance and testing as countries achieve some forms of "equivalence"; it may also have "spillover" effects to the local economy as technology and quality are achieved leading to new forms of competitive advantage which may provide a basis for a more sustainable trade in the long term.

Standards facilitate comparisons by consumers across products with common essential characteristics (Maskus and Wilson, 2000). Standards – particularly those that require independent certification – intrinsically fulfill many of the broader requirements for producers to participate in global supply chains or compete in high-value products. For example, detailed record keeping of production inputs, traceability, and third-party monitoring are also useful to improve chain management and competitiveness (Kaplinsky, 2006). When products and processes become more standardized, transparency increases and trade becomes more predictable and easy to control, thus reducing costs involved in transactions (Kaplinsky, 2006; Tander and Tilburg 2007; Busch, 2000). Standards also have technologically and innovative features embedded in them and hence the process of complying to standards lies in the transfer of advanced production capabilities to low-wage economies who in turn gain by acquiring knowledge through spillovers and "learning by doing" (Grossman and Helpman, 1989).

On the other hand however, with emerging and increasingly demanding health and safety standards over and above the governmental standards imposed by the EU, private sectors are imposing additional standards in order to protect their safety reputation and also to differentiate themselves from competitors. Buyers have also imposed many requirements informally through individual supply chains (Jaffe and Henson, 2004). Some Authors (Wilson, 2001; Wilson and Abiola 2003) have also pointed out that countries use regulation for protectionist purposes. Technical regulations may discriminate against foreign suppliers, both in their construction and in their outcomes. They may be used to gain strategic trade advantages for domestic firms over foreign competitors. Standards are often nontransparent and in some cases needlessly force firms to duplicate testing and certification costs.

In the following sections we will explore some illustrative examples related to localizing global standards in Kenyan horticulture. But first, the next section introduces the horticulture sector.

The horticulture sector in Kenya

Since 1995, production is increasing year by year in the vibrant Kenyan horticulture sector, both in exports and in the domestic market. In 2007 the production for domestic consumption stood at 1.4 million metric tons worth USD 1.1 billion. The export market experienced a 14 percent growth in 2008 to a total of USD 1.09 billion. Horticulture is currently Kenya's largest foreign exchange earner. The EU is the main market for Kenya's horticultural exports with 90 percent of all exports. Furthermore, flowers constitute about 54 percent of horticultural exports while fruits and vegetables constitute about 46 percent. There are about 1.5 million small-scale horticulture producers that produce about 70 percent of the fruits and vegetables for export and 10 percent of the flowers for export (FPEAK, 2009). Overall, the sector is extremely important for socioeconomic development in the country, since about 5 million people depend directly and indirectly on horticulture for their livelihoods.

This chapter is based on fieldwork data collection consisting of a survey of the horticulture sector carried out between February and October 2009. It covered five main regions and mostly consisted of small and medium-scale farmers including both flower and fruits and vegetable exporters. The total number surveyed included 210 respondents including farmers, middlemen and exporters. Furthermore, eighteen key informants from institutions involved in the processes of standardization also provided insights into the subject.

Figure 1   Kenyan horticultural value and standards chain

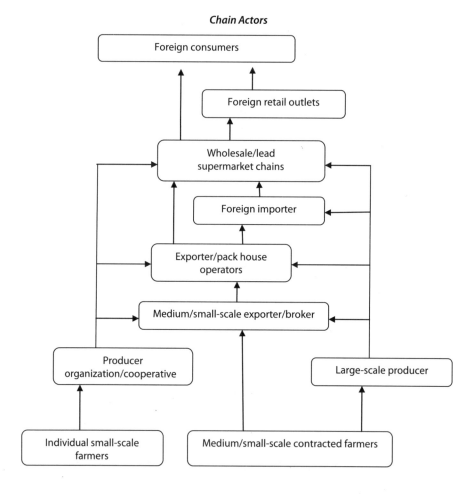

The export chain of the horticulture sector mainly consists of small and medium-scale farmers[2] at the lower end of the chain who either export directly or belong to producer groups. These farmers and their respective producer groups are contracted by exporters and other large-scale producers[3] who are exporting to large retailers in the EU or in the case of flowers, to the flower auction in the Netherlands. Exporters mainly supply seeds, equipment and financial loans for the compliance to standards; they also play an integral role in training on standards to the farmers who in turn sell their raw products to exporters. Recent developments since 2004 have seen many chain activities carried out downstream of the value chain such as sorting and grading and in some cases packing and labeling. The domestic chain on the other hand consists of middlemen also known as brokers buying from small and medium-scale producers for sale either in local supermarkets or to registered exporters (fig 1).

From the survey it emerged that producers accessing developed country markets have to conform to multiple standards ranging from mandatory – i.e. government to government – and voluntary standards which are not legally mandated but are nevertheless extremely important in order to access certain markets. Some of these voluntary standards are more generic and required by lead firms or retailers as a necessary condition for accepting orders; others are important and integral components of certain niche markets that have higher price premiums for complying producers. Table 1 below shows an overview of standards or codes of conduct to which exporters in the survey need to comply,

Table 1   Summary of compliance requirements and legal status for standards for exporters in Kenya

Compliance requirement	Legally mandated		Not legally mandated	
	Strict enforcement	Spot/sample enforcement	Required for commercial purposes	Not required but beneficial
Phytosanitary Certificate	√			
MRL Tolerances		√		
HACCP				√
Traceability			√	
GAP/Environmental				√
Social Welfare				√
Packaging Specificity			√	
Product Conformity			√	

Source: Survey data, 2009

depending on specific buyers and particular orders. While not all exporters need to comply all the time with all of the compliance criteria mentioned in this summary table, interviews made clear that most exporters need to comply with a majority of the relevant standards. In the day-to-day practice the actual detailed criteria and monitoring mechanisms of these various standards show a significant overlap in terms of intent and content, but a wide variation in terms of specific procedures. Therefore, they involve a significant amount of administrative burden, which some larger exporters obviously can handle more easily as compared to small-scale producers.

Therefore, a finding from our survey is that most of the mandatory standards are actually met at exporter level and not at the level of individual small-scale producers. In effect, we observe a hierarchy of requirements, only some of which are met at the level of large-scale exporters delivering directly to major retailers. While exporters have to obtain phytosanitary certificates and are mandated to meet MRLs, farmers are only mandated to meet GAP, traceability and social-welfare standards. Other standards such as product specificity and product conformity are predominantly met again at the exporter level, unless packaging takes place at farm level as was observed in some cases of passion-fruit packing in the Mwea/Kimbimbi area. Table 2 shows how exporters are taking responsibility for all certification requirements, while other farmers deal with only some of the requirements. Exporters try to develop their monitoring systems in a way that most of the actual compliance activities are undertaken at lower levels in the chain, while the exporters maintain overall responsibility and control.

Table 2   Compliance exporters vs. Farmers in the horticulture industry in Kenya

Compliance requirement	Exporters	Farmers including small-scale
Phytosanitary Certificate	All	N/A
MRL Tolerances	All	N/A
HACCP	All	N/A
Traceability	All	All through exporters
GAP/Environmental	All	77%
Social welfare	All	41%
Packaging specificity	All	4%
Product conformity	All	4%

Source: Survey data, 2009

Standards are used by retailers as a means of governing these chains by codifying the knowledge required to meet quality specifications (Riisgard, 2008). In turn, exporters use these standards to govern the behavior of small and medium-scale farmers that supply them with produce. In short, exporters bear the responsibility of ensuring that their products meet required standards and hence their contracted producers have to follow suit. Small and medium-scale producers therefore not only have to understand these standards, but they also have to adjust them to their local conditions; a process which may at times be demanding in terms of training, financial implications and may even act as entry barriers for smaller producers. The potentially exclusionary implications of standards also are becoming an increasingly important point of concern for development NGOs (see for example, Van Beuningen and Knorringa, 2009). Standards continue to be formulated and perceived from a "Northern" logic, which often makes it difficult for farmers to adopt and internalize specific procedures. Instead, well-intentioned standards, to protect the environment or enhance social welfare, remain alien instruments seen by farmers as instruments through which foreign buyers and major exporters exercise hierarchical control. More concretely, many of the procedures and indicators of such global standards are not suited to local conditions. Nevertheless, they are prerequisite requirements for certain markets.

At the same time, standards have positive spillover effects into the domestic market, for instance good agricultural practices are bringing improvements for producers and for the environment (Cooper and Graffham, 2009). Furthermore, standards tend to increase chain efficiency and reduce costs of transactions between different actors in the chain, thereby improving overall chain management (Tander and Van Tilburg, 2007). Wider subsequent impacts are also related to the transfer of knowledge and technology; improvement of infrastructure investments and capacity building (Cooper and Graffham, 2009).

Our survey shows that exporters also are increasingly using standards to assess and improve their quality management systems (QMS). Given the large number of smaller farmers (over 70,000) who act as suppliers to the main exporters or to producer organizations, well-functioning and locally adjusted QMSs are of crucial importance. The large number of smaller producers poses major monitoring challenges. We find that the key players in the main value chains have adopted different systems for achieving compliance and certification of smaller producers. Our survey indicates that 75 percent of interviewed farmers belong to a producer organization either formal or informal and which provided opportunities either for group certification or to obtain group contracts with exporters. 45 percent of farmers interviewed had contractual arrangements with exporters and 3 percent had contractual arrangements with producer organizations.

Moreover, lead players are also tightening their control over suppliers. Findings from the survey indicate that exporters and lead firms are increasingly playing a major role in ensuring quality throughout the chain. Contractual arrangements provide for seeds, as well as costs of compliance of standards including packaging material in some instances as well as transport costs because produce is mostly collected at the farm (see Table 3 below). In addition to this, exporters have undertaken to build structures for compliance for producer groups with whom they have contracts. Small-scale producers are closely monitored by field officers from exporting companies who offer extension services including advice on GAPs and training on standards and other requirements. Many of these exporters' functions are subsidized by development donor funding programs such as PIP/COELACP, JICA, GTZ and USAID.

We will continue with some more specific experiences that illustrate these general trends. First, a voluntary global code GlobalGAP, second an attempt to develop and implement a more comprehensive Kenyan mandatory code KS-1758, to overcome overlaps and harmonize systems, and third, a Kenyan voluntary code, KenyaGAP.

Table 3   Provision of support services by exporters through contractual arrangements

Support service	Percentage farmers
Inputs – Seeds	38
Fertilizer	8
Pesticides	8
Training on GAPs and standards	48
Upgrading – building of structures/requirements for standards	24
Compliance to standards including auditing	33
Information	57.5
Transport	88

Individual versus group certification: The GlobalGAP experience

From the perspective of including also smaller producers in certified value chains, a major distinction exists between individual and group certification. GlobalGAP (previously EurepGAP) was developed specifically for, and by, European retailers to monitor on-farm production, ensure quality, health and safety as well as addressing environmental concerns. GlobalGAP provides four different options for certification which takes care of both individual and group certifications. However, in Kenya there are predominantly two options for certification; option 1 is the individual certification and option 2 is for group certification mainly for producer organizations.[4] Under the individual certification option an individual producer applies for the GlobalGAp certificate for one or more subscopes, this usually entails putting up the required infrastructure and a quality management system (QMS) according to GlobalGAP requirements. External audit and inspection by a certification body is then done and a certificate issued thereafter if all the requirements are met. This option is mainly used by large-scale producers and exporters. Option 2 on the other hand is mainly used by small-scale producers who get certified through producer groups. In this scheme certification groups of farmers are allowed to comply as a unit but only after satisfying requirements of both external and internal Audits (see fig 2 below).

Figure 2   GlobalGAP option 2: Group certification for producer organizations

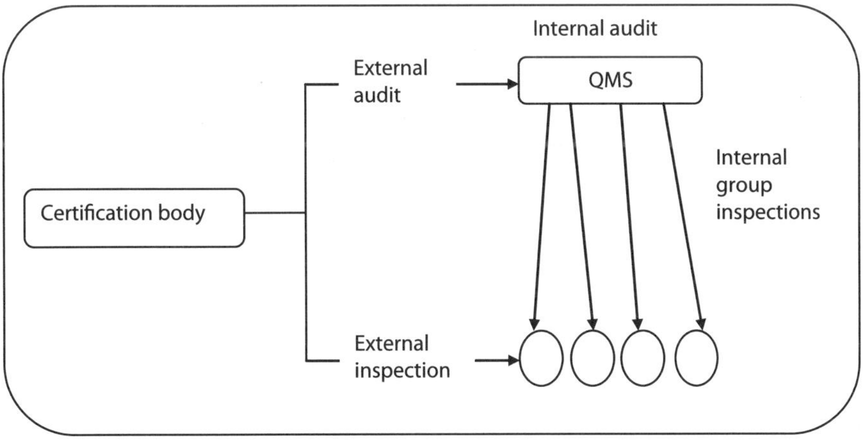

Financial requirements to obtain a "Kenyan" GlobalGAP certification are prohibitively high for small-scale farmers. These usually entail an initial cost of setting up which includes putting up the necessary infrastructure[5], additional labor requirements, additional managerial inputs and pay for testing and analysis of soils. According to data from our survey, the initial cost of setting up these infrastructures and any other additional requirements is approximately USD 1,200. Initial auditing costs are about USD 300 per day for audit fees paid to the certification body (which usually takes about two days), an auditor sustenance fee of USD 100 per day and a report fee of about USD 125 (summary Table 4 below).

Usually there is a checklist which is used for auditing and which requires 95 percent compliance for one to receive certification and once certification is received, yearly inspection and auditing is done for renewal which implies recurrent costs. Clearly it is easier for large farms to comply than smaller firms and more specifically small-scale farmers who find it more difficult to comply. This is mainly because of their financial capacity to invest in auditing and certification costs. To reduce these costs for small farms, they use a collective certification scheme (GlobalGAP option 2). Under this option, its costs approximately USD 500 per farmer to implement the Global Gap certification, about USD 400 is used as an initial cost for setting up necessary infrastructure while the rest are recurrent costs (Table 4 below).

Table 4   Summary GlobalGAP certification costs option 1 vs. option 2

Item	Option 1: Cost (USD)		Option 2: Cost (USD)	
	Nonrecurrent	Recurrent	Nonrecurrent	Recurrent
Physical infrastructure	1,200	-	400	
Auditing	-	800		50
Report fee	-	125		25
Soil testing and Analysis	-	155		25
Total	2,280		500	

Source: Survey data, 2009

It is apparent that the second option offers a cheaper alternative, especially for small-scale farmers, and therefore tends to include them in the market. Still, there also exists a third option in the Kenyan horticulture practice. Some farmers do not belong to a group and are not able to comply on their own due to financial constraints. Under this third type of arrangement these farmers supply directly to exporters who ensure quality and conformity with produce from farmers who were initially facing exclusion from the market. This type of contract farming allows these farmers to be covered through the exporters' certificate. In our survey this constituted about 33 percent of smallholders (Fig 3 below).

In this type of arrangement, the exporter has the certification and the responsibility of ensuring that the farmers with whom they have contracts are complying. In these cases monitoring is especially close, and exporters usually provide loans for putting up the QMS infrastructure and they internally audit "their" farms based on GlobalGAP criteria.

Around two-thirds of farmers interviewed believe that the requirements are unnecessarily stringent and that some do not apply to the local conditions. Most

Figure 3   GlobalGAP compliance of individual smallholders through exporters

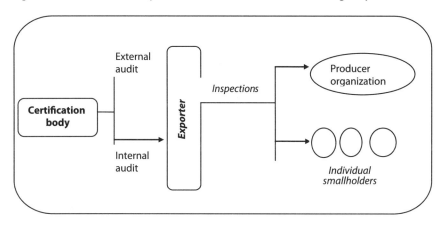

of them view the standards as lacking practical orientation to farming conditions and practical realities in terms of practices, process and techniques that uniquely characterize community farming techniques in most parts of the areas surveyed. These views reflect a lacking sense of ownership and internalization of compliance criteria, typical of how global standards are perceived by local farmers.

GlobalGAP has led to positive spillovers such as upgrading of farms and activities downstream which have invariably led to better quality management systems within the chain, consequently leading to efficiency of the supply chain. Training offered on standards has also resulted to knowledge spillovers more specifically with respect to maintaining good agricultural practices (GAP), environmental management and better record-keeping practices for farmers. Furthermore, these learning and awareness processes have stimulated the acceptance of local standards and the development of a local standards initiative known as the KenyaGap, which will be discussed below.

Localization of standards in Kenya's horticulture sector

Two examples are discussed below to illustrate challenges with an attempted Kenyan public mandatory standard and with a private voluntary standard.

KS -1758 Code of practice for the horticulture industry – A public/mandatory standard
The KS 1758 code of practice for the horticulture industry was launched in 2002 and developed by the technical multistakeholder National Food Safety Committee under the aegis of the KEBS. The code of practice originated from the Fresh

Produce Exporters Association of Kenya[6] (FPEAK) code of practice in 1996 and Kenya Flower Council[7] (KFC) code of practice in 1998, which was then harmonized as a combination of the two codes of practice. It is a code of practice that covers fruits and vegetables, as well as flowers.

Information from key informants reveals that representatives in the technical committee, consisting of staff from FPEAK, KFC, Kenya Plant Health Inspectorate Services[8] (KEPHIS), Horticultural Crops Development Authority[9] (HCDA) and the Ministry of Trade and Industry had minimal direct consultation with farmers. Representation was perceived to be taking place largely through FPEAK which mainly represents medium and large-scale exporters and farmers, as well as some of the producer organizations.

The purpose of the standard was to have a national baseline that would enable all producers to have a clearer and comprehensive guideline on the basic principles of GAPs, worker health and safety, as well as environmental concerns. The responsibility for the implementation and conformity assessment for this standard rests with KEBS. The requirements for the standard include due diligence for the safety and health of food, both for imports and exports as well as GAPs and ensuring worker welfare and addressing environmental concerns. The code of practice is harmonized with international agencies such as Integrated Crop Management UK and the Environmental Protection Agency, USA. However, this attempt at developing a comprehensive standard based on adapting global requirements to local country-specific conditions has not yet proven very successful. In fact, close to 70 percent of small-scale farmers interviewed do not even know about this code of practice. Moreover, key informants indicated that compliance requirements for this code of practice entail already having a management system in place, establishing the required infrastructure and obtaining certification for compliance which entails paying for auditors and paying for certification, so these requirements have major financial implications.

FPEAK and KFC have lobbied to make this particular standard mandatory to obtain an export license. However, next to the problems of the standard not being known to 70 percent of small-scale farmers and its rather high start-up costs, key informants indicated that another even more important reason seems to block the process of successfully implementing this standard. The many existing global standards insist upon their specific certification and auditing processes, which means the KS 1758 has not gained international acceptance. Therefore, while it could in principle be made mandatory to obtain this certificate in order to be allowed to export from Kenya, in practice it would not stimulate exports as exporters would still also need to comply with mandatory standards from specific importing countries.

The KenyaGAP initiative

A different but partly also similar illustrative example is that of the KenyaGAP initiative. The Kenyan experience with global standards led to the realization that there was a need for a more localized standard for fresh fruit and vegetables, and this led to the development of a KenyaGAP since the year 2002 (FPEAK, 2007). KenyaGAP originated from a revised code of FPEAK and incorporates principles of GAP and HACCP (FPEAK, 2007). The process of developing Kenya-GAP was consultative with most of the key industry players forming a technical committee involving KEPHIS, HCDA, the Ministry of Trade and Industry, the Kenya Flower Council (KFC) and representations from producer organizations, including individual members of FPEAK. For the sake of international recognition at that time many growers were already applying GAP standards required in European markets, in fact, some feel that it is a domesticated interpretation of EurepGAP.

Interviews with FPEAK officials indicate that the process of interpretation and benchmarking was long and tedious, taking close to two years. FPEAK invited independent EurepGAP-appointed auditors from the German standards and certification body (DAP) to audit and benchmark KenyaGAP against Eurep-GAP. KenyaGAP has therefore qualified as the first national scheme incorporating small-scale farmers concerns to acquire EurepGAP/GlobalGAP equivalence. KenyaGAP is the only scope to cover comprehensively flowers, fruits and vegetables and to have recognized third-party certification of farm production processes based on (EN45011/ISO Guide 65) product handling, processing and packaging.

KenyaGAP outlines the requirements which basically give the control points and compliance criteria, it has a checklist and interpretation guidelines. They offer flexibility on compliance criteria divided into mandatory (red), required (yellow) and recommended (green). This then leads to a multitier approach with the basic principles forming the "Bronze" Code of practice stating the minimum for all growers (new members), the Silver with slightly more stringent requirements and the Gold Code of practice for the most stringent requirements and possibly for the market leaders (e.g. continue documented reduction on use of pesticides, continue investment in drip irrigation as opposed to other forms of irrigation, investment in water-harvesting techniques, new investment towards hydroponics etc.) (FPEAK 2009).

KenyaGAP is at present the only comprehensive (vegetables, flowers, fruits) quality-assurance scheme from the African continent to have acquired Eurep-GAP/GlobalGAP equivalence. The developmental aspect of KenyaGAP is also important in that it incorporates small-scale farming techniques and concerns. It is also inclusive in that it incorporates concerns from a wide range of stakehold-

ers. It is adapted to local conditions and hence it is easier to understand and easier
to comply with. Interviews from FPEAK also indicated that the charges for certification and auditing are likely to be cheaper than for international standards.

Despite the potentially positive developments on KenyaGAP, there are still
challenges related to its implementation, dissemination and reaffirmation.
FPEAK is the scheme owner for KenyaGAP; however, the process was and still
is funded by donors such as JICA, DANIDA, USAID, COLEACP and DFID,
which raises concerns over the sustainability for this kind of arrangement. Moreover, our survey indicates that only 7 percent of small-scale farmers interviewed
know about this system of certification. FPEAK has not yet begun training and
certification of farmers as they are still laying out the process with a third-party
certification body based in Kenya. Many sector players are concerned about the
overlapping certification, especially if most exporting firms and farmers are already GlobalGAP certified. There are also issues raised concerning market penetration in the European market because GlobalGAP is a buyer-driven initiative
and acceptance of KenyaGAP may raise concerns for a number of buyers. A major remaining question therefore is whether KenyaGAP will remain a local standard for regulation of the local sector or if it really can be accepted internationally
as equivalent to GlobalGAP. At the moment it seems that KenyaGAP might
not be felt as necessary for larger producers who already possess GlobalGAP
certificates, while for the smaller producers it may be more complicated and more
costly to obtain KenyaGAP as compared to supplying through either a producer
organization or an exporter with a GlobalGAP certificate.

Conclusions

One way to enhance the developmental relevance of global standards is to develop
more localized monitoring and certification practices. The Kenyan horticulture
sector provides some interesting illustrative examples of the opportunities and
challenges related to attempts at localizing global standards. A major challenge is
that leading international buyers do not have any direct incentive to contribute to
the development of localized standards. Indirectly, all chain actors can potentially
benefit from more context-sensitive QMS, certification and auditing practices.
However, such longer-term potential benefits do not weigh up to the short-run
additional costs and potential initial confusion created by letting go of the (partly
illusionary) benefits and clarity of a globally standardized implementation of
standards. The examples show how group certification through producer organizations can be much cheaper and thus provide opportunities to avoid exclusion
of smaller and financially weaker producers. Moreover, such smaller producers

can also opt for a type of contract farming that allows them to sell their produce to larger exporters who in turn are made responsible for quality control and implicit certification of such smaller producers. Illustrative examples of attempts at localizing a mandatory public standard and a voluntary private standard show differences and similarities. A main similarity is the problem of convincing value chain actors of the relevance and equivalence of such localized standards. An important difference is that the "infrastructure" for effective monitoring and certification practices is present for private voluntary standards, but is lacking for mandatory public standards. Notwithstanding the limited success to date with attempts at localizing global standards, we believe it is worthwhile to continue searching for more developmentally relevant standardization mechanisms. While the increasing importance of standardization seems given, it remains an open question whether development scholars and practitioners can develop ways to make standardization processes more developmental.

Notes

1   Localization is the process of adapting, translating and customizing a standard for a specific market (for a specific locale).
2   Small-scale farmers have farm sizes ranging from 0.25-2 acres, whereas medium-scale farmers have farm sizes ranging between 2.5-10 acres.
3   Have farm sizes of over 10 acres.
4   Options 3 and 4 also provide for individual and group certification respectively, though this is only through a benchmarked scheme which is not yet applicable in Kenya.
5   Infrastructure includes pesticide and fertilizer storage, grading shed, cooling shed, toilet and bath, and hand-wash facilities and sanitizers.
6   FPEAK has about 200 large medium and small-scale exporters of fruits and vegetables represented either as individuals or as producer organizations.
7   KFC has about 61 flower-growing companies, mostly large and medium scale, representing more than 60% of the Kenyan flower export.
8   A regulatory agency for quality assurance on agricultural inputs and produce in Kenya. KEPHIS undertakes: Plant variety protection; seed certification; phytosanitary inspection of imports and exports and analysis of soil, water, agricultural produce, fertilizers and pesticides.
9   A regulatory agency for the development and marketing of horticultural produce in Kenya.

References

Athukorala, P. and S. Jayasuriya (2006). *Meeting food safety standards in export markets: Issues and challenges facing firms exporting from developing countries*. A paper presented at the IATRC Summer Symposium Food Regulation and

Trade: Institutional Framework, Concepts of Analysis and Empirical Evidence, Bonn, Germany, 28-30 May 2006.

Beuningen, C. van, and P. Knorringa (2009). *Inclusive improvement: Standards and smallholders*. The Hague: HIVOS and ISS.

Busch, L. (2000). 'The Moral Economy of Grades and Standards'. In: *Journal of Rural Studies* 16, pp. 321-346.

Blowfield, M. E. and C.S. Dolan (2008). 'Stewards of virtue? The ethical dilemma of CSR in African agriculture'. In: *Development and Change* 39, pp. 1-23.

Brunsson N. (2000). *A world of standards*. Oxford: Oxford University Press.

Cooper J. and A. Graffham (2009). 'GlogalGAP version 3: Threat or opportunity for small-scale African growers'. In: A. de Batisti, J. MacGregor and A. Graffham (eds.), *Standard bearers horticultural exports and private standards in Africa*.

Den Butter, F.A., S. Groot and L. Faroek (2007). *Transaction costs perspectives of standards as a source of trade productivity and growth*. Tinbergen Institute Discussion Paper available at www.tinbergen.nl.

Dolan, C. and J. Humphrey (2000). 'Governance and trade in fresh vegetables: The impact of UK supermarkets on the African horticulture industry'. In: *Journal of Development Studies* 37 (2), pp. 147-176.

FPEAK (2007). 'KenyaGAP = GlobalGAP: A first for Africa'. In: *FPEAK Newsletter Issue* 6 September to December.

Grossmann, G.M. and E. Helpmann (1989). *Endogenous product cycles*. NBER Working Paper No. W2913. Available at SSRN: http://ssrn.com/abstract=227204.

Jaffe, S. and S. Henson (2004). *Standards and agro-food exports from developing countries: Rebalancing the debate*. World Bank Policy Research Paper 3348.

Kaplinsky, R. (2006). 'How can agricultural producers appropriate greater share of value chain incomes?' In: A. Sarris and D. Hallaman, *Agricultural Commodity markets and Trade/new Approaches to Analyzing Market Structure and Instability*. FAO.

Maskus, K.E. and J.S. Wilson (2000). *Quantifying the impact of technical barriers to trade: A review of past attempts and the new policy context*. Paper presented at the World Bank Workshop, "Quantifying the trade effect of standards and technical barriers: Is it possible?" April 27.

Nicholls, A. and C. Opal (2000). *Fair trade: Market-driven ethical consumption*. London: Sage.

Okello, J. (2005). *Developing country family farmers' strategic response to developed country food safety standards: The case Kenyan green bean growers*. Paper Presented at American Society of Agricultural Economics in Carlifonia, 2005.

Riisgard, L. (2008). *Localizing Private Social standards: Initiatives in the Kenyan Cut flowers*. DIIS Working Paper 2008/20.

Tander, N. and A. van Tilburg (2007). 'Standards and market access in Indian cashew processing and international trade'. In: R. Ruben et al., *Tropical food chains: Governance regimes for quality management*. Wageningen: Wageningen Academic Publishers.

Wilson, J.S. (2001). *Advancing the WTO agenda on trade and standards: A developing country voice on the debate*. Draft paper prepared for the African Economic Research Consortium (AERC) Conference on Trade, Geneva, March.

Wilson, J.S. and V.O. Abiola (2003). *Standards and global trade: A voice or Africa*. Washington: World Bank.

World Bank (2005). *Food safety and agricultural health standards: Challenges and opportunities for developing country exports*. Poverty Reduction and Economic Management Trade Unit and Agricultural and Rural Development Department, Report No 31207. Washington: World Bank.

7   Using a Partnership to Achieve Sustainable Development of the Palm Oil Value Chain in Malaysia

Meine Pieter van Dijk

Introduction

Partnerships have become important for economic development. At the World Summit on Sustainable Development (WSSD) in Johannesburg in 2002, goals for sustainable development have been set. World leaders concluded that agricultural trade and market dynamics can play a major role in achieving sustainable development and eradicating poverty. In order to profit from trade, however, countries must ensure that their products meet the high quality standards in the field of health, food safety, social standards and environment of developed countries. Food safety and agricultural health standards can impede trade, especially for developing countries, through explicit bans on imports of particular products or through the high costs of compliance with stringent standards, which can diminish competitiveness. The combined effects of institutional weakness and rising compliance costs could contribute to the further marginalization of weaker economic players, including poor countries, small businesses, and smallholder farmers (Aksoy and Beghin, 2005). Yet in certain circumstances, the new landscape of proliferation and increasingly stringent food safety can be a basis for the competitive repositioning and enhanced export performance. Standards can also provide incentives for modernizing global value chains and help clarify the necessary and appropriate risk-management functions of government. The greater attention to good practices in agricultural value chains may not only improve export competitiveness, but also generate spillover benefits to domestic consumers. From this perspective, standards can provide the basis for more sustainable and profitable agricultural exports in the long term (World Bank, 2008).

International experience highlights the respective roles of the government and the private sector to meet challenges in export of high-value agricultural products. Public-private partnerships can be important in conducting research and capacity building to develop agricultural practices, meet the new domestic and international sanitary and phytosanitary standards (SPS), and train and assist farmers to adopt them (World Bank, 2008). Not only in the agricultural sector have cross-sector partnerships among various levels of government, business/industry, nongovernmental organizations and communities become a key strategy for economic development and improving environmental, social and community outcomes. Practical experiments with partnerships have been undertaken in numerous areas of public policy, in both developed and developing countries. These voluntary arrangements aim to reach a common objective or carry out a specific task, in which parties share risks, responsibilities, means, competences and profits. The underlying idea of partnerships is that by generating additional knowledge and resources, results can be achieved that benefit all parties and which they could not have achieved on an individual basis (Kolk et al., 2008).

The Netherlands, Malaysia and Indonesia agreed to start a partnership in the palm-oil value chain in 2002.[1] The aim of the partnership was to identify the bottlenecks in the palm-oil value chain and to improve market access for palm oil into the European Union. This complex collaborative arrangement will be analyzed. Based on the idea of "collaborative advantage" (Huxham, 1993), the governments of The Netherlands, Malaysia and Indonesia have agreed to start an agricultural trilateral partnership in 2002.[2] This partnership faced several management and governance challenges and finally the Malaysian partners decided to withdraw from the partnership. This paper reviews this partnership with a specific focus on outcomes for the palm-oil sector from a Malaysian perspective. The aim of this paper is to identify factors that affected the management of the partnership and finally to determine the contribution of the partnership to upgrading the palm-oil value chain. The objective is to draw lessons learned from this case study in order to develop knowledge on how to better manage complex partnerships in an international setting.

The paper is structured as follows: In the following sections the theoretical framework and methodology are presented. Then we present a value chain perspective on Malaysia's export-oriented palm-oil sector before discussing the partnership in that country. After providing the context of the palm-oil sector the point of view of Malaysia will be given before going deeper into the governance of the partnership and the results. Finally, we formulate lessons learned before drawing some conclusions.

The theoretical framework

Van Dijk (2008) defines a partnership as a form of cooperation between parties with similar objectives but different (complementary) qualities, which each contribute resources and share in the investment risks and suggests to separate the

basic characteristics, or defining factors from the empirical traits of the partnership (table 1). After defining PPPs in a nonambiguous way the empirical traits
can be studied in different situations.

Table 1   Basic characteristics and empirical traits of the partnership

Basic characteristics	Empirical traits of the partnership
Common objective	Level of equality or hierarchy
Some legal or informal arrangement	Level of trust
Joint activity	Level of ownership
Shared resources	Expectations
Sharing of risks	Commitment
	Complementarity
	Resources put in place
	Actual risks and their distribution
	Drivers
	Other internal or external factors affecting the success or failure of a partnership

Partnerships are based on ideas of dialogue, reciprocity, trust and sharing of
different values, knowledge and practices to realize mutual benefit. In this ideal perspective, synergy between collaborating organizations is accelerated. In
summing up the potential benefits of partnerships from an actor perspective,
Brinkerhoff (2002) suggests that partnerships may a) increase effectiveness
as actors gain access to crucial resources such as expertise and relationships;
b) lower transaction costs and improve access to information; c) enhance efficiency through the identification and exploitation of comparative advantage;
d) facilitate creative problem-solving through the joint efforts of partners with
different perspectives and expertise; and e) reduce conflict over time, as actors
realize that the costs associated with ongoing tension between stakeholders
become too high and therefore decide to cooperate. In this sense, collaboration moves beyond the purely instrumental relationships suggested by classic
resource dependency theory.

Partnerships may include many actors as diverse as business, trade unions,
university research institutions and nongovernmental organizations from different countries and cultures. Partnerships exist on different levels and have different parties (some public and some private) participating. Managing such complex
partnerships seems to be difficult in practice and specific skills are needed to
manage them (see Huxham et al., 2000; Steger et al., 2009). Partnership literature highlights that factors positively or negatively influencing the dynamics of

Figure 1   Framework for analyzing partnerships and their impact on performance

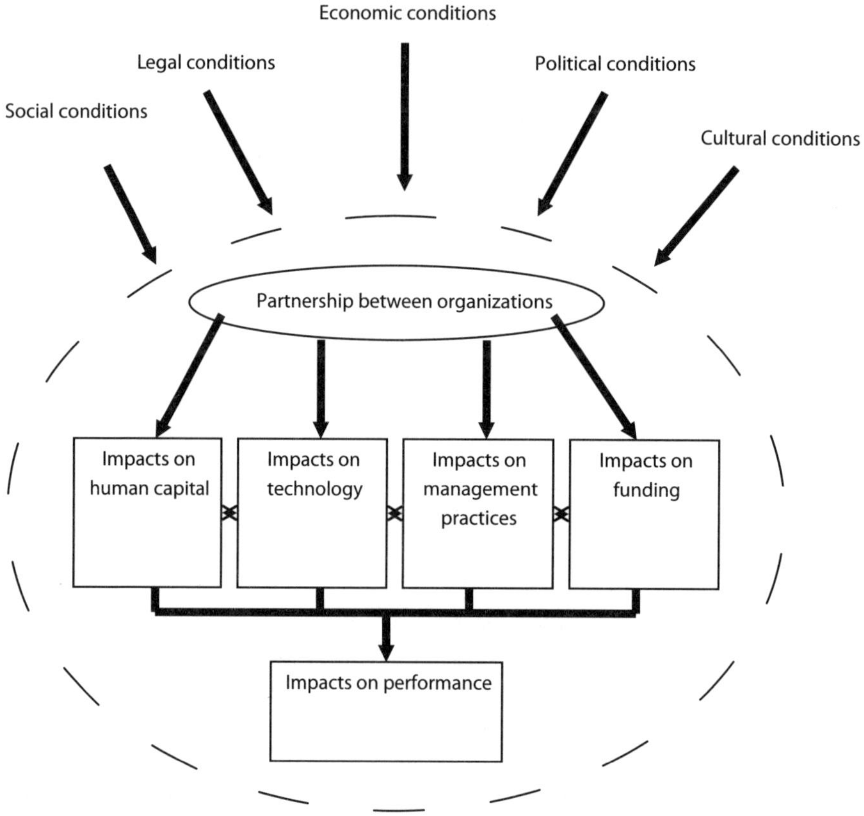

a partnership can be relevant for the overall success or failure of the partnership. Identified factors include a clear vision of the objectives, needs that can be best fulfilled through partnerships, mutual benefits, shared commitment and owner-ship, human and financial resources, good leadership, clear and enforceable lines of accountability, flexibility and effective monitoring and evaluation regimes (see OECD, 2006). These "internal factors" are in close relation with the partnership design.

Besides hostilities within the partnership, collaborative arrangements are also significantly influenced by the broader policy and institutional context (Hux-ham et al., 2000). These factors include, for instance, legal frameworks and the rule of law, democratic governance or environmental stability and flexibility. Factors in the broader development environment are often beyond the scope of individual partnerships but are frequently targeted by donors and sometimes government's reform initiatives (Brinkerhoff, 2002: 78). To get a more precise idea of the external conditions and their influence, a conceptual framework to analyze partnerships and their impact on service provision was taken into account. It has been developed by Schwartz (2008: figure 1 above) and emphasizes the role of external factors such as the legal, political and cultural factors influencing the functioning of the partnership. His model also stressed the impact of the partnership on the institutions involved, in particular due to a changing technology, a different way of managing things, or the availability of funding.

Table 2   Internal and external (enabling environment) success factors for partnerships

Internal factors	External success factors for partnerships
Partnership building	Legal framework
Commitment	Institutional framework
Relations	Development of the private sector
Governance arrangements in the partnership:	Level of development of the economy
consultative structures	Sector specific factors
Level of ownership	Policy context
Transparency	Willingness to participate
Horizontal and vertical accountability	Time horizon
Inclusiveness of stakeholders	A real need for this partnership
Trust	A sense of urgency
Clear roles and complementarity	An active private sector
Good planning	Available finance
Clear drivers: a champion in the public &	Political commitment
private sector	Cultural factors
Relevant knowledge & experience	Social conditions
Clear distribution of tasks	
Win-win situation	

Table 2 provides an overview of the major success factors based on a literature study on partnerships in the international setting (e.g. Brinkerhoff, 2002; Visseren-Hamakers et al., 2007; OECD, 2006). We assume that in the everyday practice of partnerships external and internal factors are combined in the collaborative process. Figure 2 visualizes interplay of internal and external factors in partnerships in complex settings.

Figure 2   Internal and external factors in partnerships combined

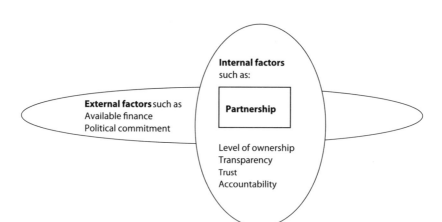

The methodology

There is not yet much experience in the review of partnerships in development cooperation. "Partnering" has to be assessed based on a) project or program results and b) process-oriented results:

a Project or program results refer to assessment of outcomes of projects implemented under the scope of a partnership.

b The process-oriented assessment is focused on the partnership governance system and aims at identifying i) synergies mobilized by the partnership; ii) obstacles in the process and ways in which partners may collaborate more effectively in the future; iii) factors that may contribute to success and scalability.

Figure 3   Framework of analysis for partnerships

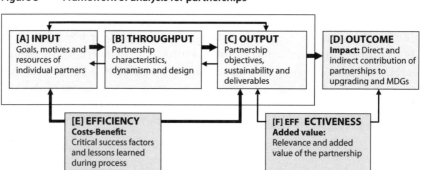

The challenge of a partnership review is to integrate the processes of collaborative arrangements into performance measurement systems. The framework of Van Tulder and Kostwinder (2007) is an example of how to integrate the analysis of the partnering process and the assessment of results. The analytical framework is based on the premise that most partnerships go through comparable stages. Basically the partnership process consists of four stages: a) input, b) throughput, c) output and d) outcome; and has two evaluative dimensions: e) efficiency and f) effectiveness (figure 3). Their approach is inspired by Pollit and Bouckaert (2000). They assume that programs (here partnership) are set up to address some specific problems. To solve those, needs are identified and inputs and resources are set up to address them. Processes are the activities taking place to transform the inputs into outputs. The outputs will then interact with the external conditions to get results hopefully addressing the starting problem.

With the help of this analytical framework and taking into consideration the internal and external factors affecting the partnership performance, this paper aims to generate knowledge on how to effectively manage partnerships in an international setting to contribute to the upgrading of an existing value chain. The case-study approach was selected because it provides the possibility to explore internal and external factors more in-depth. The chosen case study is a "multiple purpose" partnership which is based on a shared interest of actors involved, and builds on two pillars: engagement/dialogue and capacity-building (Steger et al., 2009). In the researched case the tool of partnerships was used to build local capacity and thereby improve access of palm oil to the European market. At the time of the assessment, the partnership was finalized which enabled the analysis in detail of the outcomes of the collaborative activities, as well as the identification of the external and internal factors that impacted on the performance.

The research project entailed a qualitative-performance analysis of a partnership with governmental and nongovernmental actors of Malaysia, Indonesia and The Netherlands. The research focus on the results for Malaysian actors and the Malaysian palm-oil sector allows identifying context-specific factors. The data selection process included desk research, review of partnership documents, such as minutes of meetings or project reports and semistructured interviews. The interviewed stakeholders can be divided in:
- primary stakeholders (partners) who were involved in the decision-making process on trilateral level;
- and secondary stakeholders who were mainly involved on consultative basis and in project implementation.

The interviews aimed to learn about the experience of the partnership partners in how far they consider that the partnership achieved its objectives or in how far their expectations were satisfied. For that reason we have always asked our key informants how they defined a partnership, what their objectives were to step into it and what they expected from it. Besides applying an interview technique, we decided to include a list with critical success factors (internal and external) for partnerships based on an extensive literature research. The respondents were asked to rank the items on a five-point Likert-scale based on the importance of the factors as experienced in the partnership. The ranks were compared with the results of the data analysis and the findings of the desk study. This allowed identifying factors that affected the management of the partnership and finally its performance.

We now present the case study and the findings which provide an answer to the question whether the partnership on palm oil under review has indeed successfully reached its goals and has added value for the Malaysian partners involved, as well as stimulating sustainable development in Malaysia. Finally, it enabled us to draw lessons learned from this case study in order to develop knowledge on how to better manage complex partnerships in an international setting.

A value chain perspective on the palm oil

The global value chain (GVC) concept is not new, but the global value concept came up when the discussion of the effects of globalization started and can be considered to be more encompassing than competing terms. The supply-chain concept often takes the perspective of a Western company concerned about getting raw materials and spare parts. In the same way international production networks refer to efforts to outsource and place the production of certain parts in developing countries. The commodity chains, or what the French call *filières*, are much older and come closest to the GVC. Gereffi and Korzeniewicz (1994) started using the term in its present meaning and many products which have been studied extensively under this angle are commodities, garments and textiles, leather products and electronics (Altenburg, 2006).The challenge is to develop agricultural value chains through unconventional partering while empowering local producers and stimulating local value creation. This requires a focus on innovation, while keeping an eye open for sustainability. In this contribution use will be made of previous studies concerning value chains.

The development of economic activities are put in a context of resources and markets, of local, regional and international economies, of individual entrepreneurs and clusters, and of competing in local, regional or international markets. The novel aspect of the GVC approach is that it anticipates competition and integration in the world economy. It takes into account the competition products are involved in at a worldwide scale. An export orientation is assumed in this approach, even for small and medium enterprises. Globalization is considered a win-win situation and not a zero-sum game. However, different countries, regions and cities benefit more than others from the new opportunities (Van Dijk, 2006).

Some of the major issues in the GVC literature are the role of lead firms, the issues of power in the chain and the resulting distributional issues, the low road (just based on cheap labor) or the high road of GVC competition (Guiliani et al., 2005). Theory formation has concentrated on the value chain governance situation (Humphrey and Schmitz, 2004) and not so much on how to promote competition between and within value chains, to assure a fairer distribution of the margins. The chain governance structure can be characterized as a network-styled way of governance, arm's length market relations, or as a situation of oligopoly. Sometimes one firm plays a very important role in the chain. Market power is sometimes analyzed, but it is rarely the subject of a competition regulator. They tend to focus on individual firms and not on value chains. In the case of the palm-oil value chain guaranteeing market access to the EU was the big issue. The partnership studied was established in particular for that purpose.

The export-oriented palm oil sector in Malaysia

Malaysia, a middle-income country, has transformed itself since the 1970s from a producer of raw materials into an emerging multisector economy (table 3). The agricultural sector grew on average at a rate of 1.2 percent between 1990 and 2005 (World Bank, 2008). Agriculture is no longer the most important sector of the

Table 3   Overview Malaysian agriculture data

*GDP (per capita 2008)**	*USD 15,300*
Agriculture % GDP (2003-2005)	9.2
Agriculture annual % growth rate (1990-2005)	1.2
Employment in agriculture % total (2002-2004)	14.7
Agricultural exports USD million (2003-2005)	10,562
Agricultural exports % total exports (2003-2005)	8.5
Agricultural imports USD millions (2003-2005)	5,594
Indonesian government spending % agriculture value added (2004)	12.7
Public R&D spending on agriculture as % agriculture value added (2000)	1.58
ODA to agriculture % total ODA to country (2003-2005)	0.8

Sources: World Bank (2008); *CIA (2009)

Malaysian economy, contributing 9.2% of GDP in 2008 (down from 38% in 1960) and occupying about 14.7% of employed work force in 2008 (Malaysian Ministry of Agriculture, 1998). Some of the reasons for the decline of the agriculture sector were unfavorable prices of agricultural commodities; increased prices of farm inputs; increased competition for land use; and more favorable policies accorded to the industrial sector that made investment in agriculture a less attractive alternative (Harron et al., 2001).

The Malaysian agricultural sector is dominated by industrial export crops comprising palm oil, rubber and cocoa. Agriculture still accounted for 8.5 percent of export earnings in 2008 (World Bank, 2008). In terms of total contribution to the Malaysian economy, the agricultural sector showed a comparative decline. However, in terms of absolute value, its contribution to the economy remains significant, in particular if processing is taken into consideration. Agriculture and agribusiness will continue to be significant to the economy and development of Malaysia because it provides income especially to the rural population. The rural sector is directly or indirectly dependent on agriculture.

Figure 4   Production and import of palm oil

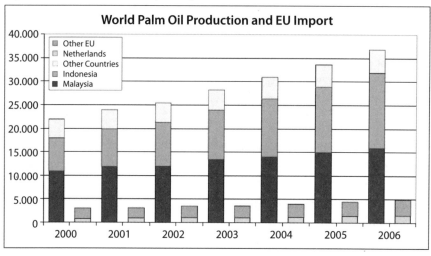

Source: MVO (2007)

Eradicating poverty and reducing regional income disparities remains a challenge in Malaysia. While the overall poverty rate declined from 22.8 percent in 1990 to 3.6 percent in 2007, the rate varies significantly by state, ranging from negligible in Pulau Pinang to a high of 16 percent in Sabah. The rates are higher in rural areas (7.1%) than in towns (2.0%) (ADB, 2008).

More than 80 percent of palm oil is produced in Malaysia and Indonesia, while over 90 percent of the world's palm oil exports originate from these countries (Figure 4). In 2008, Indonesia exceeded Malaysia as the world's largest producer and it tries to control this very important global value chain as much as possible. In 2008, Malaysian palm oil counted 47 percent of world exports. With approximately 91 percent of its total production being exported, Malaysia is currently the largest palm-oil exporter. The leading importers are China (3.6 million MT p.a.), EU (2.6 million), Pakistan (0.97 million) and India (0.56 million) (MPOC, 2009). Malaysia is very concerned about continuous access to these markets.

The palm-oil industry is the largest agricultural enterprise in Malaysia. It has evolved from just producing crude palm oil (CPO) to a more diversified industry, consisting of milling, refining and manufacturing of various food and nonfood products such as cooking oil, soaps, etc. The oil palm, dubbed the "golden crop" of the country, has witnessed phenomenal growth since the 1960s. Since its introduction, this crop has permanently changed the landscape of agriculture in Malaysia by replacing most of the rubber areas and through new area development. It has successfully enhanced the incomes of agricultural smallholders through government land schemes managed by the Federal Land Development Authority (FELDA)[3] and also other federal and state government agencies. Apart from the government programs, stable prices and sustained long-term industry profits have led the private sector to extensively venture and invest in palm oil. Malaysia currently accounts for 41 percent of world palm-oil production. Today, 4.49 million hectares of land in Malaysia is under oil palm cultivation; producing 17.73 million tons of palm oil and 2.13 tons of palm kernel oil. The industry provides employment to more than half a million people and livelihood to an estimated one million people (MPOC, 2009).

Producers who mainly consist of private estates (60%) and organized smallholders in government and state schemes (30%) usually have an in-house marketing support system to facilitate the marketing and distribution of palm oil. They have a good transportation system, and close links to refineries, crushing factories and bulk installations. The major producers also have an established network with domestic brokers/dealers who sell the processed products to the domestic market or international traders. Careful planning linked with pragmatic policies to stimulate the development of the palm-oil industry has enabled it to expand, deepen and diversify. The industry is well clustered with a whole range of business support services, product manufacturing, R&D and marketing activities in place. Apart from the three core activities (milling, refining and downstream processing), the industry is also involved in manufacturing other finished palm-oil products including vegetable ghee, margarine, shortening, soap and others. Other products that are of value but that can be considered by-products of the industry include palm kernel cake and sludge oil (Ahmad and Tawang, 1999).

In 2008, the sector was booming since record prices were paid in the world market because of a high demand for other vegetable oils, and an increasingly rich world population. The price for palm oil was above USD 1,000 per ton at a certain moment, while production cost range between USD 180 and USD 200 per ton, depending on the farm system and the location. In general the prices of close substitutes (in particular biofuels[4]), the health image of the product (in particular the percentage of cholesterol and unsatisfied fats) and the environmental image (limited CO_2 emissions and use of fertilizers and pesticides) have an impact on the demand of the product.

The Malaysian palm-oil industry is a highly regulated industry. Currently, the industry adheres to more than 15 laws and regulations including the Land Acquisition Act 1960, Environmental Quality Act 1974, Environmental Quality (Clean Air Regulations) 1978, Pesticides Act 1974 (Pesticides Registration Rules), Occupational Safety and Health Act 1977, and Protection of Wildlife Act 1972. The industry is also complying with Hazard Analysis & Critical Control Points (HACCP) and the Environmental Impact Assessment (EIA) requirements. Being sensitive and proactive on current environmental concerns, the industry is actively pursuing ISO 14000 standard series discussions and formulations notably on climate change, life cycle analysis (LCA), eco-labeling & Design for the Environment (DfE), environmental communications, and environmental management system (EMS). Policy measures for palm oil are primarily aimed at increasing productivity and quality, as well as expanding export markets. Two main institutions are responsible for the implementation of these policy objectives: the Malaysian Palm Oil Council (MPOC) and the Malaysian Palm Oil Board (MPOB).

Bottlenecks and issues for market access

a Contaminated palm oil
By the end of 1999, a few shipments of palm oil from Indonesia were found to be contaminated with diesel oil and were rejected by buyers in The Netherlands. The discovery prompted European buyers to shun Indonesia and also Malaysia, while the EU planned to recall all products containing palm oil from Indonesia. Since Malaysia is the largest exporter of palm oil in the world, any restriction such as higher nontariff seriously puts up barriers in the sector. Furthermore, Malaysian companies have invested heavily in setting up plantations in Indonesia, where the political and legal context is quite different. The contamination cases proved to be an important incentive for designing the partnership on palm oil.

b Reputation Malaysian palm oil in Europe

Various issues have weakened the reputation of particularly Malaysian palm oil in the European market. Highly publicized effects of ongoing palm-oil expansion are deforestation and the loss of biodiversity[5], increased greenhouse emissions, and the weak position of smallholders:[6]

i Deforestation and the loss of biodiversity

Deforestation in Malaysia has many causes, such as logging, cattle ranging, shifting cultivation, mining, land-use policies, and urban development. The main concern for environmental groups is the impact of palm-oil plantations on the High Conservation Value Forests in and surrounding the plantations and the loss of biological diversity, often symbolized in the diminishing population of orangutans.

ii Greenhouse emissions

Deforestation, during which carbon stored in trees is released into the atmosphere, now accounts for about 20 percent of the world's greenhouse gas emissions. Forest fires in 1997/1998 in Indonesia had a particularly big impact.

iii Food versus fuel debate

In the context of concerns for future food security of a growing global population, the large-scale production of energy by the agricultural sector has provoked severe criticism. Palm oil that is produced for fuel purposes may threaten food security because it competes with food crops for arable land, while the increased demand for palm-oil diesel drives up prices for edible palm oil.

iv Smallholder integration

There are concerns that smallholders are losing their autonomy as independent producers and becoming entirely dependent on banks, agribusiness, and the government. Moreover, 10 percent of palm oil is produced by independent smallholders (MPOA, 2005). They lack adequate technologies to comply with strict market-access regulations.

It was the concern for food safety of palm oil after incidents of contaminated palm oil from Indonesia late 1999, and the worsening reputation of palm oil in the Netherlands and other European countries that drove the Malaysian stakeholders together in the partnership.

Governance and management of the partnership

In the context of the Johannesburg Implementation Plan, the governments of The Netherlands, Indonesia and Malaysia agreed to start an agricultural trilateral cooperation in order to stimulate market access and sustainable development (amongst others) in the palm-oil sector. The instrument partnership was selected for capacity building to comply with food safety regulations and to draw attention on strengthening structures and awareness to contribute to sustainable development, not only with respect to economic issues, but also to social and ecological issues. The latter objective is based on the understanding that agricultural exports are expected to contribute directly to poverty alleviation by generating foreign exchange and creating employment, particularly in rural areas. The framework to work in a partnership aimed to improve mutual understanding of the need to effectively address both:

a Market failure to ensure continuous improvement in product and process development as well as

b Governance failure to secure accountability between decision makers, industry and society.

In 2004, partners and stakeholders together identified bottlenecks in the whole production chain and tried to find solutions, with participation of stakeholders from government, the private sector and civil society. Specific activities in the field of capacity and institution building were expected to enable countries to effectively deal with multilaterally agreed standards, and with standards related to EU-policy and legislation. Decisions were taken by a *Trilateral Coordinating Committee* which consisted of governmental representatives (partners). Stakeholders were involved in working groups which functioned as (technical) advisory groups. *National Focal Points* within the governments where identified in each country which were responsible for coordinating stakeholder involvement and project implementation. During the last meeting in November 2008, the Malaysian partners announced to step out of the partnership. The trilateral partnership therefore officially ended.

The element of multistakeholder consultation was introduced by the "Northern" partner of the partnership. The Malaysian stakeholders understood the partnership as a government-to-government partnership. As a compromise it was decided that civil-society organizations and the private sector would be involved on a consultative basis at national level. The private sector was consulted and provided advice to the governmental agencies involved in the partnership on palm oil. The industry representatives stated that the industry could make claims and that they had been involved at the project level. There was no direct involvement of smallholder representatives in decision-making processes. Nevertheless, it is not always clear how businesses were involved in drawing up and implementing proposals. Clearer definitions of the decision-making procedures and responsibilities were lacking which lead to nontransparent processes.

It was a rather new experience for the Malaysian government to involve civil society organizations in consultation processes. A distinction needed to be made between two types of NGOs, a) technical-oriented NGOs with a focus on technical knowledge; and b) social NGOs which are more oriented towards advocacy. It seemed that it was less challenging for the government and the private sector to work together with science-based NGOs. The objectives and expectations of the partnership were high and not always made explicit or shared by all parties. On the Malaysian side the initial expectation was to improve the quality of the product and in this way assure access to the EU market. In due course environmental concerns became very important in the discussion between the three partners and at the end the issue of climate change and CO_2 emissions dominated.

A Memorandum of Understanding, signed by only two of the three partners, underlies the partnership. The Malaysian partners, who never signed the Memorandum of Understanding, were not sure about the governance structure of the trilateral partnership and considered that instead of consensus, an agreement between the other partners was enough to choose a project. In general, the perception was that the available money would be allocated to projects in Indonesia, while it was not made clear to everybody why financing projects in Indonesia is easier for The Netherlands than spending money in Malaysia. In the first case it would come from the budget of Official Development Assistance (ODA), but Malaysia, given its level of development does not qualify for such support. The Malaysian partners perceived a lot of the benefits were going to Indonesia for no clear reason and felt that this eroded the feeling of ownership of the project.

Partnership projects and results

Some Malaysian project proposals (e.g. on assessing pesticide risks) did not materialize. This was explained by the Malaysian partner by a more preferential treatment for Indonesian projects, which would then be traced back to the special relation between The Netherlands and Indonesia. However, the partnership activities achieved concrete results such as:

- an extensive overview of the actual and potential contamination of palm oil with mineral oil;
- a better understanding of EU food-safety regulatory requirements;
- capacity building for laboratory workers;
- growing awareness of the high conservation value forests concept in Malaysian palm-oil stakeholders; and
- support for smallholders to implement principles and criteria for sustainable production of palm oil (based on Roundtable on Sustainable Palm Oil).

Impact of the partnership on palm oil on improved market access
Malaysian government and industry stakeholders agreed that the partnership
was successful in respect of the main objective of the partnership: food safety.
The setting of clear threshold levels, capacity building and training in Malaysia
and personal contacts through the partnership helped to improve the reputation
for Malaysian palm oil in The Netherlands and Europe.

The partners welcomed the partnership and were grateful for the implementation of projects of which the project on hydrocarbon analysis in crude palm oil
was perceived as most fruitful. In general, the partnership was understood to have
a minimal impact on the Malaysian palm-oil sector. The problem of contamination was basically experienced as an Indonesian problem and not a Malaysian
problem. From the Malaysian perspective, Malaysian palm oil is now better integrated and traceable along the value chain than Indonesian palm oil. Because
of the creation of a better reputation of Malaysian palm oil, the Malaysian partners are grateful with the outcome of the projects of the partnership focusing on
food-safety regulation and capacity building. The fact that the main problem of
traceability was solved by the partnership was perceived as the main success of
the partnership on palm oil. Capacity of governmental staff with respect to market access requirements was built up successfully. In particular the information
exchange on regulations and market conditions supported the buildup of market
intelligence. In this regard, the partnership on palm oil improved the mechanisms
to comply with food-safety standards.

Spin-off of the palm-oil partnership on socioeconomic development
Oil palm has a huge development potential for Malaysia. Meeting European food-
safety standards is a necessary condition for smallholders whose produce is being
exported to Europe. However, it is not a sufficient condition for socioeconomic
development. The new quality standards also create barriers for smallholders,
and the partnership has not generated any tangible results that make life easier
for Malaysian smallholders in the palm-oil sector.

Impact on increasing coordination and cooperation
The partnership was understood as a platform for stakeholders. The Malaysian
stakeholders highlight that through the collaboration with European actors they
got better access to institutions in Europe. Very useful linkages were developed
especially during project activities such as an analysis of samples on food safety.

The relation of Malaysian government and the palm-oil industry can be characterized as very close already before the partnership started. It is not expected
that the relation between government and the private sector changed due to the
partnership.

Effectiveness and efficiency of the partnership – the Malaysian point of view

From the Malaysian point of view the partnership on palm oil had two selling points:

a the possibility to improve the negative perception of Malaysian palm oil which existed in The Netherlands;

b the possibility for technology and knowledge transfer by Dutch experts. In this regard the partnership was understood as a unique chance to be a mechanism for developing market intelligence.

If asked what the Malaysian partners expected from the partnership the answer is usually information about the EU market, modern technology and support in developing these agricultural subsectors. The major issues changed from quality concerns to environmental concern to the effects on climate change. The real added value of the PPP was the increased awareness of the common problems. However, through the partnership the government was also getting to know the NGOs better and internationally it improved contacts in the different countries (ministers of different countries now talked to each other). The partnership helped Malaysia to deal with EU regulation and led to the removal of some of the bottlenecks.

In general, the Malaysian stakeholders appreciated the partnership on palm oil but would have preferred more outcomes. The partnership could have indeed achieved more in reaching global acceptance for palm oil. In this context, the Malaysian partners were convinced that partnering in a trilateral partnership with Indonesia – the second important palm oil exporter – and with The Netherlands, as strategic import country, could achieve more than partnering on bilateral basis.

In Malaysia NGOs were usually considered as anti-development and not consulted or involved. Civil society started the discussion about the sustainability of the palm-oil sector. Another positive outcome is better care for the environment. Some of the main players have got to know each other in that framework and understand the question of market access to the EU also has to do with the quality of the product exported. The Malaysian partners perceived a shift of the objective of the partnership from quality issues towards more sustainability. Sustainability was not a primary objective of the partnership. Sustainability became more relevant in the course of the partnership (high value forest conservation discussion). In the palm-oil case, sustainability was indirectly introduced through linkages with the Roundtable on Sustainable Palm Oil (RSPO). RSPO, a not-for-profit association that brings together stakeholders of the palm oil industry – ranging from oil-palm producers and oil processors to environmental and developmental NGOs – aims to develop and implement global standards for sustainable palm oil (see Box 1). RSPO is the most developed system in regard to sustainable palm oil. Through project implementation in the context of sustainability, linkages with RSPO were created. RSPO is a voluntary collaboration for which it is important to create awareness and interest for the mechanism. Through overlap of stakeholders involved in RSPO and consultative processes of the reviewed partnership on palm oil, the WSSD partnership managed to fasten the process of creating awareness of RSPO. Even though there is no formal direct involvement of the Malaysian government in RSPO, the trilateral partnership created indirect linkages between RSPO and the Malaysian government. The Malaysian government committed itself to support activities focusing on smallholder inclusion.

Box 1   Roundtable on Sustainable Palm Oil

Roundtable for Sustainable Palm Oil (RSPO) is an international platform through which welfare organizations and industry are aiming to make worldwide palm-oil production more sustainable. The RSPO has more than 300 members, including representatives from the entire production and processing chain of palm oil (for instance Unilever, The Body Shop, IOI/Loders Croklaan, Golden Hope/Unimills, Ahold, Shell. WWF, Oxfam-Novib). The members cover around 40 percent of the global palm-oil production. In November 2005, the RSPO defined eight principles and 39 criteria for sustainable palm-oil production. The criteria were drawn up by a special working group in which both civil society organizations and companies were represented. One of the main principles adopted for the production of sustainable palm oil is that, whatever the case may be, new plantations may not replace any "primary forest" or areas with high conservation values. The first shipment of RSPO-certified palm oil arrived in Europe in November 2008, but European demand is modest. According to the latest RSPO Trade flash the production capacity of RSPO-certified palm oil has reached 1.75 million ton. This means that per month on average 140.000 ton of certified palm oil will become available to the market (RSPO, June 2009). But less than 1 percent of the certified sustainable palm oil produced was purchased by consumers at a 10 percent premium over uncertified palm oil (PalmoilHQ, 2009). The Asian palm-oil industry blames the European food and palm oil-processing manufacturers for being reluctant to purchase sustainable palm oil (PalmoilHQ, 2009).

The analysis of the data based on the theoretical framework

This contribution aimed to identify the internal (process) and external (contextual) factors that affected the performance of the partnership. The objective is to learn how to better manage complex partnerships in a global value chain. Table 4 summarizes the relevant variables and the score of their importance by the stakeholders in the case of Malaysia.

Table 4	Relevant factors influencing the failure of the partnerships and their score
Variable	*Score in Malaysia*
Agreement about the objectives	No real agreement
Mutual benefits	Low on the Malaysian side
Ownership	Low on the Malaysian side
Transparency	Low in general
Available finance	Considered limited by the Malaysians

The first internal factor influencing the success of a partnership mentioned in table 2 is "partnership building". Our definition of a partnership (table 1) requires agreement about the objectives, but that was missing in this case. Typically, The Netherlands was thinking in terms of developing commercial relations with a middle-income country like Malaysia, while Malaysia considers The Netherlands as more developed and a country that could provide assistance to Malaysia in a number of fields, like it does to neighboring Indonesia. In fact, the objectives changed from assuring market access to achieving more sustainable production. The objectives of the partnership were not always clear to all parties in the partnership. A problem of the tripartite partnership between The Netherlands, Malaysia and Indonesia was also that the decision-making structure the partnership created (or the governance model in terms of table 2) was not clear to all parties in the project. Already the midterm review noticed the low speed at which activities were carried out and stressed that more commitment would be necessary from different parties! In general, partnerships require a certain level of responsiveness to demonstrate resilience when difficulties occur. Responsiveness is characterized by flexibility, openness and awareness about possible risks which might occur along the partnership road. These characteristics have not been developed sufficiently in the partnership under review from a Malaysian point of view. A clear governance structure should have been created and the decision-making procedures should have been explained. Communication between the different partners could have been better. This applies to contacts between the three countries, between the ministries in these countries and the private sector and between the other parties in the partnership.

Another internal factor influencing the success of a partnership mentioned in table 2 is creating a win-win situation. Considering this partnership a win-win deal requires that the mutual benefits are clear, which was not always the case for Malaysia. A clear understanding of the mutual benefits is a requirement for a successful partnership. Only if stakeholders realize the mutual benefit of the partnership, they are willing to support the collaboration with their core organizational competencies. The fact that the Malaysian partners stepped out of the partnership shows that they did not consider that the partnership had added value for them. It also shows a lack of commitment, which is the second internal factor mentioned in table 2.

The third internal factor determining the outcome of a partnership is the feeling of ownership by the relevant party. As argued, the Malaysian side did not always have that feeling and sometimes considered the partnership a deal between a former colony and its motherland. It also seemed there were too many countries involved in the partnership and too many local organizations were actively involved. This means that it was difficult to take decisions and that projects were difficult to manage, in particular if only one meeting was organized per year for the trilateral coordinating committee. Furthermore the different parties did not always agree on the major problems and clear agreements were not always reached about who should do what and when.

The final internal factor that comes out in the analysis as affecting the partnership negatively is the lack of transparency. The Malaysian partners did not always have a good picture of the available financial means and that the partnership approach means that all partners contribute resources. The partnership did not include a financial risk-sharing structure. Project funding was a recurrent issue in the partnership because the sources of funding were not always clear.

Finally, available finance, an external factor, is mentioned in table 4 as influencing the results of the partnership negatively. The Malaysian side considered that there was not enough finance available to finance the projects it desired, while most Indonesian projects could be funded. Working groups tried to reach consensus, but at the level of the partnership it seemed that an agreement between two partners was enough to get a project approved. Approval still did not mean that the finance would be available in the Malaysian case.

Also the presence of a clear driver is mentioned as a factor influencing success in table 2. Staff members interviewed mentioned that it was not always clear who was driving the partnership, or the working groups for that matter. There was a lack of leadership and steering of the process. Similarly, good planning is an important internal factor. A well-functioning intra- and interorganizational coordination mechanism is required in successful partnerships. Administrative support systems throughout the partnership process are an option. Capacity, engagement and commitment of personnel involved in management and support processes of the partnership are success factors for managing new and complex forms of collaboration. Although the experiences with capacity building were generally considered positive, the support system for the partnership was not judged as optimal.

Besides the available finance, one other external factor that played a role was the time horizon. In fact, the time frame for the cooperation was not clear to all parties. The project lasted six years and it was still not clear when the fruits would be available and how the project would continue. At the same time a number of the actors in the process had changed. In fact this was again a problem of lack of ownership of this partnership. Another contextual or external variable is the history of cooperation between public sector, private sector and civil society in the countries concerned, which made it difficult to deal with the nonstate actors in an equal way. In the following section the lessons learned of this research on how to manage specific factors impacting on partnership performance are presented.

Lessons learned

Shared objectives and explicit expectations
It is important that the objectives are shared and the expectations of all parties are made explicit. A clear vision of the objectives of the partnership and to which all involved parties would be effectively committed is of high importance. The recommendation is that partnerships need to build on a shared vision (Steger et al., 2009). The actors have to follow clearly shared objectives and expectations.

Specifying the contributions of each partner and a clear governance structure
Another lesson learned is that it is necessary to develop a clear framework for the contribution by each partner before the partnership starts by means of a thorough and realistic cost/benefit assessment. The decision structure needs to be clear and the contribution of each party should be specified from the start. Some more sophisticated coordination and administration systems are required for ensuring transparency and accountability towards all actors involved.

Considering financing opportunities
Additionally, a fund for "urgent projects" could support the implementation of projects for which the usual mechanism to search for funding is inadequate. In this context, not only financial transparency is required. Transparency requires that partners have documentation available on the decisions they have taken and the related actions, performance and outcome.

A trilateral constellation may be too complex
The lesson learned from the Malaysian side was that the trilateral constellation could not work because the partners were not financially equal. From a Malaysian perspective it was considered that Indonesia did not have facilities and capacities for effective palm-oil export. Therefore, project implementation in Indonesia was more commonly considered as relevant compared to Malaysia. The Malaysian palm-oil sector is further developed and therefore several projects were not relevant for Malaysian partners.

The corresponding recommendation is not to make partnerships too complex. Involving different actors from different countries and different backgrounds requires novel governance and management techniques. These instruments need to be developed based on lessons learned from partnerships in practice and with feedback from this kind of research. Partnerships in the international context are not necessarily based on equality, especially if one partner is from the "North" and the other partners are from the "South". To compensate for this inbuilt inequality good arrangements should be put in place for the contribution of all partners for the financing of activities.

Conclusions

Continuous market access is extremely important for the global palm-oil value chain and for Malaysia. The complex collaborative arrangement studied set up to assure access and sustainable production faced several problems and the Malaysian partners decided to withdraw from the partnership. The Malaysian partners questioned whether the partnership served a purpose after the original objective had been achieved. The complexity and diversity of the partnership meant a challenge for such a collaborative arrangement. The lessons learned stimulated the reconsideration of the Malaysian position in the partnership on palm oil and the country finally decided to use an exit option and stepped out of the partnership. The main reasons for withdrawing were a perceived conflict of interest between the two Asian partners, or in terms of Malaysia, no equality in treatment. This resulted in difficulties to achieve the implementation of desired activities. In fact, there may have been insufficient communication between the partners because of a governance structure that was too distant from the day-to-day activities.

The study showed that in particular internal variables, such as the imbalances between the resources or power of the stakeholders involved, play a role. The rules governing the partnership and the accountability systems were underdeveloped. This led to nontransparency and hindered building trust between the actors. Flaws in the institutional design challenged shared responsibility and commitment and limited the upgrading of the palm-oil value chain.

However, there were also successes. From a Malaysian perspective Malaysian palm oil is now more integrated and traceable along the whole value chain. The market-access problem has been solved and production has become more sustainable. Also because of a better reputation for Malaysian palm oil, the Malaysian partners are happy with the outcome of the projects of the partnership focusing on food-safety regulation and capacity building. The fact that the main problem of traceability was solved was perceived as the main success of the partnership on palm oil. Also the capacity of the Malaysian Palm Oil Board (MPOB) staff with respect to market-access requirements was built up successfully. In particular the information exchange on regulations and market conditions supported Malaysia's knowledge of the international palm-oil market. The partnership on palm oil improved the mechanisms to comply with food safety standards.

This case typically proves that a partnership is not successful if it does not start in the right way and the conditions for success are not fulfilled. A number of internal and some external factors contributed to the low performance of the partnership in relation to the high expectations. The output and impact are limited and some indirect positive effects were by-products, which cannot be claimed exclusively by the partnership. Success factors were usually not present in the Malaysian case. Although it was observed that from a Malaysian point of view the partnership did not manage to develop its full potential for upgrading Malaysian capacity and for providing support for the necessary adjustments in the structure and operation of this value chain, the experience allowed us to learn a number of lessons for future partnership-development activities to upgrade global value chains.

In the first place there is not really a lead firm in this chain, but rather leading stakeholders, such as the Malaysian government and the different sector organizations. Secondly, this is a producer-driven chain. Malaysia is actively trying to use its expertise in palm-oil production to increase its direct and indirect market share. It does so by investing in palm-oil plantations in Indonesia, but also in a number of African countries. Finally, it turned out that the major stakeholders engage in a partnership as long as they see the benefit (solving the access problem), but withdraw when they see they can solve other problems (sustainable production) in a different way (the RSPO). The current partnership contributed only very indirectly to the success of the developed global standard for sustainable palm-oil production. The case study does show, however, that it is possible to upgrade global value chains through partnerships and provides evidence concerning the factors influencing the success or failure of such efforts.

Acknowledgements

The author acknowledges that this paper is partly based on findings of a review assignment by The Netherlands Ministries of Foreign Affairs and Agriculture, Nature and Food Security. The views expressed in the paper are entirely those of the author and do not necessarily represent the views of the partnership partners.

Moreover, the author would like to thank Stella Pfisterer[7] and other colleagues who supported the field research in Malaysia and Indonesia and who gave their reactions to a presentation of the findings of the report on the study prepared for the two ministries.

Notes

1   This contribution is based on the following reports:
    Pfisterer, S. and M.P. van Dijk (2009). *Review of the Trilateral WSSD Partnership. Malaysian Point of View – Final Report (October 2009)*. ECSAD: The Hague.
    Pfisterer, S., M.P. van Dijk and R. van Tulder (2009). *The Effectiveness of the Trilateral Partnership between The Netherlands, Malaysia and Indonesia. Review of the World Summit on Sustainable Development Partnership Program in Palm Oil, Shrimps and fruits and Vegetables. Final report (October 2009) for the Dutch Ministry of Agriculture, Nature and Food Security and the Dutch Ministry of Foreign Affairs*. ECSAD: The Hague.

2   "Collaborative advantage" will be achieved when "something usually creative is produced that no organization could have produced on its own and when each organisation, through collaboration, is able to achieve its own objective better than it could alone" (Huxham, 1993: 22).

3   FELDA land schemes were established to provide productive land to the landless poor so they could be gainfully employed in agriculture. This land resettlement is part of the government program to enhance the income of the rural population. The government provided the entire initial establishment and operating costs of the land scheme, which was centrally managed by FELDA. Settlers were chosen from all over the country and each family was given 3.45 hectares of land, including simple housing. Of the total, 3.44 hectares were for the agricultural holding and the remaining land was for accommodation. The government also provided all the necessary infrastructure to support the growth of the area. The settlers initially worked as laborers paid sufficiently to take care of their needs. Over the years, when the holding matured and production began to bring income to the settlers, the revenue was deducted to cover all the establishment, operating and management costs of the scheme. In the end, the land was given to the settlers, although FELDA still managed the operation of the scheme (Ahmad and Tawang, 1999).

4   Palm oil benefited from substitution effects, but prices have gone down in 2009. The biomass left after pressing palm nuts is an important resource that can be used better to produce energy. Palm oil is also competing with subsidized European rapeseed.

5   The Netherlands could help Malaysia with detailed satellite imaginary technology to keep track of the intrusions on the forest and the yield predictions.

6   There are land right issues, in particular on Serawak. A Dutch NGOs (NOVIB) has programs to deal with the issue.

7   Stella Pfisterer worked for MSM at the time of the research and is currently Research Associate at the Rotterdam School of Management of Erasmus University.

References

ADB (2008).   HYPERLINK "C:\\Users\\trien001\\AppData\\Local\\Microsoft\\Windows\\Temporary Internet Files\\Content.Outlook\\A3J633L9\\www.adb.org\\Documents\\Books\\ADO\\2009\\MAL.pdf" www.adb.org/Documents/Books/ADO/2009/MAL.pdf. Manilla: Asian Development Bank.

Ahmad, T. and A. Tawang (1999). *Effects of trade liberalization in agriculture in Malaysia*. The CGPRT Centre, Working paper 57. www.uncapsa.org/publications.

Aksoy, M.A. and J.C. Beghin (2005). *Global agricultural trade and developing countries*. Washington: World Bank.

Altenburg, T. (2006). 'Governance patterns in value chains: Shaping value chains for development'. In: Altenburg (ed.), 'Shaping value chains for development'. In: *European Journal of Development Research* 18 (4), pp. 498-521.

Brinkerhoff, J.M. (2002). *Partnerships for international development. Rhetoric or results?* London: Lynne Rienner Publishers.

CIA (2009). *World Fact book*. Washington: CIA.

Dijk, M.P. van (2006). 'Different effects of globalization for workers and poor in China and India: Comparing countries, clusters and ICT clusters?' In: *Journal of Economic and Social Geography* 97 (5), pp. 463-470.

Dijk, M.P. van (2008). 'Editorial'. In: *International Journal of Water* 4 (3/4), pp. 149-159.

Gereffi, G. and M. Korzeniewicz (eds.) (1994). *Commodity chains and global capitalism*. London: Praeger.

Guilani, E., C. Petrobelli and R. Rabellotti (2005). 'Upgrading in global value chains: Lessons from Latin American Clusters'. In: *World Development* 33 (4), pp. 549-573.

Harron, M.H., M.N. Shamsudin and I.A. Latif (2001). 'Challenges for Agribusiness: A case for Malaysia'. International Symposium *Agribusiness Management towards Strengthening Agricultural Development and Trade*, Chiang Mai University: Thailand.

Humphrey, J. and H. Schmitz (2004). *Governance and upgrading: Linking industrial cluster and global value chain research*. IDS Working Paper 120.

Huxham, C. (1993). 'Collaborative capability: An intra-organizational perspective on collaborative advantage'. In: *Public Money and Management* July-September, pp. 21-28.

Huxham, C., S. Vangen and C. Eden (2000). 'The challenge of collaborative governance'. In: *Public Management Review* 2 (3), pp. 337-358.

Kolk, A., R. van Tulder and E. Kostwinder (2008). 'Business and partnerships for development'. In: *European Management Journal* 26 (4), pp. 262-273.

Malaysian Ministry of Agriculture (1998). *New Dimensions in the Third National Agricultural Policy (1998-2010)*. Kuala Lumpur: MMA.

MPOA (2005). MPOA and Sustainable Palm Oil. Presentation held at RSPO Public Forum on Sustainable Palm Oil 6. January 2006, Kuala Lumpur.

MPOC (2009). www.mpoc.org.my/Industry_Overview.aspx (accessed June 2009)

MVO (2007) *Sustainable Palm Oil Production: What is the Dutch industry doing?* www.mvo.nl/Portals/o/duurzaamheid/grondstoffenvoorziening/download/071108-MVO-FactsheetPalmNL.pdf (accessed April 2009)

OECD (2006). *Evaluating the effectiveness and efficiency of partnerships*, workshop. Paris: 12 September 2006, ENV/EPOC (2006)15.

Pollit, C. and G. Bouckaert (2000). *Public management reform: A comparative analysis*. Oxford: Oxford University Press.

Schwartz K. (2008). 'The new public management: The future for reforms in the African water supply and sanitation sector?' In: *Utilities Policy* 16, pp. 49-58.

Steger, U., A. Ionescu-Somers, O. Salzmann and S. Mansourin (2009). *Sustainability partnerships: The manager's handbook*. Hampshire: Palgrave Macmillan.

Stern, E. (2004). 'Evaluating partnerships'. In A. Liebenthal, O. Feinstein and G. Ingram, *Evaluation & Development. The Partnership Dimension. WorldBank Series on Evaluation and Development*. Vol. 6. New Brunswick: Transaction Publishers.

Van Tulder, R. and E. Kostwinder (2007). *From Idea to Partnership. Evaluating the Effectiveness of Development Partnerships – Analytical Framework*. Unpublished document.

Visseren-Hamakers, I.J., B. Arts and P. Glasbergen (2007). 'Partnership as governance mechanism in development cooperation: Intersectoral North-South partnerships for marine biodiversity.' In: P. Glasbergen, F. Biermann and A.P.J. Mol, (eds.), *Partnerships, governance and sustainable development*. Cheltenham: Edward Elgar Publishing Limited, pp. 138-170.

World Bank (2008). *Agriculture for development. World Bank Development Report 2008*. New York: Oxford University Press.

Part IV

Value Chains in the Industrial and Services Sector

8 Global Competition in the Semiconductor Industry

A Comparative Study of Malaysian and Chinese Semiconductor Value Chains

Paul Goes and Meine Pieter van Dijk

Introduction

Because of lower production costs Asian countries are very attractive to locate electronic assembly activities. Countries, cities and companies try to create sustainable competitive advantages, to achieve sustainable economic growth. Knowledge and the ability to innovate are important to achieve sustainable economic development. Continuous innovation is one of the semiconductor industry's main characteristics. Semiconductors are components that provide the memory, logic and virtually all other intelligence functions in today's electronic systems. In this chapter, a comparison between China's and Malaysia's semiconductor industry is made. This comparison is chosen because China is showing the highest economic growth figures in the region while Malaysia is one of the most developed countries in Southeast Asia and an important player in the global semiconductor industry. The study tries to answer how sustainable the economic growth figures are and whether there is a move towards higher value-added activities. Three questions will be addressed, given both countries are competing for investments in this industry. First of all, are the actual semiconductor industries in both countries competing or rather complementary? Secondly, what can we say about the knowledge economy and other competitive conditions in both countries? This leads to the final question, which of these two countries will move up in the global value chain for semiconductors?

Value chains and innovation theories

Is the Malaysian semiconductor industry affected by the economic growth of China? We combine value chain and innovation theories with empirical data on the semiconductor industry to make a comparison between these two countries.

We will analyze the effects of changing market conditions and shifting global demand and assess the importance of innovations. Knowledge is seen as key to economic growth and is also important for the semiconductor industry. Hence innovation is relevant to improve competitiveness. Firms achieve competitive advantage through innovation, defined as: "improvements in technology and better methods to or ways of doing things" (Porter, 1990). Innovation is mostly a result of organizational learning, as well as formal research and development (R&D); it always involves investment in developing skills and knowledge and usually in physical assets and marketing effort. According to Porter (1990), innovations can shift competitive advantage when rivals either fail to perceive the new way of competing or are unwilling or unable to respond. The most typical causes of innovations that shift competitive advantage are new technologies, new or shifting buyer needs, the emergence of a new industry segment, shifting input costs or availability and changes in government regulations.

Mytelka and Farinelli (2000) choose to define innovation in a broader way to avoid an overemphasis on R&D and to encourage policymakers to widen their perspective on the opportunities for learning and innovation.[1] Innovation and intellectual-capital creation is one of the most important characteristics of the semiconductor industry. According to UNCTAD (2005) innovative activity and capabilities are essential for economic growth and development. Moreover, science, technology and innovation are identified as essential in achieving the Millennium Development Goals (Sachs and McArthur, 2005). The innovative milieu is very important in the competitiveness framework and therefore cannot be missed in this study.

Figure 1   The Value Chain

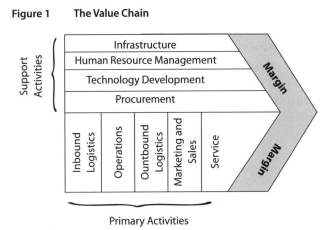

In a global economy, firms can configure their activities (assembly, manufacturing or R&D) wherever their advantage lies. We have tried to find out how competitive Malaysia and China are in the semiconductor industry. Secondly, the analysis of the semiconductor industry can be used to draw conclusions and make recommendations on how both countries can facilitate their "moving up" in the global value chain. Competitive advantage at the firm level basically depends on how companies organize and perform their activities. The activities resulting in competitive advantage differ per industry. Reconfiguring the value chain by for example relocating activities is often the reason for a major improvement in a firm's competitive position.

The value chain gives good insight in the sources of costs. Cost advantages can be realized through the whole value chain: Low-cost product developers, low-cost manufacturing, low-cost marketers and so on. The value chain is embedded in a value system, which consists of the suppliers, buyers and distribution channels. It is increasingly important for companies to manage the whole value system in order to create a competitive advantage (Porter, 1990). Multinational companies (MNCs) locate, for example, labor-intensive activities in low-cost countries. Not only labor-intensive activities are relocated, Schmitz (2006) also points to the relocation of R&D activities to Asian countries as one of the drivers of Asian economic growth.

Figure 2   Global Value Chain Semiconductor Industry

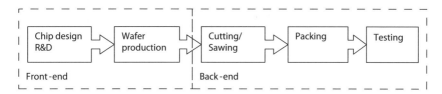

The semiconductor value chain can be broken up in front-end activities (chip design and wafer production) and back-end production (assembly and test, see figure 2). "Research and Design" of chips and "wafer production" are defined as "high-end" activities. These are mainly capital-intensive activities, with high value added and they are often performed in developed economies. The first step in the production process is the production of "wafers". Many chips are cut out of these wafers; this is where back-end activities start. These are mainly labor-intensive activities and therefore interesting to outsource to low-cost countries. Besides Japan, all East Asian countries have made their entry into the sector via the last step in the value chain, the packaging and testing of chips. The most important reason is the labor-intensive character of these activities. In general all Asian countries are moving to front-end activities but some are moving faster than others (Mathews and Cho, 2000).

Many semiconductor companies in Malaysia and China are originally from the United States (US), Europe and Japan. Many front-end activities are still located in their home country. The main reasons for keeping research and development (R&D) "at home" are: Lack of skilled labor in foreign countries and issues concerning intellectual property (IP). Important reasons for not moving existing wafer production facilities are high investment costs. A company needs to consider hidden and other costs associated with the relocation of their existing manufacturing facilities, such as productivity and revenue loss, training and retraining, hiring and redeployment cost, etc.

Numerous developments influence industries all over the world. This makes it difficult to ascertain which changes in the Malaysian semiconductor industry are caused by China. China can affect the Malaysian semiconductor industry in various ways. For example, demand for semiconductors or semiconductor-related products from China can rise because of an emerging *semiconductor-using* industry in China. Or, if the semiconductor industries in Malaysia and China are complementary, China's rise can lead to increased Foreign Direct Investment (FDI) from Malaysia in China and vice versa, which leads to increased trade between the two countries. A complementary semiconductor industry may also lead to changes in FDI and trade to and from China and Malaysia to and from other global players. An impression of Malaysia's and China's position in the global semiconductor industry can be given by analyzing trade statistics and FDI figures. Figure 3 visualizes the relations in the global semiconductor industry.

Figure 3 FDI and Trade relations

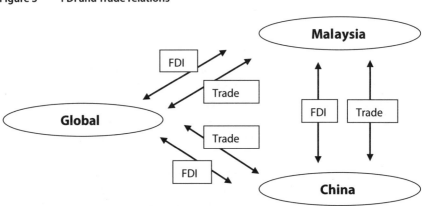

Source: Authors

A *competing* Malaysian and Chinese semiconductor industry will show contradictory changes in FDI and trade among the individual countries and in relation to the rest of the world, while trade in this industry between the two countries will decline. A *complementary* industry, however, will show similar developments in trade and FDI statistics and increasing trade and FDI between the two countries.[2] Insight in *how* the two countries relate to each other is necessary to interpret differences in competitiveness in the right manner, to draw the right conclusions and to make relevant recommendations.

Table 1   FDI and trade in competing and complementary structure: the hypotheses

Malaysia-China	Global	Between Malaysia-China
Competing	Changes in FDI and trade with global partners differ for Malaysia and China	FDI and trade between Malaysia and China decline
Complementary	Changes in FDI and trade with global partners are different for Malaysia and China	FDI and trade between Malaysia and China increase

China has two big advantages: "cheap labor" and a "big internal market". This makes China an interesting country to invest in. Will China take over markets from neighboring countries in Southeast Asia? Production factors like labor, capital, raw materials and entrepreneurship are still important but *knowledge* will be a key factor for driving growth (Economic Planning Unit Malaysia, 2000). Will Malaysia be able to continue to compete with China in an advanced sector like producing semiconductors, where the country had a ten-year lead until recently? Analyses of FDI and trade statistics that provide insight in the dynamics of the semiconductor industry in the two countries and give an indication whether the Malaysian semiconductor industry is "competing with" or "complementary to" the Chinese semiconductor industry will be presented.

Development in the semiconductor industry in Malaysia and China

Malaysian exports were always dominated by tin, rubber and palm oil. Nowadays, these products only count for 10 percent of the value of total exports. Electrical machinery and equipments, of which the semiconductor industry is also part, is the most important export sector and counts for 37 percent. This is also the most important sector in China where it accounts for 25 percent of its total exports.

Electrical machinery includes the semiconductor industry, but is also the main end-user of the semiconductor industry. Malaysia's and China's manufacturing performance is monitored by foreign companies looking for investment opportunities in low-cost countries. Especially China is an interesting country to invest in. The FDI inflows have gone up and down since 1990. In 2001, Malaysia faced a big decline in FDI inflows, probably because of the 9/11 terrorist attacks.

To understand determinants of competitiveness and to gain insight in the semiconductor industry, we will discuss the global value chain and China's and Malaysia's position in it. The semiconductor industry started in 1950 with transistors and other devices that are now classified as "discretes". In 1960, US companies like Fairchild and Texas Instruments drove the process of integration of such devices into a single chip or Integrated circuit (IC).

Figure 4   Change FDI inflow Malaysia, China, World (based on UNCTAD, 2005)

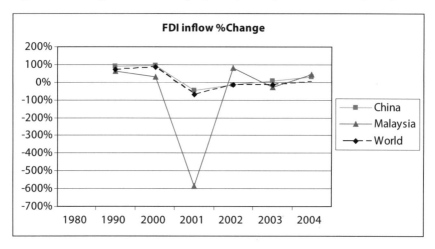

In the 1970s, Intel developed entirely new kinds of ICs, such as Dynamic Random Access Memories (DRAM) and general purpose (programmable) microprocessors. In the 1980s, chips available for use in computers, consumer products, communication devices and many more such products exploded, through the process of customization, Application Specific ICs (ASICs) and various kinds of logic chips, microcontrollers and many more of such specializations. The 1990s were an era of rapid diversification in each of these product areas. Southeast Asia did specifically well in the market segment of memory chips (Mathews and Cho, 2000). The following table provides insight in the different semiconductor segments and their share in the world market.

Table 2   Overview of the global semiconductor industry (in USD million in the first column, or as a percentage)

Forecast	2007 Amount	2004 Annual growth	2005 Annual growth	2006 Annual growth	2007 Annual growth
Americas	42,373	20.8	-1.4	1.4	8.5
Europe	47,630	22	5.2	4.8	9.6
Japan	53,753	17.5	3.3	4.4	9
Asia pac.	119,568	41.3	11.8	7.2	12.4
Total world	263,324	28	6.3	5.2	10.5
Discrete semi-products	17,999	18.1	0.5	4.7	8.5
Opto-electronics	18,231	43.8	9	8.9	11.9
Sensors	6,503	33.6	-2.6	16.9	19.8
Integrated circuits	220,592	27.7	6.9	4.6	10.3
Total products	263,325	28	6.3	5.2	10.5

Source: www.wsts.org

The table shows how Asia has become the most important region for the semiconductor industry. The Asian Pacific region displays the highest growth figures and is expected to be more important than America and Europe together in 2006. The Asian market is growing fast because it can offer competitive products in the semiconductor industry; at the same time the semiconductor end-user industry (the electronics sector) is growing rapidly which makes the region an even more attractive location.

Japan is by far the dominant producer and exporter of semiconductors. South Korea is a major producer in its own right, followed by Taiwan, while Singapore is just establishing itself as an indigenous producer. After independence from the British, Malaysia followed a conventional import substitution strategy in the 1960s but with meager results. When Singapore showed success in opening up to multinationals Malaysia followed but lagged behind a few years. Particularly the island of Penang actively pursued Singapore-style policies from the 1970s onwards. The sites of most of Malaysia's semiconductor and electronics industry are on the Island of Penang and in Klang Valley. More recent developments of the semiconductor industry in Malaysia took place in Kulim in the state of Kedah, where the first wafer plant opened in May 2006. The Malaysian government and Kedah State government worked together to set up Kulim High-Tech Industrial Park (KHTP), inspired by the Taiwanese Hsinchu Science-based Industry Park. The semiconductor industry is not only driven by FDI. Since the late 1990s, Malaysia has witnessed the emergence of local companies serving the needs of advanced semiconductor firms. Local firms include equipment suppliers, assembly and test contractors and even wafer plants.

State agencies have played an important role in shaping the overall trajectory of the semiconductor industry. Malaysia is looking for an institutional framework in which MNCs are induced to act as engines of the country's high-technology industrialization, export growth and formation of small service and component firms (Mathews and Cho, 2000).[3] The country has several front-end production facilities. Some local companies have wafer-production facilities, while most foreign companies still focus on assembly and test facilities in Malaysia. MNCs often use local suppliers for their purchases; the lower cost of their raw materials is sometimes a reason to move to Asia. The economic development in China provides opportunities for Malaysian companies to get cheaper raw materials and to be close to the end-user market. Most foreign companies praise Malaysia for their knowledge but the choice among top engineers is still too small to do product development in Malaysia. Malaysia does offer subsidies to local companies to organize extra schooling. This might help Malaysia to attract more front-end activities.

Of all East-Asian countries, China shows the greatest potential of becoming a major semiconductor power.[4] The financial and investment capabilities of Hong Kong, plus a growing electronics and IT industry, suggests that the Chinese semiconductor industry is ready for more growth. China considers electronics and IT as the driving industry for economic development, and has even created a Ministry for the Electronics Industry (MEI). China developed its own capability in discrete and simple ICs through state-owned enterprises like Huanjing Electronics, Jiangnan Semiconductor Devices at Wuxi. The MEI focuses on attracting both back-end and front-end activities (Mathews and Cho, 2000).

Whereas semiconductor MNCs specialized in back-end (assembly and test) concentrate their activities in Malaysia, wafer fabrication houses have grown in China. There seem to be over twenty production sites in China today while there are only two local enterprises and one MNC in Malaysia. The Chinese government has also launched technology parks with significant hiring of high-tech human capital. Although foreign MNCs are still hesitant to relocate critical production processes or R&D activities to China because of weak enforcement of intellectual property rights, slowly but surely investments in R&D for commodity chips increases. The big Chinese market offers firms opportunities to find the right suppliers at a competitive price.

Competing or complementary semiconductor industries?

How did the semiconductor industry in both countries develop in the last decennium? Both Malaysia and China are going through periods of high economic growth. Trade statistics in the semiconductor industry for both Malaysia and China are available, namely in the UN Comtrade for "Diodes, transistors, semi-conductors, etc."[5] Table 3 shows the import and export statistics for "Malaysia and the World" and "Malaysia and China". The figures are in USD showing the change from the previous year as a percentage.

Table 3   Malaysian trade statistics on "Diodes, transistors, semi-conductors, etc." (percentage change)

Period	Malaysia to the world	Malaysia to the world	Malaysia to China	Malaysia to China
2000	14	26	28	54
2001	-20	1	-19	26
2002	19	4	44	24
2003	14	5	21	1
2004	24	9	33	74

Source: UN Comtrade

"Malaysia-World" trade figures show a much faster growing export than imports for the semiconductor industry. The trade between "Malaysia-China" is growing fast, both export and imports are growing at high rates. The years 2001 and 2003 seem a bit odd in the whole analysis, 2001 may be affected by the terrorist attacks in New York, and 2003 may be influenced by the SARS epidemic in the South-East Asian region. Statistics for China, including China mainland, Hong Kong and Macao special administrative regions (SAR) are presented in table 4.

Table 4   China trade statistics on "Diodes, transistors, semi-conductors, etc." (percentage change)

Period	China to the world	China to the world	China to Malaysia	China to Malaysia
2000	39	36	39	47
2001	-8	-10	5	-18
2002	25	39	-15	77
2003	24	20	-4	34
2004	23	31	68	38

Source: UN Comtrade

Similar to Malaysia, the trade statistics for "China-World" show odd numbers in 2001. Import and export between China and the rest of the world show a similar fluctuation. China is growing as a producer and a user of semiconductors. Looking at the "China-Malaysia" relation, the trade value shows figures different from "Malaysia-China", but the development of the import and exports, shows a similar pattern. On the whole, trade between the two countries is growing, with explainable odd figures in 2001 and 2003. The differences between the Malaysian and Chinese trade statistics and the world import and export statistics are shown in table 5.[6]

Table 5   World trade statistics on "Diodes, transistors, semi-conductors, etc."

Period	Export world		Import world	
	Trade value	% change	Trade value	% change
2000	€ 38.065.859.334		€ 37.895.935.813	
2001	€ 29.290.847.367	-23	€ 31.434.993.188	-17
2002	€ 30.481.604.416	4	€ 32.805.103.831	4
2003	€ 38.815.274.144	27	€ 38.629.642.703	18
2004	€ 47.189.238.523	22	€ 48.841.642.336	26

Source: UN Comtrade

In 2004, Malaysia was responsible for 7 percent of the world export in the semiconductor industry, China accounted for 15 percent in the same year. The average growth of world exports in the semiconductor industry from 2000 to 2004 was about 24 percent. Malaysia's (36%) and China's (91%) growth figures for export in those years were considerably higher. Especially China went through an excessive growth. Exports Malaysia-China grew 87 percent where exports China-Malaysia grew only 45 percent. However, Malaysia still shows growth figures higher than the world market. A closer look at the trade figures between Malaysia and China shows a higher than average growth in exports from Malaysia to China. Malaysia seems to be benefiting from the economic growth in China; in that sense Malaysia's semiconductor production is *complementary* to China's.

Foreign direct investment is also used to identify whether Malaysia and China are complementary or competitive in the semiconductor industry. Unfortunately, there are no FDI statistics at the activity level. Hence, the analysis of FDI development in Malaysia and China is limited to an overview of FDI inflows and outflows at the country level, an analysis of FDI by source country and the FDI by sector. China is known for its huge growth of FDI flows. China is not only a receiver but also an investor in other countries. A big drop in FDI can be noticed again in 2001, but Malaysia was hit much harder than China (table 6, figure 4).

Table 6   Malaysian and Chinese FDI Inflows and outflows (in USD million)

		1980	1990	2000	2011	2002	2003	2004
China	FDI inflows	767	6,762	102,638	70,815	62,800	67,532	95,265
	FDI outflows	82	3278	60,268	18,241	20,052	5335	41,583
Malaysia	FDI inflows	934	2611	3788	554	3203	2473	4624
	FDI outflows	201	129	2026	267	1905	1369	2061

Source: UNCTAD (2005)

According to UNCTAD (2005) China is perceived as a high FDI performer with high potential, while Malaysia is seen as a low FDI performer with low potential. Malaysia and China both use a different classification; this makes it difficult to compare the figures. For Malaysia (table 7) the electronics and electrical-product sector is by far the most important receiver of FDI, the semiconductor industry is part of it.

Table 7   Malaysian FDI inflows by industry

Share of FDI by sector Rank	Industry	Share (%)
1	Electronics & electrical products	58
2	Paper, printing & publishing	5
3	Chemicals & chemical products	5
4	Scientific & measuring equipment	5
5	Fabricated metal products	3

Source: www.mida.gov.my

In China manufacturing is by far the largest receiver of FDI. Semiconductor production is part of manufacturing, but it is not known how big its share is (table 8).

Table 8   Chinese FDI inflows by industry

Share of FDI by sector	Industry	Share (%)
Rank		
1	Manufacturing	70
2	Lease & business	6
3	Real estate	4
4	Wholesale	4
5	Computer & software	4

Source: www.fdi.gov.cn

The country of origin of the FDI is important. Malaysia and China both show a different top 5 of most important FDI source countries. In Malaysia (table 9) the US, Asian and European involvement dominates, while in China (table 10) we find only US and Asian investors. Hong Kong accounted for 47 percent of foreign investments in China, but is not shown in the table. US, Japan and Germany are the most important foreign investors in the semiconductor industry (Cunningham and Samy, 2005). The US and Japan are both among Malaysia's and China's most important foreign investors; Germany is one of Malaysia's most important foreign investors. Taiwan is also an important investor in the semiconductor industry and China's most important source of FDI.

Table 9   Malaysian FDI inflow by source country

Share of FDI by sector	Industry	Share (%)
Rank		
1	Taiwan	20
2	USA	16
3	Korea	15
4	Japan	14
5	Singapore	6

Source: www.mida.gov.my

China as foreign investor in Malaysia is ranked in 11th place with 1.23 percent of total Malaysian FDI. About 40 percent of total China investment comes from Hong Kong SAR. Malaysia as investor in China accounts for 0.64 percent. Bilateral investments are too small to allow firm conclusions.

Table 10   Chinese FDI inflow by source country

Share of FDI by sector	Industry	Share (%)
Rank		
1	Taiwan	13
2	USA	9
3	Korea	6
4	Japan	6
5	Singapore	3

Source: www.fdi.gov.cn

The US and Japan are the most important investors in the semiconductor industry in both Malaysia and China. This indicates that both countries are competing for FDI inflows in the semiconductor industry.[7] Cunningham and Samy (2005) conclude that labor costs and the real-exchange rates are important factors to explain FDI in the semiconductor industry. In their study they show that between 1985-2002, China hosted five new semiconductor factories, while Malaysia hosted only one new foreign semiconductor factory. Both countries invested a lot in new domestic semiconductor factories. China built twelve new factories, while Malaysia built four new ones. Japan and the US have been the most important investors in the semiconductor industry, these countries are both in the top five source countries for Malaysia and China.

Developing towards higher value added

To analyze the development of the semiconductor industry in Malaysia and China and draw conclusions on how the two countries are progressing on their goals to move up in the global value chain, value-added figures are highly relevant. Unfortunately, value-added figures for the semiconductor industry are not available. The analysis is limited to the industry level.[8] Table 11 clearly shows how Malaysia successfully moved up in the value chain and realized an increase of 49.8 percent in value added per employee. China on the other hand, was less successful and even experienced a decrease of value added per employee during this period. The faster rising labor costs in China indicate a decreasing competitiveness in comparison to Malaysia, where labor costs also rose but slower than the increase of value added.

Table 11   Labor costs and value added per worker in manufacturing (USD per year)

	Labor costs (wage)			Value added		
	1980-1984	1995-1999	% increase	1980-1984	1995-1999	% increase
Malaysia	2,519	3,429	36.1	8,454	12,661	49.8
China	472	729	54.4	3,061	2,885	-5.7

Source: World Bank (2000)

Figure 5 shows the value added per worker in USD per year in the manufacturing sector in Malaysia and China from 1999 to 2004, including a forecast for 2005 to 2007. The graph is based on data for the year 1999 and the growth rate of value added in industry as shown in table 12. Malaysia has a much higher value added per worker in the manufacturing sector, which is still growing steadily. Looking at China's growth rate of value added, a higher growth in percentage is noticed. China is catching up, but compared to Malaysia it still has a long way to go.

Table 12   Growth rate of value added in industry (% per year)

	2000	2001	2002	2003	2004	2005	2006	2007
Malaysia	13.6	-3.8	4.1	7.2	7.9	6.2	6.1	6.4
China	9.4	8.4	9.8	12.7	11.1	9.3	9.8	10.1

Source: ADB (2005)

Figure 5   Value added USD per worker per year in industry

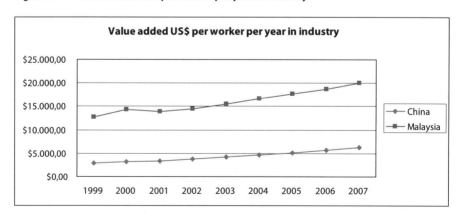

Source: ADB (2005)

Why are the value-added figures in Malaysia remarkably higher than in China and why is value added in China growing faster? We will now look at the comparative advantage of Malaysia and China in the semiconductor industry. The comparative advantage at the country level indicates how one country can perform activities at lower opportunity costs than other countries. In other words, this country is relatively more efficient in those activities. The "revealed comparative advantage indicator" is applied to the semiconductor industry of Malaysia and China.[9] Table 13 summarizes these calculations for Malaysia and China and these calculations are visualized in figure 5.

Table 13	Calculation revealed comparative advantage in the semiconductor industry (%)				
Percentages	*2000*	*2001*	*2002*	*2003*	*2004*
RCA China	136.2	155.6	165.3	149.3	152.0
Xcs/Xws	9.9	11.9	14.3	13.9	15.3
Xct/Xwt	7.3	7.7	8.6	9.3	10.1
RCA Malaysia	417.4	468.2	513.4	484.3	488.5
Xms/Xws	6.6	6.9	7.9	7.1	7.2
Xms/Xwt	1.2	1.5	1.5	1.5	1.5

Source: Authors' calculations using UN Comtrade data

Malaysia's revealed comparative advantage (RCA) is clearly higher than China's revealed comparative advantage. Hence, Malaysia is relatively more competitive in the semiconductor industry. Although China's share in the world semiconductor market is almost twice as high as Malaysia's, China would do better to focus on other activities, which have lower opportunity costs. On the basis of revealed comparative advantage, Malaysia should put more effort in developing its semiconductor industry, as they are able to produce at lower opportunity costs than China. Malaysia and China are considered latecomers in the semiconductor industry. Latecomers face high barriers in terms of technology and export markets. Developing countries have a poorer developed technological infrastructure and poorly established research, development & engineering (RD&E) institutions and educational systems. Secondly, they seem to lag behind in international marketing, because the local market tends to be less developed.

Nelson and Rosenberg (1993) argue that access to high-technology competences and a developed national innovation system (NIS) are important to competitiveness at the company level. Assistance is needed from governments for technology development and international marketing. Different mechanisms of technology leverage are applied in developing countries to enhance technology level.[10] For example, joint ventures and technology-transfer agreements are widely used.[11] How competitive are Malaysia and China in the semiconductor industry? To gain insight in the differences between the two countries and how this leads to a move upwards in the value chain, competitiveness will be measured on twelve dimensions, grouped in four different categories: Innovation, investment, economic environment and market and based on normalized scores.

Figure 6   Revealed comparative advantage China and Malaysia

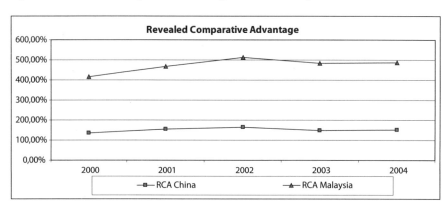

Is Malaysia's semiconductor industry complementary or competing with the Chinese semiconductor industry? On the basis of trade data for Malaysia and China the conclusion is drawn that both countries are complementary to each other. Both counties display higher growth figures than the semiconductor world market, which indicates a competitive advantage for both counties. Although the Chinese industry is growing much faster than Malaysia, Malaysia is still a net exporter to China. Both countries focus on different types of semiconductors. Analyzing trade data further, shows that Malaysia has a considerably higher RCA indicator than China. This means Malaysia has a relative competitive advantage in the semiconductor industry.

Operationalization of knowledge economy

The growing importance of innovation and R&D is stressed in new economic growth models. Whereas traditional growth models focus on providing physical infrastructure to attract firms from outside, the new economic growth models put the emphasis on the development of technology and (regional) innovation systems. We used a number of indicators to assess the competitiveness of the semiconductor industry in Malaysia and China (table 14).

Table 14   Analytical framework for competitiveness and the knowledge economy

Innovation indicators are measured by:	Economic environment to attract foreign investments in the semiconductor industry:
1 Number of patents	7 Effective Intellectual Property protection
2 Innovation Capability Index (ICI)	
3 Presence of National Innovation System	8 Sectoral flexibility of labor policies
	9 Promotion of free-trade and fair-trade policies
	10 Quality of human resources
Are Malaysia and China interesting for investors:	Competitiveness of the market is measured by:
4 R&D spending capability	11 Strength of internal market
5 Legal environment and human rights	12 Proximity to local customer base
6 Level of literacy and health	

The World Bank has developed a scorecard for the knowledge economy (Dahlman and Utz, 2005).[12] They consider four pillars of the knowledge economy: Economic and institutional regime, education and human resources, innovation system and information infrastructure, and suggest different indicators for each pillar. The dimensions selected by the authors and the corresponding World Bank data are presented in table 15. We used our own data on competitiveness: The innovation capability index (2), the strength of the internal market and the proximity to local customers (11 and 12 in table 14), both derived from our theoretical framework. We will now give a description of these categories before presenting the data for Malaysia and China in a single figure.

Table 15 shows three different values. The column "own research" presents the values as calculated in our own research, the column "World Bank" presents the values calculated by the World Bank, a one on one comparison of Malaysia and China is presented in the column "comparison". The country with the highest score gets an index of 100; the other country is calculated as follows:

$$\frac{\text{Country B}}{\text{Country A}} * 100 = \text{index country B}$$

Table 15   Values for five dimensions of knowledge economy and market potential

Own dimension	Malaysia	China	World Bank dimension	Malaysia	China	Malaysia	China
1 Number of patents per million inhabitants	79.0	100	1 Patents granted	7.65	5.15	100.0	67.32
2 Innovation capability index	100	77	2 Innovation capability index	-	-	100.0	77.0
3 Presence of national innovation system	59	100	3 Research in R&D per million inhabitants	3.19	4.47	71.36	100
4 Country's R&D spending	87	100	4 Total expenditure for R&D	5.59	7.63	73.26	100.0
5 Legislative environment of investors	100.0	58.94	5 Rule of law 2005	6.82	4.02	100.0	58.94

Source: World Bank website and authors.

The dimensions discussed in table 15 are explained below. The focus will be on the calculated scores based on our own research, while conclusions are drawn on basis of the column comparison.

Innovation

1   The number of patents granted per 1,000,000 residents
Innovation systems, whether national or regional, are defined as cooperation between private and public parties working together to initiate, import, modify and diffuse new technologies. A regional system differs from a national system, either as a geographical area or an industrial cluster. The semiconductor industry is characterized by high R&D spending, which (should) lead to high patenting numbers. According to WIPO (World Intellectual Property Organization), the "Semiconductor Devices; Electric Solid State Devices not Otherwise provided for" industry (technical field) is 5th in number of patents over 2005. This accounts for 2.5 percent of worldwide given patents.

The number of patent applications is an indicator to assess how innovative countries are: The more innovative, the more relevant inventions. To compare two countries, the number of patent applications per 1,000,000 residents is measured. Obviously, more inhabitants can apply for a higher number of patents; a considerably smaller country with the same number of applications is clearly more innovative. Both Malaysia and China are in the WIPO's top 10 ranking of development countries in number of applications.

Table 16   Top 10 ranking development countries WIPO

Country	1995	1996	1997	1998	1999	2000	2001	2002	2003	2004	2005	Pat/ mln	Inhabi- tants (mln)	Rank	Country	Pat/ Index mln
Rep. of Korea	196	306	305	510	870	1,580	2,324	2,520	2,949	3,556	4,422	90.6	48.8	1	Singapore	98.0
China	103	123	166	348	277	784	1,731	1,018	1,295	1,704	2,501	1.9	1314.0	2	Rep. of Korea	90.6
India	0	4	13	14	101	190	295	525	764	723	675	0.6	1095.4	3	Cyprus	35.0
South Africa	42	72	84	114	317	387	419	384	357	411	360	8.1	44.2	4	South Africa	8.1
Singapore	26	35	80	125	168	222	288	330	282	431	441	98.0	4.5	5	China	1.9
Brazil	67	72	95	113	115	178	173	201	219	278	275	1.5	188.1	6	Malaysia	1.5
Mexico	11	31	46	66	55	73	104	132	131	118	140	1.3	107.5	7	Brazil	1.5
Egypt	0	0	0	8	1	1	1	1	22	53	51	0.6	78.9	8	Mexico	1.3
Cyprus	3	4	4	7	7	19	38	23	28	42	28	35.0	0.8	9	Egypt	0.6
Malaysia	2	3	2	4	5	5	18	18	31	45	37	1.5	24.4	10	India	0.6

Note: Malaysia is not a PCT contracting state, applicants who are nationals and/or residents of this state (or of any other state which is not a PCT contracting state) can file a PCT application together with another applicant who is a national and/or resident of a PCT contracting state.
Source: WIPO Statistics, PCT Statistical Indicators Report, Annual Statistics 1978-2005, May 2006

China shows very high growth figures for granted patents. The number increased from only 103 patents in 1995 to 2501 patents in 2005. Although Malaysia is not a PCT (Patent Cooperation Treaty) contracting state, applicants can file a PCT application together with another applicant who is a national and/or resident of a PCT contracting state. Malaysia shows a more modest patent growth figures from 2 in 1995 to 37 in 2005. This is still a 9th rank on WIPO's "PTC and Developing Countries" list.

China has far more applications but also a much greater population than Malaysia. China has, calculations based on a population of 1.3 billion people, about 1.9 applicants per one million people. Malaysia on the other hand, reaches 1.5 applications per one million inhabitants (26 million). But the number of patents is not the only relevant indicator; some companies find the application too costly or too time consuming. The UNCTAD measures how capable countries are in the Innovation Capability Index. The innovation capability index is the second indicator used to measure "innovation".

2 Innovation Capability Index

The Innovation Capability Index (ICI) measures at the country level the innovative capabilities per country. The ICI combines the "Technological Activity Index" and the "Human Capital index", both are weighed equally. In the table below the components of the "ICI" are further clarified. The ICI is an index calculated by combining the "Technological Activity Index" and "Human Capital index", both are weighed equally (UNCTAD, 2005).

Table 17   Innovation Capability Index (ICI)

Indices	Components	Weights attached
Technological activity index	R&D personnel per million US patents grated per million population Scientific population	All three components have equal weights
Human capital index	Literacy rate as % of population Secondary school as % of age group Tertiary enrolment as % of age group	Weight of 1 Weight of 2 Weight of 3
UNCTAD innovation capability index	Technological activity index	Both indices have equal weight

Source: UNCTAD (2005)

Table 18   ICI high performers

Rank	Country	1995	Country	2001
1	Sweden	0.957	Sweden	0.979
2	Finland	0.947	Finland	0.977
3	Canada	0.947	United St.	0.927
4	United St.	0.946	Denmark	0.926
5	Australia	0.944	Norway	0.923
6	Denmark	0.934	Australia	0.920
7	Norway	0.929	Canada	0.907
8	United K.	0.914	United K.	0.906
9	Netherlands	0.912	Belgium	0.894
10	Belgium	0.911	Netherlands	0.888
11	Japan	0.906	Japan	0.885

The top 10 performers on the ICI in the world is displayed in table 18. It is dominated by North-America, European countries and Japan. The top 10 only changes in sequence between 1995 and 2001. Malaysia and China are found back among the "medium" performers in terms of "ICI". According to table 18 Hong Kong's and China's positions slightly declined. Hong Kong went from a 41st ranking in 2001 to a 45th place in 1995, while China dropped from 72nd position to the 74th. Malaysia did a better job and climbed up from the 67th position in 1995 to the 60th place in 2001.

Table 19   ICI low performers

Rank	Country	1995	Country	2001
40	Uzbekistan	0.605	Jordan	0.595
41	Hong Kong	0.593	Georgia	0.593
42	Cyprus	0.581	Chile	0.576
43	Chile	0.580	Cyprus	0.566
44	Slovakia	0.580	Uzbekistan	0.564
45	South Afr.	0.579	Hong Kong	0.563
60	Philippines	0.452	Malaysia	0.467
61	Egypt	0.449	Bahrain	0.466
62	Peru	0.448	Venezuela	0.460
63	Turkey	0.430	Peru	0.425
64	Brazil	0.421	Philippines	0.423
65	Thailand	0.413	Moldova	0.413
66	Jamaica	0.413	Qatar	0.403
67	Malaysia	0.394	Jamaica	0.395
72	China	0.393	Tunisia	0.365
73	Zimbabwe	0.351	Tajikistan	0.362
74	Iran	0.349	China	0.358

3   Presence of National Innovation System

We looked at innovation systems at country level but only in the semiconductor industry. A National Innovation System (NIS) is defined as a network of institutions in the public and private sectors, either in the context of a cluster/industry or not, whose activities and interactions initiate, import, modify and diffuse new technologies. According to UNCTAD (2005) National Innovation Systems are becoming more and more interdependent. The lack of local capabilities can limit interaction between a particular country and the rest of the world. The definition of a NIS used in this research: "The network of institutions in the public and the private sectors whose activities and interactions initiate, import, modify, and diffuse new technologies." (Freeman, 1987) A NIS is measured with the following indicators (Van Dijk, 2006):
– joint industry activities;
– public/private interactions;
– public and private expenditures on R&D;
– technology diffusion;
– number of R&D institutions;
– number of projects;
– R&D personnel.

The first three indicators; "Joint Industry activities", "Public/private interactions" and "Public and Private expenditures on R&D" are also be measured by the competitive dimension "R&D spending". A quantification of "technology diffusion" could not be found. This leaves three indicators measuring competitiveness of the NIS in Malaysia and China that can be used. Table 20 shows the number of R&D workers in Malaysia and China. Between 1996 and 2000, the number of R&D workers more than doubled in Malaysia, while in China the number of R&D workers grew by 17 percent. In the far left column, the indexes for both countries are calculated. China has 702 R&D workers per million inhabitants.

Table 20   R&D personnel in Malaysia and China

	Total pop. mln	1996	1997	1998	1999	2000	% of total workforce	R&D worker per 1 mln	Index
Malaysia	24.4	4,437		6,656		10,060	0.41	412	59
China	1314	787,000	831,200	755,200	821,700	922,131	0.01	702	100

Source: UN Statistical yearbook

Investment

Investment refers to indicators showing how attractive Malaysia and China are as countries to invest in. To be an interesting country to invest in for the semiconductor industry, the countries should provide adequate funds to improve the technological level in the country. This means the government should invest in innovation and have supporting legal, educational and health policies.

4 Country's R&D spending
R&D spending measures the country's spending on R&D as a percentage of GDP. The importance of government spending is recognized in Malaysia and China. In Malaysia, MIMOS is a government-based semiconductor company. They have R&D facilities and offer support to other companies. Furthermore, High-tech industrial parks, like TPM (Technology Park Malaysia) in Kulim, offer R&D support. However, they do not market their activities aggressively. Government investments in R&D are important to come to effective partnerships. Countries receive a higher mark when a higher percentage of GDP is spent in R&D. This dimension tries to measure whether it is effective to invest in R&D in one of the two counties. Governments can help to make the country attractive to invest in. Interviews show that in China companies are pleased with government support and investments in R&D. Surprisingly, the Malaysian-based companies would like more government involvement. This is in contradiction with "Global R&D report" where Malaysia's government's efforts are praised and "resulted in quite measurable increases in R&D intensity, growing from 0.4% of the GDP in 1998 to 0.7% in 2002."

Table 21   Sources of R&D funds in China, Malaysia, Japan, the US and the Netherlands (%)

Country	Industry	Government	Academia/ other	Funds from abroad
China	57.6	33.4	6.3	2.7
Malaysia	51.5	32.1	4.9	11.5
Japan	73.9	18.2	7.5	0.4
USA	61.2	31.3	7.3	0.0
The Netherlands	51.8	36.2	1.0	11.0

Source: Red Business Information, Global R&D report

In table 21, four sources of R&D funding are distinguished. Malay and Chinese governments are spending similar amounts as share of total R&D in the two countries. The government spending is in line with developed countries like the US and the Netherlands. Japan is the odd one in the list where the government spends only 18.2 percent of the national R&D expenditure.

Another interesting point is how cultural differences can influence the R&D spending capability. Several authors mention how it is not in the Chinese nature to invest in R&D facilities. Chinese rather copy than buy new inventions (Schulte Nordholt, 2006). This is also confirmed by interviews. Malaysian companies are not willing to investment heavily in order to produce world-class goods. According to the Malaysian newspaper The Star ("M' firms urged to invest in R&D", 4 June 2006) foreigners, however, are willing to pay for their R&D done locally.

To indicate differences between Malaysia and China in the competitive dimension "R&D spending capabilities", this study uses the amount of "R&D spending as percentage of GDP". Table 22 shows R&D spending in five different countries. Expenditures on R&D as a percentage of GDP in both China and Malaysia are not spectacular at all in comparison to developed countries like Japan or the US.

Table 22   R&D spending in different countries (in billion USD)

Country	GDP 2004	R&D 2004	R&D 2005	R&D 2006
China	7,262	108 (1.5%)	126	140
Malaysia	229	3 (1.3%)	3	3
Japan	3,745	119 (3.2%)	123	126
USA	11,200	301 (2.7%)	312	321
The Netherlands	481	9 (1.9%)	10	10

Source: Red Business Information, Global R&D report

China is spending more on R&D than Malaysia. UNCTAD (2005) and World Bank (2005) note that China is considered to be one of the most attractive countries for R&D locations (61.8%) while Malaysia is considered number 15 with 2.9 percent of the votes.

5   Legislative environment for investors

Obviously, the legal environment is important for foreign investors. Less bureaucracy and feasible regulations make it easier to invest in a foreign country. The legislative environment is measured by the following indicators:
 – policy uncertainty;
 – regulation and tax administration;
 – time dealing with officials as percentage of total management time;
 – start a business: Number of start-up procedures;
 – start a business: Time required in days;
 – enforcing contracts: Number of procedures;
 – enforcing contracts: Time required in days.

Malaysia and China are compared on these six indicators. A higher mark means an easier accessible legislative environment. Both Malaysia and China try to attract FDI by offering attractive tax levels, certain facilities, information and so on. They both prefer to attract high-tech companies and therefore regulations are made so that more technologically advanced companies get a more attractive offer.

However, it is difficult to compare Malaysia and China on this dimension. Firstly, because it is very difficult to measure the impact of regulations. Secondly, many differences within each country may exist. In Malaysia and China, for example, extra incentives, such as subsidies for education and the conditions for obtaining land, differ per region and depend on the negotiation process. China is still perceived as having a very complex legislative environment. When starting a business in China without experience, the recommended approach is to form a joint venture with a local experienced and credible partner. This helps to cut down on the learning curve. Malaysia, also because of the language, is perceived as a less complex legal environment. A number of government organizations help companies to find their way in Malaysia's regulations.

6 The level of literacy and health
The level of literacy and health is important. A sufficient pool of highly educated people is key for countries that want to focus on high-tech activities. The improvement of the educational system in order to meet industrial demand is a hot item in both Malaysia and China. In both countries the educational system is definitely improving and students are obtaining a good foundation. But in both counties the education level, necessary to execute relevant R&D activities in electronics, is not met. Companies are forced to start their own education programs to provide employees with the necessary knowledge level.

Economic environment

The economic environment is important to attract foreign investments in the semiconductor industry. We measure it using four indicators, which will now be discussed.

7 Adequacy of legal environment
An index can be calculated for "legislative environment adequacy" based on a combination of various indicators related to this topic. In table 23 we combine "regulation and tax administration" indicators with the ease of "starting a business". The figures are from the World Investment Report 2006. The general rule

for legislative environment adequacy is: The faster the better. Malaysia's legislative environment works faster and is less of a constraint than the legislative environment in China.

Table 23   Calculation of the legislative environment adequacy index

WDI 2006 Percentages Unless otherwise	Tax rates as major constraint	Time dealing with officials	Time to clear customs in days	Number of start-up procedures Jan. 2004	Number of days to start a business
China	36.8	12.6	7.9	13	48
Malaysia	21.7	10.2	3.7	9	30
Index					
China	59	81	47	69	63
Malaysia	100	100	100	100	100

Source: World Bank (2006) World Development Indicators

8 Effective Intellectual Property protection

Intellectual capital is one of the most important characteristics of the semiconductor industry. It is very important that intellectual property is protected; however, whether the IP protection is effective is difficult to measure. Effective intellectual property protection is also one of the most important factors when a company considers opening or moving a R&D facility. It is widely heard that in China, the IP protection regulations are not strict enough or too difficult to control because of the size of the country. China has the policy to protect, but allowing copying activities also helps to increase China's technological level.

The IP protection environment in Malaysia is considered better than in China, but still is a concern. Innovators often lack the knowledge about benefits of getting a patent. They consider that their design will not be protected since enforcement is low. Therefore they decide not to design but to copy instead. Since measuring the effectiveness of IP protection regulations is rather difficult, the assumption is made that "only when having sufficient IP protection, foreign companies are willing to invest in R&D". The higher R&D investments from abroad the more effective intellectual property protection tends to be.

9 Promotion of free trade and fair trade policies

When investing in a foreign country, free trade policies are clearly important. Import and export should be without any difficulties and with efficient custom operations. The efficiency of custom operations in Malaysia and China in comparison to the rest of the world can be measured by indicators such as:

Number of documents, number of signatures and time needed for custom clearance. The more efficient, the higher the rank a country gets. Both Malaysia and China are members of the APEC (Asia Pacific Economic Cooperation) and both are member of the World Trade Organization (WTO). Malaysia, Hong Kong (SAR) and Macau (SAR) have been members since 1995, China mainland since 2001. Malaysia is member of ASEAN (Association of Southeast Asian Nations) and at the moment ASEAN and China are in the process of setting up a free-trade area. This is believed to be the largest potential market in the world (The Star, "Free trade plan lauded", 11 July 2006). Next to these attempts, the US is trying to set up individual trade agreements with, amongst others, Malaysia and China.

The trade policies in Malaysia are considered one of the best in the region and are, according to the Malaysian interviewees, considered one of the most attractive points of Malaysia. Malaysia offers various free industrial zones (FIZ). FIZs are areas specifically established for manufacturing companies that produce or assemble products mainly for export. FIZs enable these export-oriented companies to enjoy minimal customs formalities and duty-free import of raw materials, component parts, machinery and equipment required directly in the manufacturing process as well as minimal formalities in exporting their finished products.

The free trade policies in China are considered somewhat protective. They serve mainly to protect China's own industries and to encourage foreign investors to invest in Chinese enterprises. Table 24 shows how Malaysia and China are doing better then the rest of the world. The higher the negative variation, the better the country performs. Malaysia's import and export regulations are less complex and faster than China's.

Table 24   Promotion of free trade and fair trade policies index (measured in necessary number of days)

Country	Documents for exports	Signatures for exports	Days for exports	Index	Documents for imports	Signatures for imports	Days for imports	Index
Malaysia	6	3	20		12	5	22	
%	-19	-73	-37	-42.9 100	11	70	-45	-34.5 100
China	6	7	20		11	8	24	
%	-19	-37	-37	-30.8 72	2	51	-40	-29.9 87

Source: World Bank (2005)

10 Quality of human resources
The semiconductor industry, both back-end and front-end production, needs skilled people. Higher value added requires better skilled workers. To attract activities with high value added a country needs to be able to provide a well-skilled labor pool. The quality of human resources is measured by the productive capacity index, which assesses physical and human resources. There is still a gap between the requirements from the industry and the offered curricula at colleges and universities.

The entrepreneurs interviewed in Malaysia all agree on the fact that operators and technicians are skilled enough but top-end engineers are lacking skills. A similar story is heard in China with the additional remark that language problems do occur. Exceptions are big cities like Hong Kong and Beijing. To compare the quality of the human resources, the gross tertiary enrollment in 2004 has been taken.

Competitiveness of the market

The final competitive dimension group is the market. Market access may be one of the main reasons to invest in a specific country. China's "Big Market" is a frequently heard argument for companies to invest in China. The competitive advantage of the (domestic) market in the semiconductor industry is measured by the strength of the internal market and by being close to local consumers.

11 Strength of internal market: Total spending capacity
Access to a big internal market is a good reason to be located in a certain country. Having a facility in this country makes it easier to do business with local companies. Local demand is not only demand from local companies but also from foreign companies active in the same market. The strength of the internal market is measured by the inhabitants times GDP in PPP per capita. China is big and has great potential. Malaysia is fifty times smaller than China but exports from the electronics sector make up 60 percent of total exports. Table 25 shows the big difference between the Malaysian and Chinese internal market.

Table 25   Total spending capability index for "strength of internal market" dimension

Country	Per capita GDP in USD	Purchasing power parity (PPP)	PPP Per capita GDP in USD	Population in million people	Total spending capability in USD	Index
Malaysia	4,825	1.6	7,720	24	188,368	6
China	1,312	1.8	2,362	1300	3,103,142	100

Source: Asian Development Bank (2005)

12 Proximity to local customer base

Being close to your end-user gives a competitive advantage to competitors who are not close to customers. The higher the mark the more an industry is able to locate close to its end-users. The main difference from the "strength of the internal market" is that specifically in China locating in the country does not necessarily mean being close to your customers. The electrical and electronics industry is the semiconductors main customer. To measure "proximity to local customer base" the share of the electronics industry of total export is measured.

Companies in the electronics industry have the tendency to cluster. Semiconductor companies will locate close to their customers. Locating an establishment in China is mostly done because of the big market and to be close to local customers. Malaysia is mostly chosen because of good skilled labor at a competitive price. The local customer base for semiconductors consists mainly of the electronics and electrical industry. For both countries, this industry is the most important in national exports. The size of the electronics and electrical industry in national exports is given in table 26. Electrical products comprise 37 percent of Malaysian export and 25 percent in Chinese exports.

Table 26	Electrical products as % of exports	
	Electrical export as %	*Index*
Malaysia	37	100
China	25	68

Source: on base of UN Comtrade

Competitive advantage leads to a move upwards in the global value chain

Do these differences in the competitive environment lead to a move upwards in the value chain? Figure 7 shows the framework we use. These competitive dimensions will give insight into how competitive Malaysia and China are in comparison to each other. At the same time, this framework shows which dimensions both countries have to work on in order to stay competitive. It has to be noted that the measured competitiveness is static rather than a dynamic competitiveness. We will test the hypothesis that the existence of an overall competitive advantage results in higher value-added productivity in this industry. In other words, the country with the competitive advantage will have a "higher position" in the value chain. The position of Malaysia and China in the value chain tells a lot about how the countries are positioned in relation to each other and how competitive they are.

Figure 7   **Dimensions of competitive advantage leading to a move upwards in the global value chain**

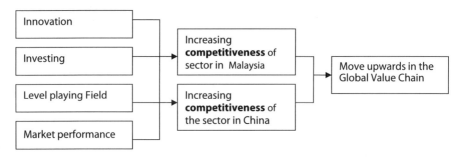

When measured by RCA, Malaysia shows a much better performance. Malaysia scores 488 percent on the RCA indictor, China "only" 151 percent. Malaysia's competitive advantage has led to a higher position in the value chain. "Value added" per employee is currently almost three times higher than China's value added in the industry sector. Malaysia is still showing steady growth figures but China is definitely doing better in her "move upwards" in the value chain.

This leads to the conclusion that Malaysia's competitive advantage in "economic environment" results at this moment in a higher value added per employee in the industry sector, but to make a "move upwards" in the value chain, Malaysia has to put more efforts in improving the dimensions "innovation" and "investing". China is catching up and already shows better value-added growth figures.

To show how the individual competitive dimensions influence total competitiveness a web is drawn for each dimension in figure 8. Malaysia is outperforming on all indicators in the dimension group "economic environment". The Chinese have the market advantage, which makes developing activities in that country very attractive.

Malaysia's and China's scores differ per dimension group. Most important differences between Malaysia and China are the "Level Playing Field" in favor of Malaysia and "Market" in favor of China (table 27).

Table 27   Score per dimension group

	Malaysia	China
Innovation	90.45	81.44
Investing	91.09	77.43
Economic environment	100.00	68.02
Market	53.00	84.00

Analyzing the competitive dimensions (figure 8) Malaysia shows a much better position on the "economic environment". Namely the "IP protection indicator" is an important difference. Secondly, the dimension group "market" is clearly in favor of China, most import dimension here is the big internal Chinese market. At the dimension "innovation" Malaysia shows slightly better results. They understand the importance of providing an innovative milieu and try to enhance their technological level through several national governmental organizations in the context of a national innovation system. Also the investment indicator is slightly in favor of Malaysia. Nonetheless, worldwide China is seen as the most attractive country to invest in (UNCTAD, 2005).

Figure 8   Competitive dimensions

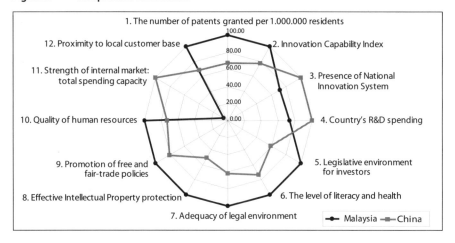

Conclusions

As far as the semiconductor value chains are concerned China and Malaysia are complementary to each other. Although the Chinese industry is growing much faster than Malaysia's, Malaysia is still a net exporter to China and is still showing higher growth figures than the world semiconductor industry. Both countries focus on different types of semiconductors. Malaysia has a considerably higher revealed comparative advantage, meaning that Malaysia has a relative competitive advantage in the semiconductor industry. Although foreign investment inflows to Malaysia remain strong, no new semiconductor firm has relocated to Malaysia since the 1990s. Some foreign semiconductor firms in Malaysia have relocated part of their operations to China and the Philippines. While China remains attractive for cost and market reasons, the lack of systemic and institutional development to stimulate upgrading is by far the prime reason why Malaysia is being bypassed for new development initiatives. Cunningham and Samy (2005) discovered that labor costs and the real-exchange rates are the two most important factors for semiconductor companies to decide on foreign investment. China has considerably lower labor costs and, according to some economists, is keeping her exchange rate purposely low.

Being both complementary as well as competing with China, Malaysia earned her current position in the world semiconductor industry and in the global value chain because of more than thirty years of experience. Mainly because China does not have as much experience and quality issues are sometimes a problem, Malaysia has to concentrate on complex chips, but has to fear its position since China is catching up fast.

Malaysia's current positions in the semiconductor industry and the value chain can be based on a better "economic environment" and more experience in the industry. Malaysia has to be aware of China catching up quickly. To remain competitive Malaysia has to make sure that enough technological knowledge is available at a good enough price. Critical dimensions that Malaysia has to keep focusing on are:

– Innovation – at this moment China shows slightly better "innovation" figures than Malaysia. In terms of the national innovation system both countries seem to lag behind. Extra investments in R&D institutions should help Malaysia.
– Knowledge – to keep students up to date, Malaysia has to support extra schooling offered by semiconductor companies. This is the way to create diffusion of knowledge. Students will then be skilled enough to add to the companies R&D.
– IP protection – although much better than China, Malaysia has to keep focusing on IP protection. IP protection is often the biggest worry for MNCs when they want to move R&D facilities.

An interesting trend for both Malaysia and China is the rise of a different type of company in the semiconductor industry. These companies focus mainly on R&D, marketing and sales and outsource the production from wafers to final chips producers. This is a great opportunity for new entrants, but they will need help from the government to find solutions for the high investment cost that come with the start-up of wafer fabrication.

Notes

1   Mytelka and Farinelli (2000) point out that innovation goes beyond formal R&D activities including:
    - Continuous improvement in product design and quality;
    - Changes in organization and management routines;
    - Creativity in marketing;
    - Modifications to production processes that bring costs down increase efficiency and ensure environmental sustainability.

2   Assumptions for this analysis are that both countries have a similar technology level and the analysis only concerns two countries.

3   Three companies in the Malaysian semiconductor industry were interviewed. Fico is a Dutch company, a supplier for back-end production activities; Infineon, is from origin German, executing back-end activities and was the first MNC to start front-end activities in Malaysia, and finally; Renesas, a Japanese company is also performing assembly and test activities. The view on the Malaysian semiconductor industry is discussed for all three companies.

4   Also in China three companies where interviewed: On semiconductors, Sharp and Lattice semiconductors. Additional received interesting comments from Infineon Malaysia about China were also used.

5   US Comtrade, the "HS 1992" classification was chosen.

6   2001 is the odd year, because of previous discussed reasons. After 2002, as a year to catch up, 2003 and 2004 showed 20% plus growth figures.

7   This is confirmed by the industry, stating in an interview that "if multinationals have to make a choice, they will probably pick China since that country offers both investment opportunities and a very sizable promising market".

8   Sources used are World Bank (2000). Table 10 shows labor costs and value added per Employee. Data from the periods 1980-1984 and 1995-1999 are compared.

9   The "revealed comparative advantage (RCA) indicator" measures the relative export performance by country and industry. RCA is defined as a country's share of world exports of a good divided by its share of total world exports. In the following example the index for country "I" good "j" is RCA = X_{ij}/X_{wj} divided by X_{it}/X_{wt} times 100%, where "X_{ij}" is exports by country "I" (w=world) of good "j" (t=total for all goods) (Deardorff's Glossary of International Economics).

10 Mathews and Cho (2000) mention: subcontracting, OEM (original equipment manufacturer), ODM (own design manufacturer), licensing, technology-transfer agreements, joint development agreements, the purchase of a company and starting a joint venture.

11 An example is that China demanded access to sensitive technology in exchange for the building of a high-tech rail between Shanghai and Hangzhou from several German companies (The Star, "Germans 'no' to tech transfer", 4 July 2006).

12 For each pillar a number of indicators are suggested and at the website the data can be collected for about 80 variables and 114 countries. Data for the most important countries can be found on www.worldbank.org/kam.

References

ADB (2005). *Asian Development Outlook 2005*. Manila: Asian Development Bank.

Asheim, B. and A. Isaksen (1997). 'Localisation, Agglomeration and Innovation: Towards regional Innovation Systems in Norway'. In: *European Planning Studies* 5 (3), pp. 299-330.

Cunningham, R. and Y. Samy (2005). *Determinants of Foreign Direct Investment: Evidence from the Semiconductor Industry*, May.

Dahlman, C. and A. Utz (2005). *India and the knowledge economy*. Washington: World Bank.

Deardorff *Deardorff's Glossary of International Economics*. www-personal.umich. edu/~alandear/ glossary/

Dijk, M.P. van (2006). *Can China remain competitive? The role of innovation systems for an emerging IT cluster in the Jiangsu province capital Nanjing*. Rotterdam: Erasmus University.

Economic Planning Unit Malaysia (2000). *Third Outline Perspective Plan, 2001-10*, Chapter 5, April. Kuala Lumpur.

EECA-ESIA (2005). *The European semiconductor industry: Competitiveness report*. Brussels: European Semiconductor Industry Association.

Freeman, C. (1997). *Technology and Economic Performance: Lessons from Japan*. London: Pinter.

Mathews, J.-A. and D.-S.Cho (2000). *Tiger technology: The creation of a semiconductor industry in East Asia*. Cambridge: Cambridge University Press.

Mytelka, L. and F. Farinelli (2000). *Local Clusters, Innovation Systems and Sustained Competitiveness*. Maastricht: UNU/INTECH Discussion Papers, October.

Nelson, R. and N. Rosenberg (1993). *National innovation systems: A comparative analysis*. Oxford: Oxford University Press.

Porter, M.E. (1990). *The competitive advantage of nations*. London: Collier Mac-Millan.

Sachs, J.D. and J.W. McArthur (2005). 'The Millennium Project: A plan for meeting the Millennium Development Goals'. In: The Lancet 365 (9456), pp. 347-353. www.thelancet.comSchmitz, H. (2006). 'Asian drives: Typologies and questions'. In: *IDS Bulletin* 37 (1), pp. 54-62.

Schulte Nordholt, H. (2006). *De Chinacode ontcijferd: Economische grootmacht Ja, Wereldrijk Nee*. Amsterdam: Byblos.

Stoneman, P. (ed.) (1995). *Handbook of the economics of innovation and technological change*. Oxford: Blackwell.

UNCTAD (2005). *World investment report 2005: Transnational corporations and the internationalisation of R&D*. Geneva: United Nations.

UNDP (2005). *Human development report.* New York: Palgrave.

World Bank (2000). *World development indicators.* Washington: World Bank.

World Bank (2004). *World development report 2004: Making services work for poor people.* Washington: World Bank.

World Bank (2005). *World investment report.* Washington: World Bank.

World Bank (2006). *World development indicators.* www.worldbank.org/data

9   Business-community Partnerships

The Link for Sustainable Local Development?

Diederik de Boer and Laura Tarimo

Introduction

Governments in African countries are struggling on how best to focus on sustainable local economic development. How can communities benefit from investments within their area? What can the government do to promote linkages between the communities and business, and what can the communities themselves do to make effective use of local investments in their region? Partnerships are increasingly being promoted as vehicles for addressing development challenges. It is assumed that partnerships contribute to economic development when they are working towards a set of policies, programs, and activities which initiate and contribute to broader processes (Pfisterer et al., 2009).

There is need for further investigation on the outcomes and impacts of partnerships, as well as the factors contributing to their effectiveness. Although the concepts of partnership and sustainable development are linked discursively, there is little empirical evidence linking the two. It is only recently that empirical evidence for the effectiveness of partnerships in the field of development became a research focus. So far the range of assessments has given rise to contradictory assessments. Some cases provide best practices (Fiszbein and Lowden, 1999), while other studies analyze more critically the effectiveness of partnerships (Visseren-Hamakers et al., 2007). The understanding on how partnerships function and under what conditions needs to be enhanced.

Sustainable local development (SLD) is the central focus of this research. Local economic development is "a process in which partnerships between local governments, community and civic groups and the private sector are established to manage existing resources to create jobs and stimulate the economy of a well defined area" (Helmsing, 2003). It emphasizes local control, using the potentials of human, institutional, physical and natural resources (Rylance, 2008). Sustainability includes the concepts of intra- and intergenerational equity and quality of life (Warhurst, 2005). Sustainable development is development that meets the needs of the present while having the intent of allowing future generations to meet their needs as well (WCED, 1987). Aspects such as equitable access to quality education and health care, and the contribution of the partnership to environmental sustainability must be taken into account.

This study will assess community-business nature-based tourism partnerships in northern Tanzania. One of the characteristics of the nature-based tourism industry is the fact that it takes place in rural areas with a lot of wildlife. However, these are often also the areas where the level of development is low; this is in contrast with the well developed tourism businesses. From an economic development point of view, the tourism businesses are important as they generate income but also generate nonfinancial and institutional impact in the communities they work in. However, the impact on the economy in communities remains limited, although economic development policies exist on paper. The results of these policies are hardly felt at the district level, and even less at the village level (Van Dijk, 2006). Moreover, these policies often do not promote a framework of collaboration between local officials and private sector companies. Yet, collaboration between such parties is necessary to solve company – but also community and district – problems, and to stimulate local economic growth.

Objectives

The main objective is to study the partnership between tourism businesses and communities in the context of the global-tourism value chain. In other words how can business-community partnerships enhance the community's participation in the global-tourism value chain and bring local economic development?

The first objective, therefore, is to examine current practices in the interplay between companies and local communities with respect to local economic development. The second objective is to study what the potential is for business-community partnerships to provide conditions for upgrading of the community's economic activities leading to higher value products and services. Hence, community-business partnerships which are more successful in improved conditions for upgrading will be selected and compared with less successful ones. The third objective relates to studying whether as a result of partnering with a private sector actor, communities have been able to upgrade to more value-creating activities, and whether this has resulted in positive financial, nonfinancial, empowerment and conservation outcomes on the whole for the community.

Research questions

The main research question is: Under which conditions community and tourism company partnerships optimize local economic development? Subquestions are:

- What are the different kinds of relations or partnerships that exist between tourism businesses and the community?
- To what extent do ground rules for collaboration in business-community partnerships influence their performance in terms of sustainable development?
- In what way do tourism business-community partnerships improve conditions for upgrading the community's activities within the global-tourism value chain?
- Are tourism business-community partnerships enabling communities to upgrade their activities, such that they participate more effectively in the global-tourism value chain?
- What are the financial, nonfinancial, empowerment and conservation outcomes of tourism community-business partnerships for rural communities?

Context, tourism and local economic development in Tanzania

Tourism tends to be an important economic sector in countries which are rich in natural resources, but economically poor. In 2008, Tanzania received 736,829 tourists who contributed over USD 65 million to its GDP (TANAPA). This is between 15-17 percent of the overall GDP, and a contribution of 25 percent to the country's foreign exchange earnings (National Bureau of Statistics, 2009). But tourism has contributed little to local development.

Despite being used as an instrument in development, the impact of tourism on improving rural livelihoods is not really being analyzed. It is argued that the link between tourism and the improvement of rural livelihoods is complex, and requires further debate. Research in this area is lagging behind (Jafari, 2001; Rogerson, 2006; Hall, 2007; Simpson, 2008). However, recently some districts and villages in Tanzania have benefited from tourism by developing collaborative arrangements with tour companies. Tourism companies choose to locate their lodges outside official National Parks in game controlled areas (GCAs), protected areas (PAs) or wildlife management areas (WMAs) which also have communities living in them. These locations are usually cheaper for both the tourist and the tour company, and tourists can enjoy exclusive game viewing far from the congestion that is to be found within the National Parks. Moreover, tourists have an opportunity to experience the culture of communities living there.

Villages allow tour companies to use an area of communal land for tourism activities and receive economic and social benefits for the village members. In turn, the villagers have the responsibility of looking after the environment and the wildlife by limiting activities such as cultivation, livestock grazing, tree cutting and illegal hunting within the wildlife areas located in their village land.[1] In exchange, communities receive compensation from the tour companies, ranging from USD 10,000 to 80,000 per year, which is often used for building schools, clinics, and providing other facilities and social services in the village (Nelson, 2008). These kinds of agreements are currently widely practiced in areas such as Ngorongoro, Longido, Simanjiro, Babati, Mbulu, and Karatu Districts within northern Tanzania. These activities provide a new source of communal income as well as a source of employment and a limited market for local goods. In 2003, for example, seven villages in Loliondo Division, had earned over USD 100,000 annually from several ecotourism joint ventures carried out on their lands. In Ololosokwan, one of the seven Loliondo communities referred to above, tourism revenue grew or remained high each year since the initiation of these agreements in 1999 (see Figure 2, Akunaay et al., 2003). This shows the potential for such arrangements between villages and tourism businesses to contribute to the economic development of resident communities in these areas.

Figure 1   Income to Ololosokwan village, in Arusha region from payments by companies

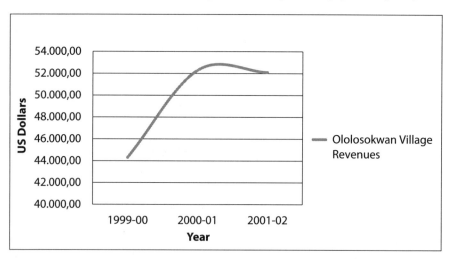

However, not all relations between investors and communities have been positive. In the same Loliondo Division, conflict arose in 2009 between a tourism investor and the community when the resident Maasai pastoralists were evicted from their settlement area so that the land could be used as a game hunting concession for a foreign tourism investor. The presence of the investor restricted the Maasai's access to grazing areas for their cattle, resulting in ongoing tension and conflict between the two parties. Some of the community members' homesteads and food reserves were set on fire by Tanzania's riot police force, leading to significant economic losses (Daily News, 10 September 2009). In this particular case, hunting-tourism activities led the villagers to suffer significant opportunity costs as economic activities which they depended upon for their livelihood were negatively affected.

Overall these cases highlight the importance of building positive relations between communities and businesses, and the need to ensure that both parties see benefits in the tourism investment. Conservation of wildlife resources is only possible when villagers see tourism as a real and viable economic opportunity. If wildlife does not generate benefits or the benefits do not reach the rural population (for example, due to a skewed distribution of the direct use value), people are unlikely to appreciate and conserve it (Arntzen, 2003).

Upgrading of tourism value chains

Barriers preventing rural communities from being included in tourism value chains

On the whole it can be observed that the major tourism enterprises in the private sector in developing countries tend to be owned by established businesses operating from urban centers, with many having a significant foreign ownership (Rylance, 2008; Mbaiwa, 2008; Massyn, 2008). The question is what obstacles do rural communities face, which prevent them from taking advantage of their surrounding natural beauty and benefiting economically from tourism?

Several factors have been identified in literature on why rural communities in Africa fail to actively take part in the tourism industry. A crucial factor appears to be the lack of access to capital for investment. Costs of borrowing from banks are very high, for example in Mozambique the interest charged for loans is 15 percent in real terms, which has resulted in 70 percent of tourism projects involving foreign investment (McEwan, 2004). A lack of access to capital also prevents entrepreneurs in rural communities from benefiting from economies of scale (Ashley and Haysom, 2008), as they are not able to supply tourism products in large enough quantities to make the activity economically viable.

Rural community members also often tend to lack the skills that allow them to participate effectively and successfully in the tourism industry. Rylance (2008) argues that government should play a greater role in the training of local community members so that they can access the tourist market. Responsibility to promote the potential of the community-based tourism market in Mozambique, for instance, has mostly been left to foreign organizations such as the Netherlands Development Organization (SNV), and the German organization Technoserve. Skills required by rural community members range from basic entrepreneurial skills to foreign language skills, as language has also been identified as a constraint to local economies accessing the tourism marketplace (Mbaiwa, 2008; Rylance, 2008).

Another problem is a lack of access to the tourism market networks (Ashley and Haysom, 2008). Means of global information sharing in rural areas are often very limited, and villagers have no clear picture of the status of demand for tourism activities, or other products in their area. They also often lack means of reaching this market to promote products from their locality.

Poor infrastructure is another obstacle. Poor road systems means that rural communities are restricted by the lack of mobility of tourists and also the lack of transfer of knowledge and skills between communities (Rylance, 2008). Tourists tend to depend on transportation provided by the tour operator which brings them to a specific location. This makes it difficult for communities to establish economic linkages with main-stream tourism activities, even when they are located in the vicinity of a popular tourism destination. Poor roads have been identified as a persistent barrier to development for local economies that exist outside of major cities (Rylance, 2008).

The issue of land rights is also important as many private sector residents (in rural areas) still do not possess title documents to prove ownership of their land/ property (Rylance, 2008). This prevents individual entrepreneurs and communities from having security in the use and lease of this resource. Moreover, without formal ownership, land cannot be used as collateral to obtain loans.

Finally, the extent to which rural communities in Tanzania are included in the global tourism value chain depends on the extent to which Tanzania itself is participating in the global tourism market. The competitiveness of the Tanzanian tourism industry is important, and factors such as air travel accessibility, accommodation, transportation and National Park entry costs on arrival, as well as the quality of the experience, will determine the number of tourists rural communities have potential access to (Pawliczek and Mehta, 2008).

Barriers preventing tourism companies from establishing backward or local linkages

It has been observed that rural communities face several obstacles, which prevent them from initiating tourism ventures themselves. The next point to consider is what opportunities exist for tour operators to create and maintain economic linkages with rural communities. Economic analyses have suggested that in many developing countries, each unit of economic activity in the tourism sector generates about 0.6-1.2 units of activity in other sectors which supply tourism (Ashley and Haysom, 2008). This means that there are potentially opportunities for rural communities to benefit from supplying their labor, as well as goods and services to the tourism sector even if they are not directly involved in supplying the tourism service themselves.

However, in this aspect rural communities also face challenges. Tourism business owners have indicated that it is too expensive for them to use smaller (local) suppliers who tend to provide insufficient quality standards and quantity capacity (Frey and George, 2008). Safety and security issues can also be a problem when dealing with local suppliers. It is argued that tourists demand international standards that smaller local businesses are often unable to offer (Frey and George, 2008). To address these challenges communities require training, and access to capital and technology to enable them to produce the required quantities, quality and level of service.

With regards to employment, it is also the case that rural communities tend to benefit only marginally from tourism. Even though some jobs are generated by the tourism sector, the well paying positions are often taken by skilled individuals from towns and cities or from overseas. This is because the majority of community members do not have the skills, which would allow them to obtain well paying jobs (Suich, 2008). Therefore the training of local communities to acquire such skills should be a priority.

Another challenge identified for creating economic linkages with local communities is that a significant financial and time commitment is required of the private sector company. For example Storm River Adventures in South Africa, which assisted local women to establish an independent catering company to supply meals to their guests, needed to have intensive input in areas such as training, mentoring, equipment, premises and administration (Ashley and Haysom, 2008). Upfront commitment and investment from the private sector business is crucial. On the positive side, the case of Spier Leisure, also in South Africa, indicates that once the business has committed to sustainability issues and placed priority in sourcing from disadvantaged groups locally, the result can be cost-saving for the business. Spier Leisure managed to see a reduction in costs of USD 15,600 (25% of previous costs) in the first year of sourcing from a local supplier they supported, while the amount invested into developing the local enterprise was a total of USD 11,300 (Ashley and Haysom, 2008).

Upgrading strategies for boosting sustainable inclusive value chains

In attempting to integrate local communities in supplying products to the tourism sector, there is a need to combine demand, supply and market intervention (Ashley and Haysom, 2008). Some initiatives have failed because they focused either on supply by working with farmers, or on demand, by working with chefs but not on both together (Torres 2003, 2004). In order to enhance employment and business gains from the tourism chain intervention is required on the supply side, such as the business environment and supporting micro enterprises. Intervention is also required on the demand side – e.g. in influencing hotels to buy locally. Finally, intervention is required in the market – to enable suppliers and purchasers to engage more efficiently in transactions (Ashley et al., 2005; Meyer, 2006).

One way to link communities with tourism activities is through partnerships. For example, in Botswana Community Trusts have been established in joint partnership with international safari companies who have the skills and experience in tourism development (Mbaiwa, 2008). It has been suggested that large-scale development is the precursor of small-scale development (Carter, 1991) hence, as tourism development proceeds, indigenous firms, industries and locals gain knowledge and experience (Mbaiwa, 2008). Over time local enterprises should be able to upgrade their products and services. In the literature four types of upgrading are recognized:

1 Process upgrading: Refers to improving efficiency in the transformation of inputs into outputs by reorganizing the production process or by introducing innovations.
2 Product upgrading: Involves adding a new quality to the product by moving into more qualitatively improved product lines, resulting in increased unit values.
3 Functional upgrading: Includes acquiring new functions in the chain (such as processing, transporting, marketing) to increase overall skill content of activities.
4 Inter-chain upgrading: Involves using the knowledge acquired in particular chain functions to move horizontally into alternative chains, which may be international, regional or local (De Boer et al., 2010, Van Wijk et al., 2009).

Through interaction with longer-established "global" firms, local enterprises gain access to technology, capital, markets, and organization which enable them to improve their production processes, attain consistent and high quality, and increase the speed of response (Gereffi et al., 2005; Humphrey and Schmitz, 2009). In the case of enterprises in rural areas in Africa access to infrastructure and land rights are also important for the upgrading of local products and services.

However, a basic requirement for upgrading is the strategic intent of the firms involved. Without intrafirm investment in equipment, organizational arrangements and people, no substantial upgrading of any kind is possible (Humphrey and Schmitz, 2009).

There is also a role to be played by local governance in fostering upgrading and competitiveness. It has been argued that market dynamics alone are insufficient to achieve competitiveness through upgrading; rather, the development and rapid diffusion of knowledge can be fostered by policy networks of public and private actors (Scott, 1996). When local enterprises are integrated into the global value chain, they are able to access more developed "global" markets (see figure 1 chapter 3, Perspectives on developing country value chains), which brings about further upgrading, as the entrepreneurs attempt to meet demands of the more developed markets.

Partnerships

Partnerships are taken to mean agreements between actors from two or more spheres of society – state, market and civil society – that are not purely transactional, but are based on the desire to fulfill some shared vision or goals (Van Huijstee et al., 2007; Pfisterer et al., 2009). From a holistic, multistakeholder point of view, partnerships should preferably involve a range of significant actors. Consequently, partnerships can be arranged among any combination of partners, including governments, nongovernmental actors, international organizations and the private sector.

For PPPs in developing countries, the equal sharing of risks, responsibilities and benefits is of particular importance. The objective of these PPPs is to accelerate sustainable growth in developing countries by working in tandem both with the public and private sector whereby the public sector focuses on developmental benefits and the private sector focuses on profitability within a corporate social responsibility (CSR) framework. PPPs in developing countries have been defined in the following sense:

A Public-Private Partnership is a voluntary joint operating agreement between actors from the public sector and non-public sector (private sector, NGOs, foundations). The partners commit to bring in their core-competencies to reach a common goal in the context of sustainable development in a developing country. All partners agree to share risks, responsibilities, resources, expertise and turnovers (Pfisterer and de Boer, 2006).

Public and private actors in developing countries have to manage, in general, high risks either in terms of economic, political or social stability. Entering into a PPP can reduce these high risks. The ideal PPP program provides an added value to a specific project/program which otherwise never could have been reached.

Therefore, the "partnership" component is the crucial factor in such a close cooperation. Partnerships for sustainable development are specific commitments by various partners intended to contribute to sustainable development and possibly to achieve the MDGs. Those partnerships are of a voluntary nature and are based on shared responsibilities of all partners involved. Moreover, successfully operating PPPs need strong partners that are committed to change and have a long-term commitment to sustain and replicate results (Sterr, 2003).

Civil society also plays an important role in PPPs. Whereas the public sector is the creator of an enabling environment for business, civil society can act as a business-development partner, connecting people at the local level with companies and their initiatives, but also acting as a "watchdog" with regard to these initiatives.

Linking the theory on PPPs and that of value chains, it is observed that PPPs potentially have a role to play in providing conditions for local communities to upgrade their services and products since through contact with the private sector and civil society groups, local communities can benefit from transfers of capital, skills, technology, infrastructure, organization etc. which facilitate upgrading.

PARTNERSHIP TYPOLOGIES

In a review of partnership typologies, Hailey (2000) identifies a "spectrum of partnerships" with one extreme having "resource", "dependent", or "conventional" partnerships, commonly defined by simple contracting relations between partners, while at the other end of the spectrum are "authentic", "active", or "reciprocal" partnerships which are marked by mutuality, trust and shared governance, dialogue and learning.

"Conventional partnerships" are commonly short term, bureaucratic, one way and unequal, with the Northern agency driving the agenda. "Dependent partnerships" are based on fixed-term blueprints with rigid roles and static assumptions, poor communication, and are commonly motivated by access to funds and individual interests (Hailey, 2000).

"Authentic partnerships" are based on trust and commitment; shared beliefs, values or culture; accepted standards of legitimacy, transparency and accountability; and common approach to gender issues (Fowler, 1997). "Reciprocal partnerships" attempt to change the traditional way of working by creating two-way, horizontal relationships based on solidarity and equality (Hately and Malhotra, 1997). "Active partnerships" are those based on a negotiated process, with common purpose, shared risks, marked by debate, learning and information exchange.

It is expected that partnerships which are "authentic", "active" and "reciprocal" as per definitions above will have the most success in enabling transfers of capital,

skills, technology, organization, thus enabling communities to upgrade their activities and to contribute to sustainable local development. Partnerships that are
short term, one way, unequal and static will be less successful in contributing to
value chain upgrading and to local development.

GROUND RULES FOR COLLABORATION, OR CRITICAL SUCCESS FACTORS FOR PARTNERSHIPS

Based on literature research: Hailey (2000), Van Dijk (2008), Pfisterer (2009),
Van Tulder and Pfisterer (2008), Van Huijstee et al. (2007), and observation in
the field, the following key principles have been clustered:
a level of commitment;
b level of transparency and accountability;
c mutual benefits.

a Level of commitment
Due to the costs of investing in a partnership in terms of the time and energy
devoted to relating to the partner, as well as adapting organizations to meet the
needs of the partner, it is expected that a longer-term commitment is more likely
to bring net benefits to the organization (or community) involved in a partnership (Ashman, 2001).

Commitment is related to the formality of the contract between partners,
whether there is a written and signed agreement. This will be a sign that the
partners share a common goal and are willing to carry out their respective responsibilities in order to achieve the goals of the partnership. Furthermore, commitment refers to the money or resources invested in the partnership by each
party. It is assumed that the higher the investments in physical and human capital
for the partnership, the higher the commitment of the partner to the agreement
and the greater the impact in terms of sustainable development. Finally, the level
of commitment can be measured through the frequency of interactions between
partners. This is particularly important from an institutional perspective. Deep
interactions between partners and a bilateral flow of information facilitates the
interorganizational learning necessary for the invention of new patterns of action
(practices), new methods of solving problems (technologies), and new under-
standings of legitimate behavior (rules) (Lawrence et al., 2002).

b Level of accountability and transparency
Transparency is linked to accountability. When an organization's decision-making and operational processes are transparent accountability is possible – internal
and external stakeholders are able to see where the responsibility lies (Jahan-

soozi, 2006). Transparency is the key requirement that will catalyze the accountability forces of peer pressure, reputation, market incentives and financial or legal commitments (Hamann and Boulogne, 2008).

In a partnership, proper accountability mechanisms are important for entrenching the terms of participation (Johnson and Wilson, 2000). Partnership accountability implies finding ways to hold each other to account, be expected to give each other an account of activities and progress, and be expected to take account of each other's needs or concerns (Caplan, 2005). A measure of how accountable partners are to each other is checking whether there are clear mechanisms in place for reporting progress with respect to the fulfillment of the obligations of each party.

A higher level of transparency of the partnership and the accountability of the partners to each other and to the general public increases the likelihood that the partnership will be successful in achieving its goals. The concept of transparency is linked to openness and is described as being both a relational characteristic as well as an environmental condition for organizational processes (Jahansoozi, 2006). Transparency is a required condition for building trust and commitment in the organizational relationship. Jahansoozi argues that trust and knowledge that what was agreed upon will actually happen is needed in order for collaboration to occur. Trust and the mutual recognition that each organization needs each other to accomplish their aims and objectives is a key element of mutual partnership (Hailey, 2000). Transparency becomes a "critical" relational characteristic when trust has declined due to a crisis or when it has been eroded over time (Jahansoozi, 2006).

Within this cluster of transparency and accountability the following factors are put together: Transparency, trust and horizontal and vertical accountability, informal relations, and governance arrangements in the partnership or consultative structures.

c Mutual benefits

Another ground rule for collaboration in partnerships is the presence of mutual benefits. Partners will be more committed to fulfilling their roles and responsibilities in the partnership when it is clear that the outcomes of the partnership will benefit each partner. It has been noted that a clear understanding of risks, identification of roles and responsibilities, and shared specific visions of each project are vital to the partnership's success (Nijkamp et al., 2002). These come hand in hand with the partners' understanding that there are some positive gains to be had from the partnership either in the form of enhanced access to resources, achieving legitimacy, becoming more efficient through relationships, or controlling asymmetries between organizations in the network (Babiak, 2008).

This variable comes from the model by van Dijk presented in chapter 7, which clusters the following factors: Mutual benefits, clear distribution of tasks, clear roles and complementarily, inclusiveness of stakeholders, level of ownership and win-win situation.

Business-community partnership models

"Business" in this study refers to a private sector company or investor. "Community" has been defined in literature as a physical location, such as a municipality or local district (Provan and Milward, 2001), or as a group which are bonded by similar interests (Babiak, 2008). The term "community" here refers to the village members living near or within the physical location where a tour operator wishes to invest in a property or tourism activity. Village members are represented formally by a village council and chairman, which make up the local (village) government. This means a partnership between a private sector investor and a village is in effect a tripartite partnership involving the private sector company, the village government which takes the role of the public sector, and civil society represented by the village members themselves.

Following a preliminary field study, three partnership models were identified in Tanzania:

1 Direct agreements (tripartite): These agreements involved a private sector investor and local government, with village members being the beneficiaries of the partnership.

2 Direct agreements (multipartite): These agreements involved a private sector investor, central and local governments, the village members as beneficiaries as well as local and international civil society organizations.

3 Indirect agreements: These agreements involved a private sector investor and central government. Local government and the village members did not have a formal agreement with the investor, but they were indirect beneficiaries of the partnership.

Sustainable local development (SLD)

Business-community partnerships are expected to contribute to sustainable local development. Sustainable local development in this research is considered from the following viewpoints identified by Spenceley (2008):

i Financial: Waged jobs, sales of goods and services and shares of collective income.

ii Nonfinancial: E.g. improved access to infrastructure, communications, water supply, health, education, security services, transportation services.

iii Empowerment impacts: Opportunities for institutional development and participation in local economic decision making.

In addition, improved practices in conservation are considered, since the sustainability of any economic venture based on tourism depends on the continued presence of wildlife over time.

iv Conservation impacts.

The four factors above make up the components of sustainable development considered from a social, economic and environmental point of view, and embracing
Elkington's (1997) "triple bottom line" approach to development, with the following objectives:
a to create longer-term economic or business impact (Profit)
b to advance the less favored groups in society or the world (People)
c to nourish the environment (Planet)

Methodology

Conceptual framework

In this study we investigate four different types of partnerships and to what extent the ground rules for collaboration, as defined in the previous section, are
fulfilled and conditions for upgrading have been shaped, and consequently impact on upgrading and sustainable development in the communities involved (see
figure 2).

Data collection

This study discusses the impacts of "nature-based tourism" on sustainable local
development. Nature-based tourism may incorporate natural attractions including scenery, topography, waterways, vegetation, wildlife and cultural heritage; and
activities like hunting. More specifically impacts of "wildlife tourism" are considered. This is a form of nature-based tourism that includes the consumptive and
nonconsumptive use of wild animals in natural areas (Roe and Dalal, 1997). Wildlife tourism has frequently been used to link wildlife management with economic
incentives to promote conservation in developing countries (Roe and Dalal, 1997).

A multiple case study approach was used to obtain the required data. Two
districts were selected in which the case studies would be carried out. These
are Longido District bordering west Kilimanjaro and covering a corridor area

Figure 2   Conceptual framework

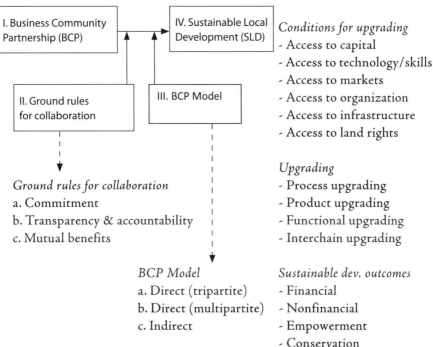

I. Business Community
Partnership (BCP)

IV. Sustainable Local
Development (SLD)

II. Ground rules
for collaboration

III. BCP Model

Conditions for upgrading
- Access to capital
- Access to technology/skills
- Access to markets
- Access to organization
- Access to infrastructure
- Access to land rights

Upgrading
- Process upgrading
- Product upgrading
- Functional upgrading
- Interchain upgrading

Ground rules for collaboration
a. Commitment
b. Transparency & accountability
c. Mutual benefits

BCP Model
a. Direct (tripartite)
b. Direct (multipartite)
c. Indirect

Sustainable dev. outcomes
- Financial
- Nonfinancial
- Empowerment
- Conservation

linking Kilimanjaro National Park with Amboseli National Park in Kenya, the second district was Babati located around Tarangire National Park in Tanzania. Criteria for selecting the districts were that they are located in a rural location in northern Tanzania, that they possess areas of wildlife in which tourism activities took place, and that each of the existing partnership models, i.e. direct (tripartite), direct (multipartite), as well as indirect agreements, could be found within the district selected. Studying the cases in two districts provides a means of comparison and an opportunity for identifying some external factors that influence the performance of partnerships that are not considered in the current framework.

Based on the conceptual framework outlined above, the data required was related to information on the type of business-community partnerships existing in the villages, the level of fulfillment of ground rules for collaboration for each partnership studied, and the subsequent impact on local economic development measured in terms of outcomes, i.e. revenues, jobs, sourcing of products and conservation, as well as the extent to which the partnership provided conditions for upgrading in the tourism value chain.

Data was collected using semistructured in-depth interviews with ten differ-ent actors involved in business-community partnerships per case. Theoretical sampling was done to ensure that all stakeholder groups, i.e. value chain actors and facilitators were represented. Stakeholders interviewed include the investor (tour operator), members of the village government council, village members, dis-trict government representatives, NGO representatives, and central government representatives in order to gain their perspectives on the tourism ventures under study. Visits to the research sites further facilitated access to information on the ventures as they allowed access to visual evidence of the outcomes of the partner-ship and perspectives of the different stakeholders.

Respondents were always willing to participate and share information. However, language barriers and the difficulty of explaining concepts to indi-viduals living in the margins of society implied that information documented was often from the elite members of the community, e.g. village leaders, com-munity-based organization leaders, leaders of producer groups, wildlife au-thorities in the district and central government as well as some NGO officials. Perspectives from the poorest community members were therefore not always easy to obtain.

Results collected from the interviews are presented in a table showing the performance of each partnership case relative to each other in terms of ful-filling ground rules for collaboration, improving conditions for upgrading, causing the upgrading of the community's activities economies, and finally in the overall sustainable development outcomes. Rankings were made based on stakeholder perceptions of the level of meeting ground rules, improving condi-tions for upgrading, upgrading as well as meeting development outcomes. For each partnership case a ranking of HIGH, MEDIUM or LOW was given for all the variables tested according to the respondents' perception of the partner-ship's performance, and on the basis of the researcher's assessment of the per-formance of each partnership case relative to the performance of other cases studied.

Analysis

Business-community partnership models in northern Tanzania

As shown in the conceptual framework, three models of business-community partnerships were identified in northern Tanzania, which will now be discussed.

Direct (tripartite) agreements between a private sector investor and local gov-ernment, with village members being the beneficiaries of the partnership. In this model a tour operator and the village government come to an agreement such that the tour operator can use an area of the village land for tourism activities. In return the tourism company compensates the village by paying a leasing fee and/or an agreed upon fee per tourist bed per night. The village in return takes responsibility of ensuring that the area where the tour operation is carried out is secure, and that no activities are carried out that are incompatible with tourism activities. The village is responsible for controlling tree cutting, cultivation and livestock grazing in these areas.

Direct (multipartite) agreements between a private sector investor, central and local governments, the village members as beneficiaries, as well as local and international civil society organizations. A case of this type of partnership is the wildlife management areas (WMA) partnership model. The Tanzanian government established WMAs through the Wildlife Policy of 1998, with the objective of involving local communities in conservation of wildlife areas. WMAs bring together the following partners:

Central government, or the Tanzania Ministry of Natural Resources and Tourism through the Wildlife Division (WD). The government drafts regulations that monitor tourism activities which are carried out outside of National-Park areas, and it is also the agency which collects revenues generated from tourism in these areas. The WD is generally responsible for the conservation of wildlife in these areas, and is expected to provide vehicles and human resources for antipoaching activities.

Villages voluntarily enter into WMA agreements, and are required to give up certain uses of a particular area of their land, e.g. cultivation, residential housing, herding for the purpose of wildlife protection and conservation. In return villages receive a share of revenues obtained from tourism activities carried out in their village area. Tour operators make an agreement with the Community-based organization (CBO) of a WMA to use a portion of land to set up a tented lodge for tourists. They invest in physical property, and are involved in promoting the area for tourism activities. They offer compensation to villages, usually based on a bed-night fee recommended by the WD.

District governments are involved in an advisory role through a conservation advisory committee of the WMA. The District in collaboration with the WD also plays a role in controlling poaching. NGOs such as the African Wildlife Foundation (AWF) and SNV – a Netherlands development organization, play a facilitation role in building human and technical capacities for the villagers in areas such as resource management planning.

Indirect agreements: Hunting-tourism partnerships. In this model agreements are made between a hunting company and the central government. The village is not directly involved in making a formal agreement with the tourism investor. The tour operator makes payment for the use of a hunting concession directly to the Wildlife Division, and a portion of the revenues is delivered to the district government. Some of these funds are intended for village development, however it is up to the district government to decide on and coordinate the use of these funds. The district provides antipoaching services in collaboration with the hunting company, which sometimes provides resources, e.g. vehicles or personnel. The hunting company may also contribute to community development by providing funds and/or facilities directly to the village, but this tends to be carried out voluntarily and driven by the level of CSR practices by the tourism company.

The impact of business-community partnerships on sustainable local development

As mentioned in the methodology, three partnership models were studied in two districts to find out their contribution to improving conditions for value chain upgrading, the extent to which they meet ground rules for collaboration, their contribution to the upgrading of local economic activities, and finally in bringing sustainable development outcomes within the communities they operate in. Below are findings from the research and a discussion of the impact of each partnership case on the variables mentioned.

VALUE CHAIN UPGRADING USING BUSINESS-COMMUNITY PARTNERSHIPS

The data shown in Table 1 point to the fact that the business-community partnerships investigated contributed to improving conditions for value chain upgrading in a few areas. For example, the most significant area of contribution of the partnership was in allowing access to capital, which was medium in both cases of the first model of partnership, i.e. of direct agreements between the tour operator and a village. Capital in both communities was provided in the form of money payments per tourist bed nights which went up to USD 50,000 per year in one case, as well as donations from some philanthropic tourists.

Access to markets was also provided in the model of direct agreements between companies and villages. For example, in Longido district tourists visiting the village would be encouraged to visit a Maasai family boma, make a contribution to the family and buy handicrafts made by the women, hence a medium level of sourcing was observed. In the Babati-district case of direct agreements studied there were also some sales of vegetable and meat products to the lodge, although the volume of sales was small, and sales were also not regular. However, relatively speaking, sales were higher in this case compared

Table 1   Conditions for upgrading

	LONGIDO District			BABATI District		
	Model I (Direct agreements)	Model II (WMA)	Model III (Hunting)	Model I (Direct agreements)	Model II (WMA)	Model III (Hunting)
Access to capital	MED	LOW	LOW	MED	LOW	LOW
Access to markets	MED	MED	LOW	MED	LOW	LOW
Access to technology/ skills	LOW	LOW – MED	LOW	LOW	LOW	LOW
Access to organization	LOW	HIGH	LOW	LOW	HIGH	LOW
Access to infrastructure	LOW	LOW	MED	LOW	LOW	MED
Access to land rights	MED	MED	MED	MED	MED	MED

to others studied; hence, a medium level of sourcing was attributed. When a WMA was initiated in Longido, the tourism investor continued to encourage tourists to visit the boma in the village and there were some jewelry sales. In the Babati-WMA case, some villagers' perceptions were that links had been weakened with the investor once new regulations were put in place that saw tourism activities being regulated by central government, and which prevented direct agreements from being made between the investor and the community. Overall sourcing of products was low in the hunting model, as the number of clients was small in the first case, and the perception was that the clients' quality requirements could only be reliably met by using produce from town. In the second case, relations were very weak with the village and no business links had been established yet.

The findings show that in all models, little access to technology was facilitated by the partnerships, e.g. in areas such as marketing information and tourism-service skill transfers. Such transfers would occur if there were high levels of employment in positions that enabled the workers to learn new skills. Although there was some employment in the direct agreements and WMA partnership models, the numbers were low – on average four people per lodge from the village, and the jobs often were not managerial or skills-based due to the low level of skills and knowledge available in the community. In the Longido-WMA cases, training was taking place for an accountant and manager, hence capacities were being built in these areas, but numbers were still low. In the hunting model there was a low level of employment per village in both districts due to low numbers of hunting tourists in general. In Longido, the hunting tourism investor was responsible for maintaining relations with sixteen different villages, which resulted in only a couple or so workers being employed by the company per village.

Access to organization was highest in the WMA model of partnership in both districts studied. This is because the process of forming a WMA requires involvement of the whole village and the formation of a community-based organization with members from all villages involved in the WMA. These processes contributed to building links between village members over the issues of the use of natural resources available in their village land and the sharing of benefits obtained from such uses. Importantly, this model of partnership also contributed to building links across villages, as WMAs tend to incorporate several villages spanning the targeted conservation area. This provides opportunities for villages to exchange information on good practices in wildlife use and conservation. The other two models of partnership did not contribute significant changes to the level of organization within the community, although they may have strengthened the capacity of existing systems of governance which took the responsibility of managing relations with the tourism investor.

In all partnership models and cases access to infrastructure was a result of tourism development in general. For example, paved roads leading to National Parks greatly benefited villages which were located in the vicinity of these parks. However, in the Babati hunting case, it was observed that feeder roads were constructed to serve a lodge located in a remote area, which resulted in the community benefiting as well. Tourism partnerships have also generally improved access to land rights in rural areas. Both in the direct agreements model and in WMAs the villages had been provided with an incentive to obtain a land title deed in order to secure legal rights to allow them to make agreements with private investors over the use of an area of land and its natural resources for the purpose of income generation for the village and the business.

On the whole, it is observed that conditions for upgrading were provided by the direct agreements partnership model in the specific area of allowing the community access to capital, while the WMA partnership model allowed the community access to organization. Conditions for upgrading were low or nonexistent in the hunting model, and particularly in the Babati case, which showed the weakest relations and lowest level of interaction between the tourism investor and the village.

GROUND RULES AND THE PERFORMANCE OF THE BCP IN VALUE
CHAIN UPGRADING

Table 2   Ground rules for collaboration

	LONGIDO District			BABATI District		
	Model I (Direct agreements before 2007)	Model II (WMA)	Model III (Hunting)	Model I (Direct agreements before 2007)	Model II (WMA)	Model III (Hunting)
Level of Commitment	MED	MED	Voluntary	MED	LOW	None
Transparency/ accountability	MED	MED	LOW	MED	MED	LOW
Mutual benefits	HIGH	MED	MED	HIGH	LOW	LOW
Number of tourist beds per year	MED: 1574 in 2005	MED: 2197 in 2009	LOW: 579 in 2009	HIGH: 4848 in 2007	HIGH: 3857 in 2008	HIGH: 4900 in 2009

Table 2 shows the extent to which each partnership case met ground rules for collaboration. The results show that the ground rules were consistently met in the direct agreements model in both districts at a MEDIUM or HIGH level. In both cases studied the partners had signed a written contract or made a verbal agreement, and met from time to time to discuss their respective responsibilities and to make payments for use of the village land, showing a significant level of commitment. Frequent contact between partners often led to additional benefits to the village in certain areas, e.g. the investor would gather funds from donors to assist in village-development programs. Payments were made via a bank account for which village members could request the balance, thus the procedure allowed for a certain level of transparency. Both parties seemed to be satisfied in general with benefits gained from the partnership.

The three ground rules for collaboration were met in the WMA partnership model, but only adequately. In Longido, the village showed commitment by following through the lengthy process of setting up a WMA. Transparency on funds collected would be ensured by publication of revenues earned from tourism by the community-based organization. However, benefits to individual villages were low considering a significant proportion of earnings was retained by the central and district governments while the remaining amount needed to be divided by up to ten villages constituting a WMA. In the Babati WMA case, the level of commitment was low due to dissatisfaction with the lack of process and lack of involvement of all community members in establishing the partnership, as well as a lack of agreement over benefits sharing.

In the hunting model few ground rules for collaboration were met except when the investor had decided to adhere to socially responsible practices. It was observed that the current policy framework does not sufficiently encourage investors in hunting to establish relations with villages in which the investor has a hunting concession. Establishing a partnership with the village is therefore at the complete discretion of the investor. In the Longido case the investor had a strong social-responsibility ethos and this reflected in the level of commitment and benefits passed on to the villages. In the Babati case there were hardly any linkages established between the tourism investor and the village. The level of commitment, transparency and accountability and mutual benefits were all low in the latter case.

It was observed that conditions for upgrading were hardly met in the Babati hunting case, where ground rules of collaboration had not been met. On the other hand, and as noted in the previous section, some conditions for upgrading were provided in the direct agreements partnership model, i.e. access to capital, and in the WMA model, i.e. access to organization. These findings are consistent with the proposition that meeting ground rules for collaboration is a prerequisite for a partnership to improve conditions for value chain upgrading.

THE PERFORMANCE OF THE BCP IN CONTRIBUTING TO VALUE CHAIN UPGRADING

Table 3 shows the extent to which each partnership contributed to the upgrading of the community members' products and services. In the previous discussions it was observed that the direct agreements partnership model in both districts had the highest level of commitment of the tourism investor and the community to the partnership. It may be assumed that such levels of commitment are more likely to lead to close links between the investor and the village to be developed. Such links would be conducive to transfers of capital, skill and technology to community members which could then facilitate the upgrading of their economic activities.

However, the research shows that the impact of individual partnerships in facilitating the upgrading of the village's economic activities is limited. The level of upgrading in the Longido case of direct agreements was low; in contrast to the Babati case studied which showed a medium level of upgrading. An explanation for this difference lies in the fact that the Babati case was located in an area near a National Park where the tourism volume and traffic were higher, and where the community had a longer history of having awareness of tourism, and of providing products and services to this sector. Hence capacities of community members and

Table 3   Upgrading

	LONGIDO District			BABATI District		
	Model I (Direct agreements before 2007)	Model II (WMA)	Model III (Hunting)	Model I (Direct agreements before 2007)	Model II (WMA)	Model III (Hunting)
Process upgrading – reduction in costs of production or increased productivity	LOW	LOW	LOW	MED	MED	LOW
Product upgrading – an improvement in the quality of products	LOW	LOW	LOW	MED	MED	LOW
Functional upgrading adopting new functions, e.g. providing accommodation in addition to a local tour	MED	MED	LOW	MED	MED	LOW
Intersectoral upgrading – production / supplying of a service in a different sector	MED	MED-LOW	LOW	MED-LOW	MED-LOW	LOW

enterprises in providing tourism services were higher in the Babati case than in the Longido one. This was evidenced by the presence of producer groups such as women groups focusing on jewelry, basket and mat making in Babati, which were absent in the Longido case of direct agreements model. The women in Babati had also established links with a consultant from the African Wildlife Foundation, who assisted them with developing skills and using more innovative processes in their craft. Moreover, in Babati the village had the advantage of being in the proximity of other tourism investments which were outside their village area but close enough that the investors sourced some products from them. The level of product- and process upgrading was relatively better in the Babati village compared to others studied even when the partnership model changed to a WMA.

It may therefore be deduced that the medium level of upgrading of economic activities in Babati was a result of linkages developed with several actors in the tourism sector rather than just the single investor located in their village. This alludes to the concept of "embeddedness" referred to in partnership literature, where it has been suggested that the higher level of connectedness and linkages a partnership has with other actors in society, the better the performance of the partnership in improving institutions (Lawrence et al., 2002). Embeddedness has been defined as the degree to which a collaboration is enmeshed in interorganizational relationships (Dacin et al., 1999; Granovetter, 1985).

It should be mentioned that a second case of a direct agreement partnership was observed in another location in Longido district. This was a partnership between a local tourism investor, the Tanzania Tourism Board, which is a body of the central government, the local community of Longido village members, and an NGO, the Netherlands development organization (SNV), which provided support for a short period of time. This partnership case differed from the previous direct agreement cases mentioned as it involved a Tanzanian investor and the tourism product offered was a combination of nature and cultural tourism together. In this partnership case the levels of product, process, functional and interchain upgrading were MEDIUM, MEDIUM, HIGH and MEDIUM respectively. The higher levels of upgrading observed in this case can be attributed to the level of linking with local businesses and activities, which was high. Overbookings of tourists in the investor's lodge during peak periods meant that local guest houses benefited from providing the additional accommodation demanded. The village owned a camping site which was used by some tourists arriving in the village. This can therefore be classified as functional upgrading. A crafts women's group supported by a local NGO also benefited from selling their handicrafts to tourists to supplement their income from farming or livestock keeping. As this is a new sector of work for the local women this upgrading can be classified as intersectoral upgrading. The high level of linkages with local businesses was partly facilitated by the location of this investment, which was in a town setting with a number of established businesses. This setting is different from that observed in the first village studied of Elerai where the number of established local businesses was smaller.

The findings above indicate that BCP models which allow for close links to be developed between the investor and community will be most effective in allowing community members to upgrade their economic activities. Partnership cases where ground rules for collaboration were not adequately met, as in the Babati hunting case, had very few linkages established between the investor and the local community or entrepreneurs; consequently, there was no evident transfer of capital, skills or technology to the local community. However, the findings also suggest that establishing linkages with other actors and businesses within the sector and outside of the partnership itself is equally important if a significant impact in terms of upgrading is to be achieved.

THE PERFORMANCE OF BCPS IN CONTRIBUTING TO SUSTAINABLE LOCAL DEVELOPMENT

As observed earlier the direct agreements led to greater transfers of capital in both districts, which the villagers used for ameliorating infrastructure and services in the village. In Longido the village used the funds obtained from the partnership to construct a village office, some classrooms for the primary school and also to support secondary school students with school fees. The same was observed in the Babati case of direct agreements. The financial services and infrastructure outcomes were therefore relatively high for both cases of this model.

Table 4   Sustainable development outcomes

	LONGIDO District			BABATI District		
	Model I (Direct agreements before 2007)	Model II (WMA)	Model III (Hunting)	Model I (Direct agreements before 2007)	Model II (WMA)	Model III (Hunting)
Revenues	HIGH	MED	MED	HIGH	MED	LOW
Employment and training	MED	HIGH	LOW per village	MED	HIGH	LOW
Local procurement	LOW	LOW	LOW	MED	MED	LOW
Increased access to services / infrastructure	MED	MED	MED	HIGH / MED	LOW	LOW
Stimulation of good governance / institutional development	LOW	HIGH	LOW	MED	HIGH	LOW
Conservation	MED	HIGH	MED	MED	HIGH	LOW

Table 4 shows the performance of each partnership case in bringing about economic, financial and nonfinancial outcomes, empowerment, governance and conservation outcomes.

Outcomes in terms of improved access to good governance and conservation practices were higher in the WMA model in both districts. The formation of a community-based organization with representatives from each village led to the establishment of a body independent from the village government, which monitored the villages' use of available natural resources and wildlife, and benefits sharing from these uses. The process of forming a WMA required the involvement of the entire community through village meetings. Such a process allows communities to organize themselves around the focus issues of wildlife use and conservation, and in the process build a wealth of social capital. It is therefore expected that this partnership model will have a significant impact in areas such as community empowerment, encouraging good governance and conservation practices. Indeed results show the WMA cases in both districts had the best performance in these areas. In Longido, conservation efforts were strengthened as village members in collaboration with neighboring villages developed a system of scouting the surroundings to prevent tree cutting as well as wildlife poaching. The Babati WMA case offers a different story as the village had been in conflict over the WMA and was in the process of demanding that they be allowed to exit the agreement. Nonetheless, the Babati community provided a case of village members – because of the existence of the WMA, demanding a higher level of awareness regarding the agreement and processes involved, and of the community mobilizing to resolve existing issues.

In the Longido hunting case, it was observed that some economic and service/infrastructure benefits were passed on to community members. This can be attributed to the investor's commitment to a socially and environmentally responsible ethos. Such an ethos was absent in the vision of the tour operator in Babati. This coupled with a policy framework that does not sufficiently encourage the investor to establish links with the community means that exchanges between the investor and the village were nearly non-existent in Babati, and consequently there were no positive outcomes to be noted from the presence of a foreign investor in the village land.

The partnership model which meets ground rules for collaboration and enables transfers of capital, skills and technology to the community will have the greatest positive outcome for local development, while the model that allows access to organization or to the mobilization of social capital has the greatest institutional impact, specifically in areas such as encouraging good governance and conservation practices.

Conclusions and recommendations

Business-community partnerships provide opportunities for local sustainable development by improving conditions for value chain upgrading. The more frequent the relations between the business and the community and if based on respect of both parties, the better the chance that communities are able to integrate easily in the value chain. On the other hand, businesses also thrive better because building good relations with the community often provides the business with more wildlife as the villagers are then more inclined to see the operations as a real partnership with a win-win situation for both parties. As a result there is more trust between the parties involved. So, mutual benefits from the partnership is an important requisite for local sustainable development. In this respect successful partnerships form the basis for the transfer and the upgrading of knowledge (technical and organizational), as well as a source for new entrepreneurial ideas, such as basket weaving, handicraft making, tour-guide services, accommodation services, etc. And a successful partnership could also arrange for an increased financial input in the communities which then is sometimes used for physical and social infrastructure upgrading, which creates a basis for further local development.

However, the extent to which conditions for upgrading are improved depends on the current level of local development. The higher the capacities of individuals, entrepreneurial groups and local government, the better the community is able to tap into opportunities brought by the presence of an investor for their own development. This study looked at three different partnership models: direct tripartite agreements, direct multipartite agreements (WMAs), and indirect agreements (hunting). Local economic development as discussed above is only guaranteed when the ground rules for collaboration have been met, so commitment and ownership, mutual benefit, and transparency are a prerequisite for the partnership to contribute to sustainable local development. It is important that there is direct, and frequent relations between the business and the community, and that the partnership is based on mutual benefits. As a result only the partnership models in which the community and the business can relate directly with each other will be successful from a financial and nonfinancial point of view. However, from a conservation (and empowerment) point of view it can be concluded that the direct relations between the villagers and the business is less important. In the WMA partnership model often six or more villages are involved in order to guarantee larger areas of nature to be protected. The protection is done by a special CBO with representatives from the combined villages which creates empowerment. However, this conservation effect is short-term. If villagers get only nominal amounts of financing in exchange, the interest of the villagers for the partnership is bound to deteriorate and over time the area will develop neither economically nor in terms of conservation. A partnership can only be successful if the benefits are mutual to both parties, but they should also be substantial in a way that at least some tangible results can be shown to the community members every year. It is recommended to define this more specifically, but that within the partnership a maximum number of beneficiary communities or a minimum amount of earnings per year per village should be set. Too many villages in a partnership make it difficult for ground rules for collaboration to be met, and create an imbalance in benefits received by the parties involved.

We recommend four things. In the first place to create a fund for local tourism development. If the ground rules for cooperation are met and if the right format of partnership has been chosen, even then local tourism upgrading could be prone to risks, such as the fact that natural disasters might strike the area or a political upheaval might disrupt the number of tourists coming per year. Compared to local business, international tourism businesses often have more capital and could even have lodges in different countries in order to mitigate these risks. But also from a positive side, capital for tourism upgrading is often easier to generate by the business than by the community entrepreneurs. It is therefore recommended that a local tourism development fund is established which could cater for both positive and negative external influences.

Secondly, it is desirable to set a maximum number of villages per WMA, or a minimum amount of earnings from tourism per village per year. Direct relations and substantial mutual benefits are a prerequisite for sustainable development. In order to generate a substantial minimal benefit the appropriate number of villages per WMA should be determined and implemented, otherwise the effect on local sustainable development becomes negligible and will finally have a negative impact on the partnership.

Then there is a need for clear policy and practices which encourage and support local benefits from tourism. Out of the study it becomes clear that government policy can be a crucial element in encouraging linkages between local and global tourism businesses. The recent focus of the Tanzanian government on wildlife management agreements has some positive aspects for sustainable development; however, financial benefits need to be enhanced. Local skills and capacities need to be developed such that local businesses participate successfully in the global tourism market.

Another observation is that transparency is an important aspect for achieving development through tourism. The government should set the tone and lead the way in being open and transparent on how money from tourism is disbursed at various levels. Moreover, the open relation between the business and the government should also focus on mutual benefits and the benefits should be substantial in a way that people at the local level can clearly see value in tourism.

Finally, there is a need for some guidelines on corporate social responsibility (CSR). Businesses which had socially responsible practices and were actively involved in community development achieved better relations with the village members, which resulted in improved cooperation in areas such as preventing poaching and looking out for the security of tourists and their property in the area. The community felt that attention was being given to them directly and as a result community members seemed to be more inclined to work in a positive way with the business. This led to both parties – the community and the business – benefiting from positive relations. However, guidelines on what is "responsible" practice, and how companies can adopt such practices, are lacking in Tanzania. It is therefore recommended that such guidelines are developed to enable more tour companies to benefit from building positive relations with communities in their investment area.

Note

1   Villages are the basic unit of local governance and administration in Tanzania (Nshala, 2002). All members of a village community compose the village assembly, which elects a village council and a village chairman. Village councils in Tanzania can act as corporate bodies, and are capable of owning property, suing and being sued, and entering into contracts with other parties on behalf of the village assembly according to the national legislation on local governance (Nelson, 2008).

References

Akunaay, M., F. Nelson and E. Singleton (2003). *Community based tourism in Tanzania: Potentials and perils in practice*. Paper presented at the Second Peace Through Tourism Conference 7-12 December 2003, Golden Tulip Hotel, Dar es Salaam.

Arntzen, J. (2003). *An economic view on wildlife management areas in Botswana*. CBNRM Network Occasional Paper 11, CBNRM Support Programme SNV/ IUCN.

Ashman, D. (2001). 'Civil society collaboration with business: Bringing empowerment back in'. In: *World Development* 29 (7), pp. 1097-1113.

Ashley, C. and G. Haysom (2008). 'The development impacts of tourism supply chains: Increasing impact on poverty and decreasing our ignorance'. In: A. Spenceley (ed.), *Responsible tourism, critical issues for conservation and development*, pp. 129-156.

Ashley, C., G. Haysom, C. Poultney, D. McNab and A. Harris (2005). *The how to guides: Producing tips and tools for tourism companies on local procurement, products and partnerships. Volume 1: Boosting procurement from local businesses.* London/Johannesburg.

Babiak, K. (2008). 'Criteria of effectiveness in multiple cross-sectoral interorganizational relationships'. In: *Evaluation and Program Planning* 32, 1-12.

Caplan, K. (2005). *Multi-stakeholder partnerships: Accountable to whom?* Presentation at NGO Forum, London, March 2005.

Carter, E. (1991). *Sustainable tourism in the Third World: Problems and prospects.* Discussion Paper 3, University of Reading, Reading.

Dacin, M.T., M.J. Ventresca and B.D. Beal (1999). 'The embeddedness of organizations: Dialogue and directions'. In: *Journal of Management* 25,3 pp. 17-356.

Daily News (2009). News article on Loliondo Masai evictions, September 10.

De Boer, D., A. Muller, R. van Tulder, M. Noor, D. Timmer, P. van Putten, F. Fortanier, J. van Wijk and V. van der Linden (2010). *A 'Rough Guide' to partnerships for development.* Utrecht: ICCO.

Elkington, J. (1997). *Cannibals with forks: The triple bottom line of 21st century business.* Oxford: Capstone Publishing Ltd.

Fowler, A. (1997). *Striking a balance: A guide to enhancing the effectiveness of nongovernmental organisations in international development.* London: Earthscan.

Frey, N. and R. George (2008). 'Responsible tourism and the tourism industry: A demand and supply perspective'. In: A. Spenceley (ed.), *Responsible tourism: Critical issues for conservation and development.* London: Earthscan, pp. 107-128.

Gereffi, G., J. Humphrey and T. Sturgeon (2005). 'The governance of global value chains'. In: *Review of International Political Economy* 12 (1) February, pp. 78-104.

Granovetter, M. (1985). 'Economic action and social structure: The problem of embeddedness'. In: *American Journal of Sociology* 91, pp. 481-510.

Hailey, J. (2000). 'NGO partners: The characteristics of effective development partnerships'. In: S. Osborne (ed.), *Theory and practice in international perspective*, p. 311.

Hall, C.M. (2007). 'Editorial. Pro-poor tourism: Do "Tourism exchanges benefit primarily the countries of the South"?' In: *Current Issues in Tourism* 10 (2/3), pp. 111-118.

Hamann R., S. Woolman and C. Sprague (eds.). *The business of sustainable development in Africa: Human rights, partnerships, alternative business models*, University of South Africa, pp. 54-82.

Hately, L. and K. Malhotra (1997). *Between rhetoric and reality: Essays on partnership in development.* Ottawa: The North-South Institute.

Helmsing, A.H.J. (2003). 'Local economic development: New generations of actors, policies and instruments for Africa'. In: *Public Administration and Development* 23, pp. 67-76.

Humphrey, J. and H. Schmitz (2007). 'How does insertion in global value chains affect upgrading in industrial clusters? In: *Regional Studies* 36 (9), pp. 1017-1027.

Jahansoozi, J. (2006). 'Organization-stakeholder relationships: Exploring trust and transparency' In: *Journal of Management Development* 25 (10), pp. 942-955.

Jafari, J. (2001). 'The scientification of tourism'. In: V.L. Smith and M. Brent (eds.), *Hosts and guests revisited: Tourism issues of the 21st century*. New York: Cognizant Communication.

Johnson, H. and G. Wilson (2000). Biting the Bullet: Civil Society, Social Learning and the Transformation of Local Governance, *World Development* Vol. 28, No. 11, 1891-1906.

Lawrence, T.B., C. Hardy and N. Phillips (2002). Institutional Effects of Interorganizational Collaboration: The Emergence of Proto-Institutions, *Academy of Management Journal*, Vol. 45, No. 1, 281-290.

McEwan, D. (2004). *Study of Economic Potential of Tourism in Mozambique: Transfontier Conservation Areas (TFCA) and Tourism Development Project*, Ministry of Tourism, Mozambique, February.

Massyn, P.J. (2008). Citizen Participation in the Lodge Sector of the Okavango Delta in A. Spenceley (ed.) *Responsible Tourism, Critical Issues for Conservation and Development*, Earth Scan, London p. 205-223.

Mbaiwa, J.E. (2008). The Realities of Ecotourism Development in Botswana in A. Spenceley (ed.), *Responsible Tourism, Critical Issues for Conservation and Development*, Earth Scan, London p. 205-223.

Meyer, D. (2006). Caribbean tourism, local sourcing and enterprise development: Review of the literature, PPT working paper no. 18, Pro-poor tourism partnership, UK.

Nelson, F. (2008). Livelihoods, Conservation and Community-based Tourism in Tanzania: Potential and Performance, in A. Spenceley (ed.) *Responsible Tourism, Critical Issues for Conservation and Development*, Earthscan, London, pp. 305-321.

Nijkamp, P., M. van der Burch and G. Vindigni (2002). Comparative institutional evaluation of public-private partnerships in Dutch urban land-use and revitalization projects, *Urban Studies*, Vol. 39 No. 10, 1865-80.

Nshala, R. (2002). *Village Rights Relating to Land Management, Tourism, and Tourist Hunting*. Unpublished report of the Lawyers' Environmental Action Team.

Pawliczek, M. and H. Mehta (2008). Ecotourism in Madagascar: How a sleeping Beauty is Finally Awakening in in A. Spenceley (ed.) *Responsible Tourism, Critical Issues for Conservation and Development*, Earth Scan, London p. 41-68.

Pfisterer, S. and De. de Boer (2006). *Comparative Analysis of Public Private Partnerships in Germany, the Netherlands and the United Kingdom*, Maastricht: Expert Center for Sustainable Business Development Cooperation.

Pfisterer, S., M.P. van Dijk and R. van Tulder (2009). *Partnerships for Sustainable Development – Effective? Evidence from the horticulture sector in East Africa.*

Provan, K.G. and H.B. Milward (2001). Do networks really work? A framework for evaluating public-sector organizational networks, *Public Administration Review*, 61 (4), 414-424.

Roe, D., N. Leader-Williams and B. Dalal-Clayton (1997). Take Only Photographs, Leave Only Footprints: The Environmental Impacts of Wildlife Tourism, *Wildlife and Development Series*, No 10, International Institute for Environment and Development, London.

Rogerson, C.M. (2006). Pro-poor local economic development in South Africa: The role of pro-poor tourism, *Local Environment*, vol 11, no 1, 37-60.

Rylance, A. (2008). Local Economic Development in Mozambique: An Assessment of the Implementation of Tourism Policy as a Means to Promote Local Economies in A. Spenceley (ed.) *Responsible Tourism, Critical Issues for Conservation and Development*, Earthscan, London, p. 27-39.

Scott, A.J. (1996). Regional motors of the global economy, *Futures* 28, 391-411.

Simpson, M.C. (2008). An integrated approach to assessing the impacts of tourism on communities and sustainable livelihoods, *Community Development Journal*, vol 43.

Spenceley, A. (2008). 'Impacts of wildlife tourism on rural livelihoods in Southern Africa'. In: A. Spenceley (ed.), *Responsible tourism, critical issues for conservation and development*. London: Earthscan, pp. 159-179.

Sterr, M. (2003). *The impact of business linkages on sustainable development: An assessment of four European partnership programmes*. Leicester.

Suich, H. (2008). 'Tourism in transfrontier conservation areas: The Kavango-Zambezi TFCA'. In: A. Spenceley (ed.), *Responsible tourism, critical issues for conservation and development*. London: Earthscan, pp. 187-203.

Torres, R. (2003). 'Linkages between tourism and agriculture in Mexico'. In: *Annals of Tourism Research* 30 (3), pp. 546-566.

Torres, R. (2004). 'Challenges and potential for linking tourism and agriculture to achieve Pro-poor Tourism Objectives'. In: *Progress in Development Studies* 4 (4), pp. 294-318.

Tulder, R. van, and S. Pfisterer (2008). *From idea to partnership: Reviewing the effectiveness of development partnerships in Zambia, Columbia and Ghana. Findings from a review of six partnerships from "A Call for Ideas" by DGIS*. The Hague: DGIS.

Van Dijk, M.P. (2006). *Managing cities in developing countries: The theory and practice of urban management*. Cheltenham: Renmin University Press/Edward Elgar.

Van Dijk, M.P. (2008). 'Public-private partnerships in basic service delivery: Impact on the poor. Examples from the water sector in India'. In: *International Journal of Water* 4 (3/4), pp. 149-159.

Van Huijstee, M.M., M. Francken and P. Leroy (2007). 'Partnerships for sustainable development: A review of current literature'. In: *Environmental Sciences* 4 (2): pp. 75-89.

Visseren-Hamakers, I.J., B. Arts and P. Glasbergen (2007). 'Partnerships as a governance mechanism in development cooperation: Intersectoral North-South partnerships for marine biodiversity'. In: P. Glasbergen et al. (eds.), *Partnerships, governance and sustainable development. Reflections on theory and practice.* Cheltenham: Edward Elgar.

Warhurst, A. (2005). 'Future roles of business in society: The expanding boundaries of corporate social responsibility and a compelling case for partnership'. *Futures* 37, pp. 151-168.

WCED (1987). *Our common future. World Commission on Environment and Development.* Geneva: UN.

Wijk, J. van, V. van der Linden and D. de Boer (2009). *Economic impact of NGO-private sector partnerships for value chain eevelopment in West Africa.* ECSAD/ICCO.

Part V

Conclusions: Upgrading Value Chains in Developing Countries

10 Upgrading of Value Chains in Developing Countries

Jacques H. Trienekens and Meine Pieter van Dijk

Introduction

The title of this book is: Linking local producers to international markets by developing global value chains. We have given a number of examples in the previous chapters and emphasized that upgrading value chains in developing countries will increase the benefits these countries derive from being linked to world markets. China is probably the country that has benefited most from globalization, in the sense of increasing its exports and import technologies and currently buying whole companies abroad (Van Dijk, 2006). We started in chapter 1 with a Chinese consultant who indicated that developing countries need to have more control over global value chains to benefit more from their own products. That is exactly what China is practicing when it is investing in mining or other industries in Africa (Van Dijk, 2009), or when a Chinese company bought the famous IBM PC company in 2005 with its worldwide marketing network, to push China's relatively unknown computer trademark Lenovo on the world market. More control allows a country or its companies to earn more money and makes upgrading of these value chains easier. Upgrading value chains in developing countries is the topic of this chapter.

After some basic theoretical insights in chapters 1-3, this book has presented a number of cases of value chains of developing countries. This final chapter will review the upgrading strategies in these value chains. First, it will define the options for value chain upgrading, distinguishing four different strategies:

1   upgrading through an increase of value added;
2   upgrading by improving market access;
3   upgrading through better value chain governance structures; and
4   upgrading through partnerships.

These categories are derived from the elements of the framework for value chain analysis developed in chapter 3. Further, as suggested in chapter 1, attention will be paid to the major role of partnerships in upgrading processes.

Subsequently the upgrading options that are discussed in the various chapters in this book will be discussed one after another. Some of the cases focus on how to improve typical conditions/constraints for upgrading: Market access, infrastructures, and economic and social institutions. Others focus on different value chain upgrading options. We combine this analysis with a discussion how to handle value chain upgrading constraints.

Upgrading in developing-country value chains

In defining value chain upgrading options we have built on the work of Gereffi (1999), Kaplinsky (2000), Humphrey and Schmitz (2002), Nadvi (2004), Giuliani et al. (2005), and Gibbon et al. (2008). Gereffi's (1999) definition of upgrading is: "... a process of improving the ability of a firm or an economy to move to more profitable and/or technologically sophisticated capital and skill-intensive economic niches."

McDermott (2007: 104) defines upgrading as: "the shift from lower-to higher-value economic activities by using local innovative capacities to make continuous improvements in processes, products and functions." The two definitions emphasize different aspects, but do not mention the importance of making these value chains more sustainable. In for example chapter 8 and 9, we have emphasized that upgrading is also an opportunity to make these value chains more sustainable.

Kaplinsky (2000) gives four directions for economic actors to upgrade: Increasing the efficiency of internal operations, enhance interfirm linkages, introducing new products and changing the mix of activities conducted within the firm. Building on Kaplinsky and others, Pietrobelli and Saliola (2008) define the following upgrading options: Entering higher unit value market niches, entering new sectors, undertaking new productive functions and in all cases enlarging the technological capabilities of the firms.

In most cases upgrading of value chains is achieved through attention for multiple business aspects, such as combined attention for product and process upgrading or collaborative product upgrading in combination with contractual arrangements. For instance Roy and Thorat (2008), in their study of the Indian grape cooperative Mahagrape, conclude that upgrading capabilities were largely related to the combined attention for innovative marketing in export markets and concurrent provision of technical assistance, inputs and (market) information to the farmers.

In the following four subsections we will discuss upgrading through increase of value added in the chain, upgrading of market access possibilities and upgrading of governance structures. Thereafter the role of partnerships and actors of chains will be discussed.

Upgrading through increase of value added

Most approaches to upgrading found in literature focus on upgrading of value-added production. This can take various forms:
- upgrading of products (and packaging);
- upgrading of processes;
- functional upgrading (in-sourcing production or distribution functions);
- intersectoral upgrading (product differentiation).

Upgrading of marketing or promotion activities is in most cases in the literature included in product upgrading. Product and process upgrading are most common in developing countries value chains; functional and intersectoral upgrading occur less as most developing countries' producers are still commodity suppliers for Western value chain partners. Giuliani et al. (2005, referring to Humphrey and Schmitz, 2002) show that although inclusion into global value chains may facilitate product and process upgrading, "... firms become tight into relationships that often prevent functional upgrading and leave them dependent on a small number of powerful customers." (see also Kaplinsky and Morris, 2002). For example, Schmitz (1999) showed for the shoe industry in Sinos Valley in Brazil that, although product and process upgrading led to improved product quality, response times and flexibility, limited attention to functional upgrading and horizontal collaboration between producers restricted the sector from further growth. In these value chains the in many cases Western lead partner stimulates product and process upgrading, but not functional upgrading, as this would mean that value-adding activities move from Western countries to the developing countries' producers.

Upgrading of value added in products is always related to (potential) demands in a market. As pointed out in chapter 2 these can be related to intrinsic (product quality, composition, packaging, etc.) and extrinsic product attributes, which are related to typical process characteristics. In the last decennia attention from Western consumers for these extrinsic characteristics has increased considerably, leading to companies to increase their attention for corporate social responsibility, ranging from attention given to issues such as labor circumstances as well as animal welfare. This has boomed the introduction of CSR principles by Western industries and retailers and offering opportunities for value-added niche-market production by developing countries' producers. Figure 1 depicts key dimensions of such CSR principles in the food value chain. These are dimensions on which producers and value chains can focus when trying to upgrade extrinsic product attributes.

Process upgrading focuses on the one hand on upgrading the product, on the other hand on optimization of production and distribution processes. The latter includes introduction of new technologies such as automated production and packaging lines, cooling installations and modern transportation technology as well as improved communication facilities in the supply chain such as internet connection, GPS systems or the intense use of mobile phones in production and transportation planning. An interesting case example is given by Francis and Simons (2008), who describe how the processes of the Argentina-UK red-meat value chain are continuously improved via programs of waste identification, quantification and root cause elimination, to facilitate continuous learning within this value chain.

Figure 1   Dimensions of corporate social responsibility in the food chain (adapted from Maloni and Brown, 2006)

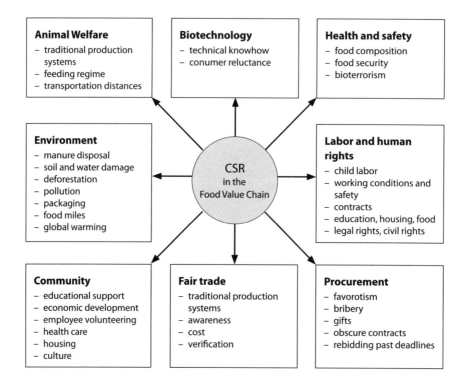

As mentioned before, a key issue for developing-country producers is functional upgrading, i.e. to perform value-adding activities in developing countries, instead of just being commodity producers of products to be upgraded in the country of the Western customer. In the production stages of the value chain, functional upgrading can also take place in intermediary functions, such as in the export sector, where exporters can achieve a role in collection, category management, packaging and sales of products (Dolan and Humphrey, 2000). The developments in the apparel sector as described by Gereffi (1999) are a typical example of how value-adding activities have been moved from developed to developing countries leading to new and more fine-meshed industry structures globally. Similarly, Tokatli and Kizilgun (2004) discuss how in some cases developing countries' (clothing) producers can achieve functional upgrading towards higher rent-giving activities. They portray the transformation of a Turkish contractor, Erak Clothing, into an original brandname manufacturer and retailer. The company created its own brand, Mavi Jeans, in 1991, which is now sold at more than 3,000 sales points, and five directly owned flagship stores.

Although primary processing activities, such as assembly of cars and processing of fruit juices are increasingly moved to developing countries, specialized processing, branding and marketing are still located in developed countries. Lowering of tariffs through the new agreements in the World Trade Organization and market differentiation by developing country producers can support further development of value-added production in developing countries.

Upgrading of market access possibilities

The aim to improve market access may imply upgrading of horizontal as well as vertical relationships focusing on taking part in the right market channel. As discussed in chapter 3, collaboration with horizontal partners may include joint purchasing of production inputs, joint use of production facilities and joint marketing of products. Moreover, in its most sophisticated form, horizontal collaboration might result in product differentiation (intersectoral upgrading). Many studies on developing-country value chains focus on upgrading of horizontal relationships through the formation of producer associations or cooperatives (e.g. Roy and Thorat, 2008; Bijman, 2007; Rammohan and Sundaresan, 2003).

An interesting example of regional upgrading is given by Fisman and Khanna (2004) who describe how the establishment of business groups in underdeveloped regions in India may support the entire development of the region. Large business groups attract supporting industries that can stimulate economic development. They can spread the costs of infrastructure buildings over more assets than a single firm. These improvements at the same time make it more enjoyable for skilled workers to live in the area. Also rotation of skilled workers is commonly used by the groups. Group firms often have an extensive supplier network that also serves them in more remote locations. They have offices in cities where the financial sector is well developed. Groups usually have good government contacts to facilitate land-intensive projects. Establishment in less developed regions is often supported by tax reductions.

Upgrading of vertical relationships should focus on being part of the right channel aiming at the right market. Developing-country value chains are now increasingly trying to differentiate their market outlets which make them less dependent on their current customers, often Western retailers or industries. However, chapter 3 has shown how difficult it is, in particular for small producers to move to another market channel. Alternatively developing country producers might look for channels to easier accessible markets, such as South African fresh-food producers accessing emerging economy markets in Asia, Brazilian pork aiming at the Russian market, where quality and safety demands are less severe than in the European Union, or mango producers from Burkina Faso that aim at the Niger home market instead of at the European market (Nadvi, 2004; Trienekens and Willems, 2007; Trienekens et al., 2009; Humphrey, 2006).

An important condition for upgrading is the consistent ability to meet standards as defined by the market. In particular in the food value chain these standards have become conditional for market access for developing country producers. Muradian and Pelupessy (2005) discuss the need for new standards in the coffee sector that can offer producers opportunities for value-added production, since the abolishment of the International Coffee Agreement and national coffee boards. However, although adherence to one of the many new voluntary standards provides for at least a certain degree of market access, it does not necessarily mean upgrading. Contrary, Tander and Van Tilburg (2007) describe how Indian cashew-nut producers tried to upgrade their product by introducing Western retail standards in their production processes. In this case, however, the proactive behavior of these producers did not pay off because Western supermarket chains in the end proved to be more interested in low costs than in good quality (at least for this product), leading to downgrading of production to previous conditions. Therefore, careful investigation of market opportunities and solid contractual agreements are imperative to successfully combine upgrading with access to new markets.

Upgrading of governance structures

Modern market-oriented chains have the tendency to become shorter as intermediaries between producers and downstream-chain parties become superfluous because of the emergence of direct trading relationships between large producers (or producer groups) and downstream parties (e.g. Bair and Gereffi, 2003). This means the development towards more integrated governance structures in these chains, such as establishing long-term (formal) contracts or going for vertical integration (Williamson, 1999). An example is the transformation of export-oriented producers to producer-exporters in some countries (e.g. table grape producers in South Africa) in order to lower transaction costs and exert full control over the supply chain. Intercompany governance relationships in these chains are often enforced by (transaction-specific) investments of processors or exporters (such as investments in cold stores, seeds, pesticides, credits) to decrease delivery uncertainty and increase quality and quality consistency of the product.

Quality standards and certification are in particular relevant for business relationships in food chains and are often included in contracts. Quality standards can be used in every governance relationship, from spot market to vertical integration (Williamson, 1999). However, in vertically integrated companies certification by an independent party is of less importance, although the use of standards may be required.

Contracts can be divided in the classical version of a comprehensive contract (where everything is fixed ex ante for the entire duration of the contract, covered by the law of contract) or a relational version (allowing for gaps not closed by contract law, embedded in a social system of relationships and subject to continuous renegotiations). Because there is no such thing as a "complete" contract – especially not in developing countries with weakly developed institutional structures – many companies tend to prefer relational contracts implying interpersonal relationships and trust.

Horizontal collaboration between actors is in many cases considered as an important enabler of value chain upgrading. Mesquita and Lazzarrini (2008), in their study of the impact of network relationships on market access find that strong network ties between companies help substitute for the lack of a strong institutional setting to support arrangements between companies and in value chains. SMEs can exploit complementary competencies, share knowledge, technologies and inputs and develop greater responsiveness to global demands, and attain greater export levels as a result.

Lu et al. (2008), in a study into the relationship between social capital (Guanxi in China) and performance of vegetables chains, finds that producers with tighter social relationships with other economic actors in the value chain tend to be more successful. Moreover, he shows that relationships considered traditional in these communities are of great importance to get access to modern markets.

Other studies focus on the role of clusters in upgrading. Gibbon (2001: 349) finds that cluster-based upgrading demands an external push to be successful, such as a linkage to export networks. Giuliani et al. (2005) study relationships between clustering and innovation focusing on Latin American cases. They find that product and process upgrading may be strongly supported by knowledge and technology in related industries (e.g. plants and seeds). Also public-private action through business-government-research institute collaboration can support innovation and upgrading processes in these clusters. However, Murphy (2007) shows in a study on the Tanzanian furniture industry in Mwanza that insufficient government support and lack of collaboration due to mistrust (steeling of ideas) prevent cluster development. This links to the issue of institutional changes necessary for value chain upgrading.

Role of partnerships and actors for change

Upgrading in value chains can only be achieved through partnerships: Private-private, public-private, public-public. Nonchain actors can facilitate upgrading processes either by providing technological, organizational, political and educational support or by changing the macrocultural discourse in general. For instance, in his case study of the upgrading process of the Argentinean wine industry, McDermott (2007) describes how the government facilitated the farmers in training and research and development (R&D) and launched new collaborative arrangements among public and private actors. Also in other studies the presence of a third, external, party is mentioned as a major enabler of change and upgrading. For example, Perez-Aleman and Sandilands (2008) in their analysis of the sustainable production program of Starbucks, show the power of NGOs that brought about significant changes in the purchasing policies of Starbucks and also point at the presence of an independent external certification organization in the upgrading process of the value chain. Riisgaard (2009) points at different "actors for change" in defining and upgrading labor standards in the East African cut-flower industry: In Tanzania the lead is taken by the labor unions, while in Kenya NGOs are the key players in the upgrading process. He also underlines the important role of Western retailers setting up corporate social responsibility (CSR) standards for their developing-country suppliers.

However, evidence in the literature on the positive role of third parties in upgrading is far from conclusive. For example, Hanna and Walsch (2008) in their study on cooperation among small manufacturing firms conclude that networks developed with the help of brokers were less successful than networks operated by the companies themselves. They show that networks developed with the aid of brokers focused on reducing costs and enhancing business processes, whilst firms developing their own networks focused on the ability to coordinate skills and joint targeting of market opportunities. This case shows that it is not only the parties that collaborate that enlarge chances of success but also the focus of their joint upgrading efforts.

Actors for change may include other value chain actors than the lead firm, e.g. retailers, industry, producer cooperative, or nonchain actors, such as governmental organizations, NGOs or other parties in the business environment of the chain, such as banking institutions or service providers. This shows that the initiative may come from the government or from the private sector.

For example, government legislation, regulations and policies may support value chain upgrading by (McDermott, 2007):
- providing market access through negotiating lower barriers for (international) trade;
- supporting physical infrastructure development to achieve a smoother flow of products through the value chain (better roads and distribution facilities, such as storage of products and better communication infrastructures);
- supporting knowledge infrastructure development by setting up good functioning education systems and providing training facilities;
- giving value chain actors access to production technology through import subsidies, and providing access to credits;
- providing a stable economic and political climate.

Business practices and business policies may support value chain upgrading by (e.g. Ruben et al., 2007; Gibbon, 2001):
- setting standards (quality, labor, environmental, trade, etc.);
- streamlining the value chain through better communication and planning;
- setting up of vertical governance mechanisms that facilitate a smooth flow of products and better distribution of value added;
- setting up horizontal governance mechanisms to improve the power balance in the value chain and enhance the bargaining position of small producers;
- support technology development.

Value chain upgrading in the cases presented in this book

This section will reflect on the upgrading options that are discussed in the various cases presented in this book.

The case study on sorghum-beer value chains in chapter 4 integrates in its analysis conditions for value chain upgrading and value chain upgrading opportunities. On the one hand it puts emphasis on how public private partnerships, including businesses, NGOs and government organizations are able to deal with infrastructural and institutional constraints for upgrading and on the other hand upgrading of value added (product, process, functional, interchain and marketing), inclusion of smallholders' challenges for organizational arrangements on value chain level are discussed. This case shows clearly how an analysis of the constraints for upgrading and an analysis of upgrading opportunities can be combined in one study.

The case in chapter 5 on biofuel value chain development in Namibia focuses on shaping the right conditions for upgrading the value chain. It indentifies typical gaps in the institutional and policy framework and proposes development options in the force field between government and private actors, trying to enhance economic and social development but at the same time considering ecological effects that may impact on long-term sustainable development of the sector. In this way it focuses on factors outside the chain, i.e. the role of policies and institutions and the wider institutional environment. Typical examples discussed are rural-development policy in relation to food security; labor policies (such as wage regulations); environmental issues and land tenure issues. In this chapter the role of public-private partnerships and multistakeholder involvement is underlined. They can ease value chain constraints and stimulate upgrading of this value chain.

Chapter 6 pictures the development of local standards in Kenya and pays attention to product and process upgrading. Moreover, it gives an interesting example of functional upgrading on a sector level, as the design of (local) standards is outsourced to the developing countries subsector. Moreover, implementation of standards requires, but also enables, development of a solid supplier's network, strengthening the channel and the organization of smallholders. In this sense standards are a form of governance. With regard to the conditions for upgrading, the chapter includes a discussion on national and international certification institutions that on the one hand restrict, by setting the standards, upgrading through product and process diversification, but on the other support and stimulate the development of local standards.

Chapter 7 again focuses on conditions for value chain upgrading (i.e. to bring sustainable palm oil to the Western market). It addresses market-access challenges and institutional differences such as business norms and cultural values, between supplier countries (Indonesia and Malaysia) and the receiving country (The Netherlands). The discussion circles upon the public-private partnership with businesses, NGOs and governmental organizations of all three countries involved. Thereby it clearly pictures the complexities of partnerships that aim at upgrading of (international) value chains: Imbalances in power relationships, information asymmetries and opposite goals of parties. The case underlines the importance of clear arrangements and procedures to govern the partnership because otherwise the upgrading process may not lead to the desired sustainable production.

Chapter 8 is about market competitiveness, economic institutions and infrastructures in an industrial sector, where it compares the Malaysian and Chinese semiconductor industries.

Both countries focus on different types of semiconductor industries. The chapter pictures both (international) value chains and analyzes typical parameters for value chain efficiency and value chain effectiveness, such as cost price, labor inputs and R&D expenditures. In this way two value chains are compared in-depth at the sector level, which can then be used to upgrade the industry.

The case in chapter 9 is about how partnerships between tourism business and local communities improve the conditions for upgrading in the tourism value chain in Tanzania. It pays attention to how different types of value chain upgrading have taken place, what important conditions for single value chains were and how upgrading contributes to local economic development. The chapter not only analyzes some major conditions for upgrading and upgrading itself, but also how upgrading impacts on local economic development, i.e. whether upgrading has resulted in positive financial, nonfinancial, empowerment and conservation outcomes on the whole for the community. It is another example of an effort to develop more sustainable value chains.

The learning case in chapter 11 (annex) on the banana value chain focuses on various value chain upgrading options, in particular on an increase of value added through process improvement (quality and logistics), product diversification, functional upgrading by encapsulating typical distribution and processing functions and development of new market channels. Moreover, the importance of better organization/governance of the supply network (smallholders), who have to be integrated in the value chain, is underlined. Although the focus is on the development of the value chain, also attention is given to factors that impact on the upgrading process, like market possibilities for different products, infrastructural limitations and possibilities and the policy environment.

Conclusions

Analyzing global value chains can be considered a new methodological tool for understanding the dynamics of economic globalization and international trade. Bolwig et al. (2010) argue that poverty and environmental concerns should be integrated in value chain analysis. This sometimes requires value chain restructuring involving various actors and realizing asymmetrical power relations between them.

All cases in this book present a typical perspective and they show the diversity of approaches to value chain upgrading. The examples range from articles focusing on upgrading of products and processes (value-added upgrading) to articles focusing on improving market access and infrastructures and relaxing institutional constraints, and articles integrating both an analysis of the conditions for upgrading and the actual upgrading process in the value chain.

References

Bair J. and Gereffi G. (2003). 'Upgrading, uneven development, and jobs in the North American apparel industry'. In: *Global Networks* 3, pp. 143-169.

Bijman, J. (2007). 'The role of producer organisations in quality-oriented agro-food chains; an economic organisation perspective'. In: R. Ruben, M. van Boekel, A. van Tilburg and J.Trienekens (eds.), *Governance for Quality in Tropical Food Chains*. Wageningen: Wageningen Academic Publishers, pp. 257-278.

Bolwig, S., S. Ponte, A. du Toit, L. Riisgaard and N. Halberg (2010). 'Integrating poverty and environmental concerns into value chain analysis: a conceptual framework'. In: *Development Policy Review* 28 (2), pp. 173-194.

Dolan, C. and J. Humphrey (2000). 'Governance and trade in fresh vegetables: The impact of UK supermarkets on the African horticulture industry'. In: *Journal of Development Studies* 37 (2), pp. 147-176.

Fisman, R. and T. Khanna (2004). 'Facilitating development: The role of business groups'. In: *World Development* 32 (4), pp. 609-628.

Francis, M. and D. Simons (2008). 'Value chain analysis in the UK beef foodservice sector'. In: *Supply Chain Management-an International Journal* 13 (1), pp. 83-91.

Gereffi, G. (1999). 'International trade and industrial upgrading in the apparel commodity chain'. In: *Journal of international economics*, 48, pp. 37-70.

Gibbon P. (2001). 'Upgrading primary production: A global commodity chain approach'. In: *World Development* 29 (2), pp. 345-363.

Gibbon, P., J. Bair and S. Ponte (2008). 'Governing global value chains: An introduction'. In: *Economy and Society* 37 (3), pp.315-338.

Giuliani, E., C. Pietrobelli and R. Rabellotti (2005). 'Upgrading in global value chains: Lessons from Latin American Clusters'. In: *World Development* 33 (4), pp. 549-574.

Hanna, V. and K. Walsh (2008). 'Interfirm cooperation among small manufacturing firms'. In: *International small business journal* 26, pp. 299-321.

Humphrey, J. and H. Schmitz (2002). 'How does insertion in global value chains affect upgrading in industrial clusters?' In: *Regional Studies* 36, pp. 1017-1027.

Humphrey, J. (2006). 'Policy implications of trends in agribusiness value chains'. In: *The European journal of development research*18 (4), pp. 572-592.

Kaplinsky, R. (2000). 'Globalisation and unequalisation: What can be learned from value chain analysis'. In: *Journal of Development Studies*73 (2), pp. 117-146.

Kaplinsky, R., M. Morris et al. (2002). 'The globalization of product markets and immiserizing growth: Lessons from the South African furniture industry'. In: *World Development* 30 (7), pp. 1159-1177.

Lu, H., J.H. Trienekens, S.W.F. Omta, and S. Feng (2008). 'The value of guanxi for small vegetable farmers in China'. In: *British Food Journal* 110 (4/5), pp. 412-429.

Maloni, M.J. and M.E. Brown (2006). 'Corporate social responsibility in the supply chain: An application in the food industry'. In: *Journal of Business Ethics* 68, pp. 35-52.

McDermott, G.A. (2007). 'The politics of institutional renovation and economic upgrading: Recombining the vines that bind in Argentina'. In: *Politics and Society* 35 (1), pp. 103-144.

Mesquitta, L.F. and S.G. Lazzarini (2008). 'Horizontal and vertical relationships in developing economies: implications fro SMEs access to global markets'. In: *Academy of Management Journal* 51 (2), pp. 359-380.

Muradian, R. and W. Pelupessy (2005). 'Governing the coffee chain: The role of voluntary regulatory Systems'. *World Development* 33 (12), pp. 2029-2044.

Murphy, J.T. (2007). 'The challenge of upgrading in African industries: Socio-spatial factors and the urban environment in Mwanza, Tanzania'. In: *World Development* 35 (10), pp. 1754-1778.

Nadvi., K. (2004). 'Globalization and poverty: How can global value chain research inform the policy debate?' In: *IDS Bulletin* 35 (1), pp. 20-30.

Perez-Aleman, P. and M. Sandilands (2008). 'Building value at the top and the bottom of the global supply chain: MNC-NGO partnerships'. In: *California Management Review* 51 (1), pp. 24-48.

Pietrobelli, C. and F. Saliola (2008). 'Power relationships along the value chain: Multinational firms, global buyers and performance of local suppliers'. In: *Cambridge Journal of Economics* 32, pp. 947-962.

Rammohan, K.T. and R. Sundaresan (2003). 'Socially embedding the commodity chain: An exercise in relation to coir yarn spinning in Southern India'. In: *World Development* 31 (5), pp. 903-923.

Riisgaard, L. (2009). 'Global value chains, labor organization and private social standards: Lessons from East African cut flower industries'. In: *World Development* 37 (2), pp. 326-340.

Roy, D. and A. Thorat (2008). 'Success in high value horticultural export markets for small farmers: The case of mahagrapes in India'. In: *World Development* 6 (10), pp. 1874-1890.

Ruben R., M. van Boekel, A. van Tilburg and J. Trienekens (eds.) (2007). *Governance for quality in tropical food chains*. Wageningen: Wageningen Academic Publishers, pp. 309.

Schmitz, H. (1999). 'Global competition and local cooperation: Success and failure in the Sinos Valley, Brazil'. In: *World Development* 27 (9), pp. 1627-1650.

Tander, N. and A. van Tilburg (2007). 'Standards and market access in Indian ca-
shew processing and international trade'. In: R. Ruben, M. van Boekel, A. van
Tilburg and J. Trienekens (eds.), *Governance for quality in tropical food chains*.
Wageningen: Wageningen Academic Publishers, pp. 211-238.

Tokatli, N. and O. Kizilgun (2004). 'Upgrading in the global clothing industry:
Mavi jeans and the transformation of a Turkish firm from full-package to
brand-name manufacturing and retailing'. In: *Economic Geography* 80 (3), pp.
221-240.

Trienekens, J.H. and S.W. Willems (2007). 'Innovation and governance in international food supply chains: The cases of Ghanaian pineapples and South
African grapes'. In: *International Food and Agribusiness Management Review* 10
(4), pp. 42-63.

Trienekens, J., B. Petersen, N. Wognum and D. Brinkmann (2009). *European
pork chains: Consumer-oriented production and distribution*. Wageningen: Wageningen Academic Publishers, pp. 288.

Van Dijk, M.P. (2006). 'Different effects of globalization for workers and poor in
China and India, Comparing countries, clusters and ICT clusters?' In: *Journal
of Economic and Social Geography, Dossier Globalization and workers* 97 (5), pp.
463-470.

Van Dijk, M.P. (ed.; 2009). *China's new presence in Africa*. Amsterdam: Amsterdam University Press.

Williamson, O.E. (1999). 'Strategy research: Governance and competence perspectives'. In: *Strategic Management Journal* 20, pp. 1087-1108.

A Learning Case of a Local Value Chain

The Banana Subsector in Arusha Municipality and Arumeru District: Producing Banana Beverages

Match Maker Associates Ltd

Introduction

This study was conducted in order to develop a real-life case of banana beverages. The case was developed in preparation for the value chain development (VCD) course, which is designed and facilitated by Match Maker Associates Limited (MMA).[1] The banana beverages case was selected due to its great potential for learning, i.e. the application of the methodologies and tools provided in the first week of the VCD course, and because the value chain is only active within the region of Arusha. Hence, it enables course participants to visit the major actors and stakeholders in the chain.

Methodology and limitations

This case study was developed through consultations and interviews with various stakeholders in the banana subsector within Arusha municipality and Arumeru district. In addition to primary data, also secondary data obtained from the internet and subsector actors was used. There were no specific limitations that hindered the development of this case study.[2] This case study is to be regarded as a "living document". It implies that the authors will continue improving the case on the basis of the evolving subsector dynamics, contributions of the VCD course participants, the feedback from the VCD panel and other key actors in the chain and by the comments of peers in VCD.

Structure of the chapter

As the case is meant for learning purposes, its structure follows the curriculum of the VCD course. The authors feel that it may benefit the "learners" to follow the structure as this enables them to cover all the key elements of the VCD course. The chapter is divided in two parts. The first part covers the subsector definition and analysis and the second part addresses the value chain identification and analyses. It is concluded by strategies for value chain upgrading, and a number of specific recommendations for value chain development.

Subsector analysis and development

A subsector can be defined by either a raw material or a final product/service for a particular market. A subsector is broadly defined to include all the firms that transact with each other in order to supply a particular set of products or services to final consumers. A subsector can include producers, processors, input suppliers, exporters, retailers, etc. In this study, we will define the subsector as "Banana subsector in Arusha Municipality and Arumeru District: With emphasis on banana beverages".

Porter's model was used to analyze competition in the market for bananas for making banana beverages. The model analyzes competition using four forces: Potential market (new) entrants, buyers of banana beverages, suppliers of banana, and substitutes of banana beverages.

Figure 1   Presentation of Porter's model

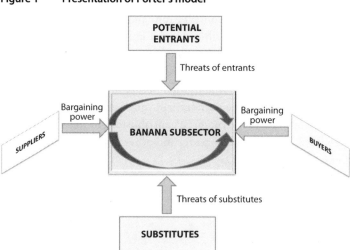

Low entry barriers permit easy entry of small-scale processors into banana-beverage processing. Entry barriers present themselves in the form of technology and capital requirements. There is widespread local knowledge of processing banana beer from ripe bananas. Also capital requirement for investment in small-scale processing is low, although investment in medium-scale processing requires substantial capital. As far as substitutes are concerned, in Arusha Municipality and the neighboring Arumeru district, there are two main competing brands of banana beer (i.e *Raha* from Banana Investment Limited and *Kibo* from Bhunu Mbundi Company Limited). There are also about seventy small-scale producers of banana beer spread all over the country. A local banana beer called *Mbege* poses a stiff competition to *Raha* and *Kibo* although many low-income consumers now prefer bottled banana beers.

Raha beer was intended for the lower and middle-income consumers. With all the substitutes, Raha is for many reasons still the most preferred brand. Raha is certified by Tanzania Bureau of Standards (TBS), it has good taste, and a good packaging and appearance. In addition, Raha is said to give less or minimal "hangover symptoms" because it is perfectly blended.

Banana Investment Limited (BIL) uses suppliers (traders) who traverse the rural markets, buy bananas from the rural markets and supply the factory. Also some farmer groups have been able to bulk and supply bananas to the factory of BIL. Important to note is that suppliers of bananas to BIL factory follow a schedule and each supplier delivers 6 tons a day on specific days allotted to them. Suppliers face stiff competition from the small-scale processors who in most cases hike prices of bananas in the local markets.

Production system in Arusha municipality and Arumeru district

Predominantly, local production technologies are used. The majority of the farmers own small farm sizes of at most four acres. There are few estate farms owning more than eight acres. Production is rain fed. Seasonal variations in yield are a key feature of the production systems. High production is noticeable during rainy seasons and low production in seasons when rain is scarce. In the area, both dessert and cooking (plantain) bananas are grown. More than six different varieties of bananas exist. The most common varieties include *Matooke, Mkonozi, Kisukari, Kimalindi, Pazi, Kisimiti, Mshare* and *Ndizi Ng'ombe*. It can be estimated that in most parts of the Arusha and Kilimanjaro regions of Tanzania, over 60 percent of farm produce of bananas feeds into the brewing industry. Banana contributes a significant part of family household incomes. In some homes banana is the most important crop grown, occupying the largest percentage of household land and contributing most to the family income when compared to all crops grown.

Key actors and functions

Subsector actors are categorized as secondary and primary actors. Primary actors are those directly involved in the production, marketing, processing, distribution trade and consumption of bananas and its products. Secondary actors are not directly involved in the functioning of the subsector but they (secondary actors) offer support services and create favorable environments for the banana production and marketing businesses in which primary actors are engaged. Table 1 below provides a brief description of primary actors and their functions.

Table 1   Summary description of primary actors

Actor	Activities / functions	Description
Smallholder Farmers (SHF)	Input supply	Owns on average 2 acres of banana plantation Uses simple tools (hand hoes and machetes for production) Relies on rainfall for production
Medium Scale Farmers	Production	Own on average four acres
Smallholder Farmer Groups (SHFG)	Bulking and trading	Currently there are five groups (consisting of at least five farmers) bulking and supplying bananas to BIL Groups are given technical advice/ extension services by BIL
Traders	Bulking and trading	BIL contracts traders to buy and supply banana to its factory Traders are supported with credit to increase their operating capital
Banana Investment Limited (BIL)	Processing and distribution	Currently the leading processor of banana is processing 6 tons of bananas a day BIL has three brands of banana drinks (Raha, Malkia sweet wine and Meru dry wine) It operates in 10 regions of Tanzania Has 750 clients (distributors) & is targeting middle- and low-income consumers

Table 1   **(continued)**

Actor	Activities / functions	Description
Bhunu Mbundi Company Limited (BMCL)	Processing and distribution	A competitor of BIL and second largest processor of banana beverage in Arusha region BMCL is currently processing 2 tons of bananas a day
Local Brewers	Processing	Many of them are located in the rural neighborhoods of Arusha municipality and Arumeru Districts They pose a stiff competition for ripe bananas for brewing banana beverages
Beverage dealers	Wholesaling	BIL and BMCL use a network of distributors in and around Arusha municipality Most of them are wholesalers stocking other types of beverages as well Some of them are supplying banana-beverage products to rural retailers
Local brew pubs; Food service (Pubs, bars and restaurants)	Retailing	Retailing of banana beverages is done by local pubs targeting very low-income consumers and food service pubs targeting middle-income consumers
Low-income consumers; medium- and high-income consumers	Consumption	Two categories of consumers of Banana beverage products, low- and medium-income consumers

Secondary actors

The Seliani Agriculture Research Institute (SARI) was identified to be undertaking research in the banana subsector. SARI supported some farmers to access tissue-culture banana varieties from Nairobi. The office of the Regional Agriculture Advisor (RAA) in Arusha and the office of the District Agriculture and Livestock Development Officer (DALDO) of Arusha and Arumeru districts have the mandate to plan for and enhance agriculture development in the district. Services, which can be provided by the office of the DALDO, include extension services and market-information services. Also district agriculture-development strategies are the mandate of the district-agriculture offices.

Business enabling environment

The National Strategy for Growth and Reduction of Poverty (NSGRP) popularly known by its Swahili acronym as MKUKUTA and the Agricultural Sector Development Strategy (ASDS) are currently guiding the agricultural development programs in Tanzania. As NSGRP and ASDS are at a national level, they likewise govern the implementation of agricultural development programs in Arusha municipality and Arumeru Districts.

The National Strategy for Growth and Reduction of Poverty[3], or MKUKUTA is a five-year national strategic design for promoting economic growth and poverty reduction across all sectors of the economy, including the agricultural sector. It provides a framework for focusing policy direction and thrust on economic growth and poverty reduction in various sectors of the economy. It does this by categorizing poverty in terms of income poverty and nonincome poverty and setting specific goals (defined as outcomes to achieve broader goals) and operational targets (outcomes with specific timeframes and quantitative targets). The agriculture sector has been clustered under those sectors that are expected to focus on promoting growth and reduction of income poverty. The operational targets for the agricultural sector under MKUKUTA include the following:

- increased agricultural growth from 5% in 2002/2003 to 10% by 2010;
- increased growth rate for livestock sub sector from 2.7% in 2000/2001 to 9% by 2010;
- increased food crops production from 9 million tons in 2003/04 to 12 million tons in 2010;
- maintaining a strategic grain reserve of at least 4 months of national food requirement;
- secured and facilitated marketing of agricultural products.

As with MKUKUTA, the Agriculture Sector Development Strategy (ASDS) is the agriculture's strategic blueprint for the development of the sector. The specific goals, priority operational targets and strategies are similar to MKUKUTA's because the ASDS was used as one of the main inputs in the preparation of MKUKUTA. ASDS strategic objectives include a) creating and enabling a favorable environment for improved productivity and profitability in the agricultural sector; and b) increasing farm incomes to reduce rural income poverty and ensure household food security. The ASDS identifies the following five strategic priority areas:

1 strengthening the institutional framework to facilitate partnerships and coordination in developing the agricultural sector;
2 creating a favorable environment for commercial activities;

3 public and private partnerships in improving agricultural support services;
4 strengthening marketing efficiency for agricultural inputs and products; and
5 mainstreaming agriculture in the decentralized planning process under the local government authorities (LGAs).

The Agriculture Sector Review (ASR, 2006) pointed out that there is a plethora
of agriculture-related policies that are not necessary consistent with one another
and are also not fully in tune with MKUKUTA and the ASDS. Efforts are being
made to upgrade some of the policies, e.g. agriculture and livestock sector policy
and develop new policies, e.g. agricultural marketing policy in response to the
present governing economic environment.

The Agriculture Sector Development Program (ASDP) formulated in 2003
is the main instrument to implement the agriculture sector development strategy
(ASDS). The objective of the ASDP is to increase productivity, profitability, and
farm incomes by a) improving farmers' use of and access to agricultural knowledge, technologies, marketing systems and infrastructure; and b) promoting agricultural private investment. The development of the ASDP started shortly after
the adoption of the ASDS in 2001, but program development was not completed
until June 2006.

The ASDP comprises of three pillars that correspond to the five strategic areas of intervention:
1 investments at district and field level to support the design, implementation of
   district agricultural development plans (75% of Sector Public Funds);
2 investments at national level to support the formulation and management of
   policy interventions, the institutional framework and national support services (20% of public funds); and
3 investments that mainstream crosscutting and cross-sector issues (5% of public funds).

Most of the ASDP funding goes to the district level where implementation happens. The ASDP activities at district level are based on the District Agricultural
Development Program (DADP). Planning for delivery of extension services and
investment in agricultural infrastructure takes place in the DADPs following a
participatory planning process from grassroots level to the district. This exercise results in proposals for projects and priority areas for interventions. The
proposals are submitted to District Agricultural Sector Advisory Committee
(DASAC) meetings in which stakeholders (from villages and wards) and civil
society organizations (NGOs, CSOs) operating in the district area participate.
The draft plan and budget of DADP developed from this process are submitted
to the full Council for approval as a part of the District Development Plan and

Figure 2   Subsector map of banana beverage

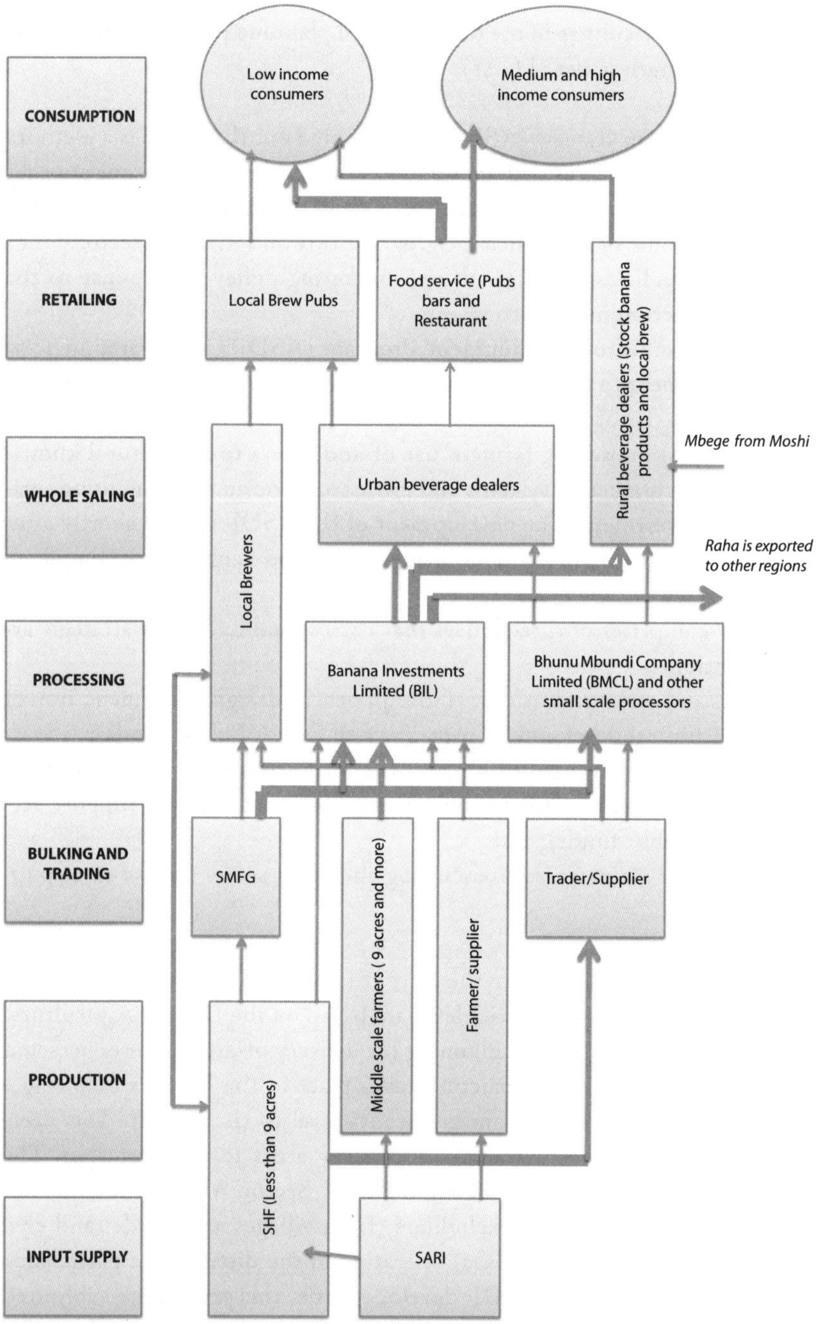

CONSUMPTION

Low income consumers

Medium and high income consumers

RETAILING

Local Brew Pubs

Food service (Pubs bars and Restaurant)

Rural beverage dealers (Stock banana products and local brew)

Mbege from Moshi

WHOLE SALING

Local Brewers

Urban beverage dealers

Raha is exported to other regions

PROCESSING

Banana Investments Limited (BIL)

Bhunu Mbundi Company Limited (BMCL) and other small scale processors

BULKING AND TRADING

SMFG

Middle scale farmers (9 acres and more)

Farmer/ supplier

Trader/Supplier

PRODUCTION

SHF (Less than 9 acres)

INPUT SUPPLY

SARI

Budget (DDPB). It is the priority areas of development that receive funds and support from the DADPs.

The implementation of ASDS is overseen by MAFS, the Ministry of Cooperatives and Marketing (MCM) and the Ministry of Water and Livestock Development (MWLD) at central level, while the Prime Minister's Office-Regional Administration and Local Governments (PMO-RALG) is responsible for coordinating the LGAs. LGAs have the primary responsibility for implementing the ASDS actions in their respective districts. These ministries will have the role of setting the right policy and regulatory framework and developing mechanisms to ensure their effective implementation at national and local level. In addition, they are responsible for coordinating the various actors within the sector. Furthermore, implementation of the ASDS will require close coordination amongst these ministries and other government institutions.

Subsector map

In this section, a subsector map will be presented and a description of the channels will be given. A subsector map is a diagrammatic presentation of the subsector. It may not be very detailed as to show all activities and players in the subsector. Nevertheless, it serves the intended purpose of enabling a reader to visualize the primary actors in the subsector and their various roles and functions. Figure 2 is a graphical presentation of the subsector map.

Three channels are identifiable: a) The Local Brewers channel b) Banana Investment Limited (BIL) Channel and c) Bhunu Mbundi Company Limited (BMCL) channel. Detailed explanations of these channels can be found below.

Figure 3   Channel I: Local brewers channel

In this channel, input supply and production of bananas is by Smallholder Farmers (SHF). Traders and sometimes Smallholder Farmers Groups (SHFGs) collect and sell bananas. Local brewers process the bananas into *Mbege* – a local banana beer. This channel is informal, but it is estimated it takes at least 50 percent of bananas sold in the markets. Banana beer coming from this channel is sold to primarily low-income consumers.

Figure 4   Channel II: Banana Investment Limited (BIL) channel

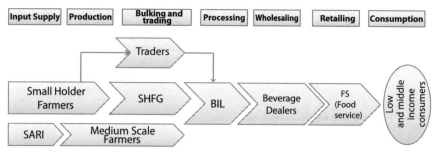

In channel II, the input supply is by SARI and Smallholder Farmer (SHF). Production is by SHF and Medium Scale Farmers (MSF). Collecting and trading is by traders, SHFG and Medium Scale Farmers. In some cases traders buy raw bananas and ripening and pealing is done from BIL, at the cost of a trader. BIL does the processing, distribution/wholesaling is by beverage dealers, retailing by Food Services (FS) and consumption is by both low- and middle-income consumers. This channel takes up to 6 tons of ripe bananas daily. It can be estimated that this channel consumes more than 30 percent of ripe bananas that goes into banana beer and wine processing around Arusha municipality and Arumeru District. In Arusha low-income people consume BIL products. Out of Arusha medium- and high-income people consume BIL products.

Figure 5   Channel III: Bhunu Mbundi Company Limited channel

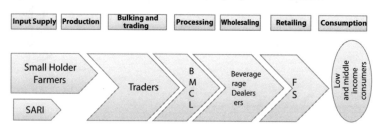

In channel III, SARI and Smallholder Farmers are involved in providing inputs. Smallholder Farmers undertake production of bananas. Traders collect bananas and processing by BMHL. Wholesaling/distribution is done by beverage dealers and retailing by the food-service sector. Low-income consumers are the target market for banana beer brand *kibo*. This channel takes 2 tons of ripe bananas a day and Kibo beer is the main product produced in this channel.

Profitability analysis

A profitability analysis was done for farm level, trade or supplier level, beer wholesaling and retailing. Details for the profitability analysis at the farm and the supplier levels are presented below. The assumptions at the farm level are:
- costs for first plowing (an acre) is estimated at Tanzanian Shilling TZS 16,000;
- costs for seedlings (for planting an acre, i.e. 166 seedlings) is estimated at TZS 1,000;
- costs for digging holes (166 holes) is estimated at TZS 100 per hole;
- 9 tons of fertilizer is needed at planting time. Costs for the 9 tons of fertilizer is estimated at TZS 150,000;
- costs for applying fertilizer is estimated at TZS 300 per hole and there are 166 holes to be dug;
- total costs for watering young banana plants is estimated at TZS 20,000;
- costs for weeding is estimated at TZS 16,000 each time and weeding is done three times a year;

Profitability at Farm Level (1 acre)

Costs in TZS	Year 1	Year 2	Year 3	Year 4	Year 5
Fixed Costs					
Land preparation	16,000				
Seadlings (166)	166,000				
Digging holes (166)	16,600				
Planting	16,600				
Watering	20,000				
Variable Ccosts					
Fertilizer for an acre (9 tons)	150,000	75,000	75,000	75,000	75,000
Applying fertilizer	49,800	24,900	24,900	24,900	24,900
Weeding	48,000	48,000	48,000	48,000	48,000
Harvesting costs (yearly estimate)		10,000	10,000	10,000	10,000
	247,800	157,900	157,900	157,900	157,900
Revenue (2nd Year for up to 5 Years)					
Rainy Season		184,000	184,000	184,000	184,000
Rainy Season		600,000	600,000	600,000	600,000
	0	784,000	784,000	784,000	784,000
Gross Profits	-247,800	626,100	626,100	626,100	626,100
Gross Margin	0.00	125.22	125.22	125.22	125.22

- costs for harvesting is estimated at TZS 10,000 each time the harvesting is done;
- harvesting starts after a year. In the first year there is no harvest, hence no income for the farmer.

Profitability at Suppliers Level	Tanzanian Shilling = TZS
Costs	
Buying Bananas	TZS 1,765,000
Transport Costs	TZS 250,000
Loading	TZS 24,000
Offloading	TZS 12,000
Total Costs	TZS 2,051,000
Revenue	
Selling Bananas	TZS 3,882,000
Gross Profit	**TZS 1,832,000**
SGM	**47%**

Assumptions for the profitability analysis at the supplier level:
- A basket of bananas costs TZS 3,500 when banana is plentiful and 6,500 when banana is scarce. Average price for a basket of bananas is TZS 5,000.
- A basket of bananas weighs between 16-18 kilograms (average weight of a basket of bananas is 17 kg).
- A trader needs about 353 baskets to fill a 6-ton truck.
- Hiring a truck of 6 tons costs averagely TZS 250,000.
- Four people load a 6-ton truck and the trader pays each of them TZS 6,000.
- Off loading is done by three people and a trader pays each person TZS 3,000.
- Selling price of bananas ranges between TZS 9,000 to TZS 13,000 for a basket of 16-18 kilograms. Average price is TZS 11,000.

Assumptions for the analysis of profitability at wholesale/distribution level are:
- Profitability calculation is done for a crate of banana beer.
- The cost of a crate of beer when buying from BIL is TZS 6,000.
- The selling price for a crate is TZS 6,500.

Profitability at Wholesale/Distribution Level	
Costs	
Buying Banana beer (1 crate)	TZS 6,000
Revenue	
Selling Banana beer (1 crate)	TZS 6,500
Gross Profit	**TZS 500**
SGM	**8%**

Assumptions made for the profitability analysis at the retail level are:
- Profitability calculation is done per crate of banana beer sold.
- The wholesale price of a crate of beer when buying from wholesaler is TZS 6,500.
- The selling price for a crate is TZS 8,500 (each bottle is sold at a retail price of TZS 350).

Profitability at Retail Level

Costs	
Buying Banana beer (1 crate)	TZS 6,500
Revenue	
Selling Banana beer (1 crate)	TZ S8,400
Gross Profit	**TZS 1,900**
SGM	23%

Assumptions for the profitability analysis for local brewing (*Mbege*):
- One bucket of banana and a quarter of a bucket of millet makes three buckets of Mbege.
- A bucket of banana costs between TZS 5,000 and TZS 10,000.
- A half a bucket of finger millet grains costs TZS 2,000.
- Firewood worth TZS 9,000 is used to make 12 buckets of Mbege, in about four cycles. On average to make three buckets of Mbege, one would need firewood worth TZS 2,250.
- The selling price for a bucket of Mbege is TZS 6,000. Three buckets would cost TZS 18,000.

Profitability Local Processors

Costs	
Average price of banana	TZS 7,500
Buying millet	TZS 2,000
Firewood	TZS 2,250
Total costs	TZS 11,750
Revenue	
Selling banana beer (3 buckets)	TZS 18,000
Gross profit	**TZS 6,250**
SGM	35%

MATCH MAKER ASSOCIATES LTD

From the above profitability analysis, it can be concluded that banana cultivation and sale is highly profitable for a farmer. Also a banana trader makes significant revenue (47%). However, the wholesale/distributor earns the lowest gross margin (8%).

Subsector dynamics

In this section we will discuss subsector constraints and opportunities and subsector driving forces. Table 2 below presents a summary of subsector constraints and opportunities.

Table 2   **Subsector constraints and opportunities**

	Constraints	Opportunities
Production/management	Production is rain-fed and hence it fluctuates, posing a constraint for farmers to guarantee contracted markets Banana pests and diseases, e.g banana weevil, Panama disease, ciga end rot and vermin (mole) reduce farm yields and consequently production, causing farm revenue losses Limited knowledge and skills in crop husbandry Absence of marketing infrastructure	BIL provides extension services for farmer-groups clients and hence opportunities for farmers to learn and improve farm management and production There is knowledge of organic methods to control banana pests and diseases. This knowledge can be shared among farmers to increase their knowledge and skills on pest and disease control Opportunities for entrepreneurs to invest in tissue-culture laboratories to produce good planting materials for farmers There is an opportunity for BIL to link its extension services to SARI and this will increase its quality of its extension service
Market access	Small individual independent farmers operating in isolation of each other are unable to bulk their produce and hence cannot access premium factory prices	With the support from BIL, farmers are being organized in groups to enable them bulking their produce and access factory price. This initiative can be replicated by other individual farmers There is a present market for banana varieties for brewing and also large-scale farms have the opportunity to enter into a contractual arrangement to supply BIL, thus guaranteeing a market for their products

Table 2 (continued)

	Constraints	Opportunities
Infrastructure/technology	Poor access roads especially on the hilly slopes which become impassable during rainy seasons, which limits farmers' access to markets for bananas Poor methods of storage (sometimes in contaminated bags) and transportation of bananas, which sometimes lead to reduction in quality or rejection of bananas delivered to the factory, resulting in losses for the trader	There are various processing technologies internationally, which are replicable in the local context
Finance & risks	Limited sources of finance, especially for traders, limits traders' capacity to buy bananas and therefore limited credit poses a problem of slow growth of the market for farmers' produce Limited source of credit for farmers to expand farm production	Presence of a credit facility from BIL which traders/suppliers can access is an opportunity for the suppliers to seize and use to increase their businesses
Policy enabling environment	There is no known policy that affects production and expansion of processing of banana	The government agriculture-development policy of enhancing processing and value addition for agricultural products is a favorable factor for the development and expansion of the BIL and other processing companies

Driving forces

The tense competition for inputs (bananas for making a local brew, like *mbege*, *Raha* and *Kibo* and over seventy other local types of banana beverages) pushes up prices for bananas. BIL uses suppliers to source inputs but sometimes suppliers also face stiff competition in the markets for bananas. The small-scale processors, many of them working in the informal sector, unfairly distort market prices, yet they do not guarantee the market for farmers produce. Small-scale farmers (many farmers fall in this category) are not risk averse and are not looking for a permanent market for their produce; rather, they are looking for high prices in spot markets, consequently increasing the competition.

There has been an expanding market for banana beverages (currently the national market is about 40 million people) with prospects of an East African market (of about 100 million people). The expanding market poses an opportunity for local processors (e.g. BIL and others) to increase production in order to meet the market expansion. The expansion in the market will pull production, an incentive for farmers to increase the production of bananas. However, farmers can only benefit from the expanded market by increasing their turnovers as prices of banana (per kilo) is unlikely to increase much because the production costs of banana beverages incurred by the processors is not coming down, meaning that processors are not willing to pay more for a kilo of ripe bananas.

Subsector development strategies

a Financing for subsector development
Financing is instrumental to increase production, purchase and marketing and to increase processors capacities. As such, the following needs to be done:
— Stimulate innovation towards development of financial products suitable for farmers by putting in place relevant incentives and rewards to such innovation.
— Enhance a forward and backward linkage arrangement (contracting) between farmers and the processors as this kind of arrangement can enhance farmers' access to finance.
— Develop an arrangement through which suppliers are supported by the processors to access advances or short-term loans to buy bananas and also finance their business expansion.
— Using appropriate mechanisms, institute a medium for a large-scale financing scheme through which processors can access financing to expand their firms and increase processing capacities.

b Pest and disease management and control
Pest and disease management and control is necessary to increase yield and farm productivity and incomes of farmers. Increased productivity means farmers will reap more from the same acreage they have. For effective pest and disease control, the following is recommended:
— Provide regular and routine extension advice to farmers. Advice should focus on relevant and practical solutions to disease and pest control.
— Train farmers in proper agronomy and best practices for banana cultivation, which brings best yields. Farmer Field School (FFS) have been redefined and applied in differing ways. However, a system through which farmers can be trained in best agronomy would go a long way to equip farmers with problem-solving skills.

c Farmer institutional organization
Farmer organization and positioning into a system where they can bulk and supply their produce is recommendable. Experience has shown that well organized farmers can buy bananas from others (who may not be in groups) and supply to the upstream market. When supplying to the factory, farmers will earn a higher average price of TZS 11,000 per basket, which now they are selling at an average price of TZS 5,000. Sound Farmer Groups (FGs) can be a solid base for production, yet at the same time also act as suppliers to upstream markets, usually lowering the procurement costs and bringing efficiency in flow of products. Recommendations for farmer institutional organizations are as follows:
– Strengthen the existing farmer organization by supporting their internal processes of governance and conflict resolution.
– Encourage activities that bring farmers cohesion and organize farmer field days.

d Market deepening and widening
Recommendations are as follows:
– Foster initiatives aiming at market deepening through increasing the efficiency of the banana marketing chain from rural production areas to urban processing zones.
– Foster market widening through exploring regional market expansion and searching for cross-border markets.

e Research and development of varieties with good qualities for brewing
The research revealed that there are many varieties of bananas grown in Arusha region. Of these varieties only those varieties with high sugar contents are suitable for brewing. The study recommends long-term research to develop and multiply varieties of bananas, which are suitable for brewing.

Value chain analysis and development

We identify value chains by looking at the key element of value chains, i.e. economic gains, governance and market-focused collaborations. This section will give a brief explanation of what these key elements of value chains are. An assessment of the channels, using the value chains elements will also be made.

a Economic gains
Economic gains are concerned with the generation and distribution of returns arising from the various functions, e.g. design, production, packaging, marketing,

and recycling in the chain. Economic gains are brought about by competition in the market and the need for the entrepreneur to innovate in order to survive in a competitive market.

b Market-focused collaborations

Collaboration of value chain participants is key and is usually market focused. This is one of the distinguishing features of a value chain from other traditional business relationships. Market-focused collaboration is when different business enterprises choose to work together to produce and market products and services in an effective and efficient manner in order to meet the needs of targeted consumer(s).

c Governance

Governance ensures that interactions between firms along a value chain exhibit some reflection of organization rather than being random. Value chains are governed when parameters requiring product, process and logistic qualification are set which have consequences up and down the value chain encompassing bundles of activities, actors and functions. Coordination usually involves managing these parameters; however, it does not require that a single firm is responsible for it. The value chain's governance role is usually undertaken by a chain leader who preferably is strategically located and fully knowledgeable with the dynamics of the chain.

The following subsection will assess in detail the identified channels, and assess whether these channels qualify to be value chains.

Assessment of primary channels

Channel I: Local brewers channel
Limited innovations and limited gains exist in this channel. Brewing local banana beer using the traditional knowledge and skills has existed for a long time and is part and parcel of the livelihood of some people. Farmers are not collaborating to produce for specific markets and neither are processors (local brewers) purposely and deliberately targeting any market. There is no evidence of market-focused collaboration among farmers producing bananas for brewing or among processors.

In addition, small-scale producers of local brews are not growth oriented and are not showing any prospects for growth. Most local pubs are buying *mbege* in bulk from Moshi and consumers prefer the pubs with a better ambiance. No evidence of value chain governance was seen in this channel. In fact, small-scale processors of the local banana beer are all working independently of each other. There is no evidence of any coordination of their activities.

Channel II: Banana Investment Limited (BIL) channel

Elements of economic gains are existent in this channel. Banana Investment Limited is leading the chain and providing innovations (e.g. developing new brands, getting TBS certification, innovation in packaging from wooden crates to plastic ones, etc.), which are currently driving the chain. Gains from market expansion are trickling down to benefit suppliers and farmers in the form of a guaranteed market for farmers' and suppliers' produce and a higher factory-landed price, especially for suppliers. It was noted that the market for products of BIL products in some places (e.g. Dar es Salaam, Morogoro, Dodoma and Mwanza) has grown by 100 percent last year due to efficient distribution channels, good packaging and recently effective promotion activities.

Elements of market-focused collaborations are existent. Currently, BIL have innovated to contract farmers to supply bananas. Also BIL has been working with suppliers and sometimes advances credit to them to enable them to deliver efficiently as scheduled. Suppliers are aware of the quality of the bananas and are working together with the farmers to keep the quality high.

Governance has to do with ensuring the chain functions effectively, and that actors take responsibility of their actions. Elements of governance exist in the sense that poor packaging of banana supplies by traders is punished. Contaminated bananas are rejected at the factory and this puts pressure on suppliers to ensure supplies are delivered in uncontaminated bags and in hygienic conditions. Also, BIL is monitoring wholesalers to ensure that they do not hike the price above the regulated TZS 350 for a 300 ml bottle. The incentive for retailers is the TZS 500 profit they get from selling a crate of BIL products.

Channel III: Bhunu Mbundi Company Limited channel

BMCL is a fairly new entrant into the formal processing. As such the company has not yet fully established its networks of suppliers, and the management is sourcing bananas from open markets. The company has yet to establish its supply networks.

From the descriptions of the channels with reference to the value chain criteria as listed above, it can be concluded that the channel of Banana Investment Limited meets all the criteria of a value chain. The following section will present a mapping of the value chain and a description of the value chain feasibility.

Value chain mapping and feasibility

We now present a mapping of the value chain. The value chain map is drawn on the premise that SARI will provide research services to develop and propagate banana varieties most suitable for banana beer production. Smallholder farmers and medium-scale farmers will increase production. Smallholders should be organized in groups in order to be able to bulk and deliver their produce to the factory gate. In such an arrangement where farmers are organized, it is also possible for them to access credit or mobilize local credit. Traders will continue to buy and supply bananas from smallholder farmers who are not in groups. With increased business BIL should be able to give distributors fair profit margins from their sales.

But for the value chain to be feasible, lucrative and beneficial to the chain actors, support services have to target research and development of the banana varieties most suitable for banana wine production, provide credit advances to traders for business expansion, give support to strengthen farmer groups and invest capital for finance acquisition of equipments for expansion.

Figure 6   Banana Investment Limited – Value Chain Map

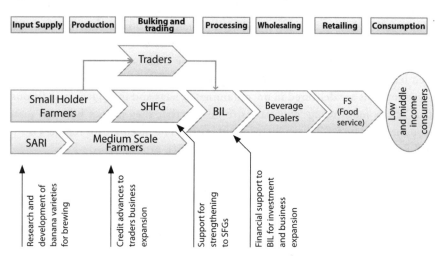

Emerging value chains – future

From the subsector map above, Bhunu Mbundi Company Limited (BMCL) presents an emerging value chain. Discussion on the limitations of this chain is presented above. This channel has prospects of growing into a formidable value chain.

In the analysis of the critical success factors, we address what BIL needs to achieve in order to participate in both the local and regional markets (order qualifying critical success factors or CSF). Analysis is also extended to look into factors, which will make BIL succeed to gain bigger portions of the market (order winning CSF). Analysis is made for two market segments: a) Low-income markets segment and b) medium- and high-income market segments.

A summary of the analysis of the critical success factors is presented in table 3.

Table 3   Summary of critical success factors (CSF)

Market segment	Order qualifying (CSF)	Order winning (CSF)
Medium- and high-income	Volumes of supply to upcountry markets (the beer should not run out) Consistency in supply with definite schedules for routes Trust and degree of collaboration among chain actors (suppliers are very critical)	Tastes and preference of consumers (it causes less hangover) Quality (reflected in labeling and the packaging with TBS certification) Terms of supply – there is need to give some profit margin to distributors and retailers
Low-income market segment	Competitive price Quantity Consistency supply	The price for the product (low-income consumers prefer a price of TZS 300 as opposed to TZS 350).

Value chain upgrading strategies

In this section, a number of upgrading strategies are recommended:

a Process related
- Speed up the upgrading of the production process to meet the growing regional and national markets. BIL is in the process of expanding production and should increase its production line in time to meet the growing demand for its products.
- BIL should enhance communication with its suppliers and ensure that suppliers are free to discuss terms, especially when bananas are hard to find or when the suppliers have fallen victim to unscrupulous farmers.
- At the farm level, emphasis should be put on increasing the production and productivity so that yields can increase from the current 9 tons/hectare to a level closer to the potential yield of 30 tons/hectare.

b *Product related*
- So far two new products, *meru* and *melkia* wine, have not gained similar popularity as *raha*.
- Reduce the formula, which produces a lot of gas in the beers. Excessive gas is said to lead to breaking bottles.
- Stronger bottles are recommended, especially for the packaging of the beers.
- BIL should consider investment in the production of Banana Juice.

c *Function related*
- Backward linkages with bigger farms will secure large and timely deliveries of inputs and reduce the dependence of small-scale farmers and fluctuations in the market.
- Increasing the number of suppliers and terms of business given to the suppliers will increase effectiveness in the delivery of bananas by suppliers.

d *Marketing related*
- Many distributors have hailed timely delivery of *raha*, ways to increase motivation of distributors should be sought.

Notes

1   A list of acronyms can be found at the end of the chapter.
2   Obviously, the authors would have wished to have more time for the field study, the analysis and the compilation of the study but this constraint is a normal feature in the consultancy/training industry.
3   Extracted from the Tanzanian Agriculture Sector Review 2006, p. 6.

About the Authors

Diederik de Boer is working at the Maastricht School of Management (MsM). At MsM he is the Head of the Sustainable Development Centre and the Director of Round Table Africa. He is also the coordinator of the Expert Centre for Sustainable Business and Development Cooperation. He got a Master in Public Administration from the University of Leiden/Rotterdam and a Master of Business Administration from Nimbas/University of Tilburg. His research interest focuses on Business – Community Partnerships in developing countries.
deboer@msm.nl

Michael Brüntrup (PhD in agriculture) works since 2003 for the German Development Institute/Deutsches Institut für Entwicklungspolitik (DIE) on topics related to agriculture and rural development, trade policy and food security. His geographical focus is Subsahara Africa. Before joining DIE, he worked for several years as a free lance consultant for impact assessments and evaluations in the fields of microfinance, gender, resource and agricultural economics for various NGOs, German development cooperation and international agricultural research institutes. His recent work includes studies on the impact of the World Trade Organisation's rules on African agricultural policies.
michael.bruentrup@die-gdi.de

Meine Pieter van Dijk is an economist and professor of Water Services Management at UNESCO-IHE Institute for Water Education in Delft, professor of entrepreneurship at MSM and professor of Urban management at the Institute of Social Studies of the Erasmus University in Rotterdam. He is member of the research schools CERES and SENSE. He worked on and in developing countries since 1973 for NGOs, the Asian Development Bank, the Inter-American Development Bank, the World Bank, different bilateral donors and UN agencies. His recent books are on the new presence of China in Africa (Amsterdam: University

Press, 2009) and Managing cities in developing countries, the theory and practice of urban management (2006, Cheltenham: Edgar Elgar).

m.vandijk@unesco-ihe.org

Paul Goes is an economist who studied 'Urban, Port and Transport Economics' at the Erasmus University in Rotterdam. He did a comparative study of the Malaysian and Chinese Semiconductor Industry answering the question; "what is the 'China effect' on the Malaysian Semiconductor industry and how can Malaysia remain competitive in this industry?" Paul has been working in the Malaysian semiconductor industry since 2006, gaining experience in addition to his theoretical understanding.

paulgoes2@hotmail.com

Raoul Herrmann is a research fellow at the German Development Institute/ Deutsches Institut für Entwicklungspolitik (DIE) in Bonn and a PhD student with the Institute for Environmental Economics and World Trade at Leibniz University of Hannover, both in Germany. His research is on the socio-economic implications of large-scale agro-industrial biofuel investments in Sub-Saharan Africa. He studied economics, business administration, and agricultural economics at the University of Hohenheim in Germany.

raoul.herrmann@die-gdi.de

Peter Knorringa is Professor of Private Sector & Development at the Institute of Social Studies, Erasmus University Rotterdam, the Netherlands. His research focuses on the role of private sector actors in development processes. An economist by background, he has over 20 years of experience in research, teaching, capacity development and advisory work. His areas of specialization are small enterprise development, industrial clustering, value chain analysis, local economic development, industrialisation; role of trust, networks and social capital in development; development relevance of fair trade, ethical trade, and Corporate Social responsibility; survival business and income and employment generation as part of (urban) poverty alleviation; monitoring and evaluation of Civil Society interventions in the areas of work mentioned above.

knorringa@iss.nl

Herma (van der Laarse-)Kwakkenbos is Corporate Social Responsibility consultant at Schuttelaar & Partners. She graduated in 2008 in International Business Administration at the Erasmus University, Rotterdam. She finalized her Master of Science in Business Administration – Global Business and Stakeholder Management – with distinction in 2009. Her (research) interests include

chain responsibility, value chain development and development cooperation. Her expertise is sustainability, sustainability reporting and corporate communication.
hkwakkenbos@schuttelaar.nl

Victor L. van der Linden (MSc) is educated in both International Business and Development studies. Victor has worked as a researcher and a practitioner on: value chain analysis and development, setting up partnerships for smallholder inclusion in value chains, cooperative arrangements between the private/public/civil society sector in 8 countries in East and West Africa, as well as in India. Currently Victor works for a Dutch development NGO in West Africa as value chain advisor to its Fair and Sustainable Economic development program.
victor.van.der.linden@icco.nl

Match Makers Associates Ltd Private Sector Development Consultants, PO Box 12257, Arusha Tanzania.
info@mma-ltd.com

Gloria Otieno is a PhD student at the Institute of Social Studies, Erasmus University Rotterdam, the Netherlands. Her PhD is on 'Standards and Trade: The case of Kenya's Horticultural Exports Industry'.
otieno@iss.nl

Laura Tarimo joined Round Table Africa in Arusha in December 2009 after completing a MSc in Philosophy at the University of Edinburgh. She completed her undergraduate studies in Economics with a focus on Development Economics and a minor in Environmental Studies at Middlebury College, USA. Previously, she worked as a teacher of Economics and Business Studies at the United World College of South East Asia in Singapore where she taught students at IB Level and IGCSE Level.
katarina@mma-ltd.com

Jacques H. Trienekens is coordinator of Value chain research at SDC of Maastricht School of Management and associate professor at Management Studies Group of Wageningen University. His research interests include (international) food chain and network management, including value chain research in developing countries. He received a PhD in Food Chain Management at Wageningen University in 1999. From 2000 to 2003 he was, part-time, Director Program Management at Agri Chain Competence centre, an organization that facilitates public-private food chain development projects. He has been a visiting professor at University of Bonn in Germany and University of Pretoria in South Africa.

Furthermore, he has been a member of the board of directors of International Food and Agribusiness Management Association (IAMA) from 2004-2010. He is editor and managing editor of Journal on Chain and Network Science and International Food and Agribusiness Management Review respectively, and has published in a variety of peer reviewed international journals.

jacques.trienekens@wur.nl

Ronald S.J. Tuninga is Professor of Management and Director of the PhD Program at the Open University of the Netherlands. He is also a Visiting Professor of International Management and Marketing at Hult International Business School. As of May 2011 he is the Honorary Chair of the Faculty of Assessors of AMBA. From 2008 until 2011 he was the Vice-chair of the Board of Trustees of AMBA. Until 2009 he was the Director Dean and Professor of International Business and Marketing of the MSM.

tuninga@xs4all.nl

Jeroen van Wijk is Associate Professor in Business and Development at Maastricht School of Management (MSM). His research concerns public-private partnerships related to value chain development and institutonal change in emerging economies. He co-chairs the value chain track of the Partnerships Resource Centre, located at the Rotterdam School of Management. He has been teaching the courses Business in the Global Arena, Value Chain Analysis, and Qualitative Research Methods and Skills for MSM. Jeroen studied sociology at Leiden University and international relations at the University of Amsterdam where he received his PhD (1999) with a dissertation on the impact of intellectual property protection in food crops. From 1989-1999 he worked as researcher at the University of Amsterdam, and as Editorial Board member of the Biotechnology and Development Monitor. Between 1999 and 2009, he was employed as lecturer in Business and Development at the Rotterdam School of Management of Erasmus University.

jcac.wijk@msm.nl

Index

Agricultural 10, 13, 21, 23, 25-26, 53, 56, 58, 69, 71, 73-74, 76, 78-79, 84, 93-97, 103-104, 109-110, 117, 125, 129, 137-138, 144-147, 149-150, 153, 256-257, 265

Agriculture 26-27, 45, 71, 73, 79, 92-94, 96-97, 109, 145-147, 159, 255-257, 265

Beer 10, 25, 71-72, 75-78, 82-84, 245, 253, 260-263, 268-272

Biofuel 9-11, 13, 16, 20-25, 89, 93, 107, 148, 246

Bottom Of the Pyramid (BOP) 17, 20, 24, 31-37, 40-41, 43-44

Business development model 10

Certificate 124, 127-128, 130, 132

China (Chinese) 9, 27, 147, 165-170, 172-196, 237, 246

Cluster 13-15, 17, 22, 28-29, 43-44, 48, 51, 144, 147, 182, 186, 193, 212-213, 243-244, 256

Competition 13, 19, 22-23, 38, 89, 144-146, 165, 252-253, 255, 265, 268

Competitive(ness) 10, 12, 16-18, 22-23, 27, 31, 33, 36, 38, 44, 48, 53, 59, 63, 90-92, 100, 102, 120-121, 137, 165-167, 169-172, 174, 177, 179-181, 186, 188, 192-196, 206, 209, 246, 268, 271

Compliance 13, 53, 74, 119-120, 123-126, 128-131, 137

Consumer 9, 13, 18-19, 24, 32, 36, 39, 41, 46, 49, 53, 60, 91, 120, 122, 137, 154, 170, 192, 239, 252-255, 258-261, 268, 271

Contract 11, 16-18, 20, 46-47, 54-58, 63, 74, 76-77, 81, 84, 100, 103, 107, 111, 125-126, 128, 133, 188, 211, 221, 229, 240, 243, 254, 269

Cooperation 12, 15-17, 19, 26, 72, 109, 138, 142, 149, 152, 156-157, 182, 184, 191, 210, 228, 244

Cooperative 11, 20, 22, 43, 49-50, 53, 56-58, 81, 83, 109, 122, 238, 241, 245, 259

Corporate Social Responsibility (CSR) 32, 34, 40, 209, 218, 228, 239-240, 244

Credit 21, 47, 57, 59, 61-62, 73, 76, 79, 81, 83-85, 100, 102-105, 110, 243, 245, 254, 265, 269-270

Distribution 12-13, 17, 19-20, 24-25, 38, 43, 44, 47-48, 50-52, 54, 56, 58-60, 82, 91-92, 94, 97, 102, 104, 106, 110, 139, 141, 145, 147, 167, 205, 213, 239-240, 245, 247, 254-255, 260-262, 267, 269

District 202-203, 213-226, 251-253, 255-257, 259

Empower 20, 36, 85, 144, 202-203, 214-215, 225-227, 247

Environment 11, 17, 19, 27, 33-35, 43, 45, 47-48, 53, 57, 60-64, 71-72, 74-75, 81-83, 85, 89-93, 98, 100, 104-105, 107-110, 119, 123-126, 129-130, 137-138, 140-141, 148-149, 151, 153, 180-182, 188-190, 193-196, 202, 204, 208, 210, 212, 214, 226, 240, 245-247, 254, 256-257, 265

Farmer 10-12, 16, 21-22, 25, 38-39, 49, 71-85, 92-93, 95, 97-100, 102-106, 108-111, 119, 122-132, 137-138, 208, 238, 244, 253-255, 257-262, 264-271

Food processing 18, 53

Food security 11, 25-26, 73, 89, 90-93, 106-108, 110, 149, 159, 240, 246, 256

Ghana 25, 71-72, 75-85

Global Value Chain (GVC) *passim*

Government *passim*

Horticulture 26, 119, 121-124, 128-129, 132

Indonesia 26, 138, 143, 145-149, 151-153, 155-157, 159-160, 246

Infrastructure 18, 21, 23, 25, 50, 53-54, 57, 59-62, 64, 85, 96, 100, 125, 127-128, 130, 133, 166, 179-181, 206, 208, 210, 215, 219-220, 225-227, 238, 241, 245-247, 257, 264-265

Innovation 20-24, 33, 55, 60, 72, 74-75, 144, 165-166, 179-182, 184, 186-187, 194-196, 208, 244, 266, 268-269

Institution 15, 25, 27, 32, 35-36, 43, 45, 47-48, 54, 57, 60-64, 71-75, 78, 80-81, 84-85, 89-93, 102, 108-110, 122, 137, 139-141, 148, 150, 152, 158, 172, 179, 181, 186, 196, 201-202, 211, 214, 224, 226, 238, 243-247, 256, 259, 267

Integration 12, 19, 24, 38-39, 46, 54-55, 62, 80, 101, 144, 149, 170, 243

Intermediary 21, 50, 58, 76, 81, 85, 241

Jathropa 16

Kenya 26, 52-53, 119, 121-124, 126-133, 215, 244, 246

Link(age) 9, 16, 20, 37, 38, 40, 49, 63, 78, 201, 203, 208, 214, 243, 264, 266

Local 9-15, 17, 19-22, 25, 32-34, 36-38, 40, 46, 48, 51, 57-63, 69, 71-72, 74-80, 82-84, 89, 92-93, 101-102, 107, 109, 120, 123, 125, 128-130, 132, 143-144, 156, 171-172, 179, 181, 186, 189, 192-193, 195, 201-204, 206-211, 213-218, 223-228, 237-238, 246-247, 251, 253, 255, 257-260, 263, 265-266, 268-271

Malaysia 26-27, 137-138, 143-160, 165, 167-196, 246

Manufacturer (manufacturing) 10, 51, 147, 167-168, 170, 175-176, 178, 191, 241, 244

Market access 13, 18-19, 25-27, 50, 57, 59, 62, 100, 119, 138, 145, 148-149, 152-153, 155, 158-159, 192, 237-239, 241-247, 264

Marketing 16-17, 21-22, 24, 49-50, 57, 59, 61, 63, 76, 91, 99-102, 147, 166, 179, 196, 208, 219, 237-239, 241, 245, 254, 256-257, 259, 264, 266-267, 272

Multinational (MNC) 11, 18, 29, 31-32, 35, 43-44, 46, 71, 167

Namibia 25, 89-91, 93-97, 99, 101-105, 107-110, 246

National 10, 12, 14, 17, 22-23, 25-26, 35, 43, 57-58, 60, 73, 78, 82, 90-92, 94-96, 102-103, 109-110, 119-120, 129-131, 150, 179, 181-184, 186-187, 193, 195-196, 203, 206, 215, 217, 220, 222, 242, 246, 256-257, 259, 265, 271

Netherlands 16, 26, 56, 75, 123, 138, 143, 146, 148-149, 151-153, 155, 159, 185, 187-188, 206, 217, 224, 246

Non-Governmental Organization (NGO) 17, 19, 32-33, 35, 60-61, 71-72, 75-83, 85, 91, 93-94, 96, 98, 102, 108, 125, 138-139, 143, 151, 153, 209, 216-217, 224, 242, 244-246, 257

Outgrower 11, 16, 18, 20-21, 78, 80-81, 83

Palm nut (oil) 10

Partnership 11-12, 17, 20, 22, 25-27, 32, 35, 37, 40, 71-85, 111, 137-145, 148-159, 187, 201-203, 205, 208-228, 237-239, 244-247, 256-257

Plantation 11, 16, 20, 63, 148-149, 154, 159, 254

Poor 10-12, 20-23, 31-33, 54, 61, 72, 78, 89, 92, 94, 96, 106, 110, 137, 179, 203, 206, 210, 216, 265, 269

Poverty 10, 16, 20, 31, 33, 37, 46, 52, 72-73, 92, 94, 96, 105-106, 109-110, 137, 146, 150, 247, 256

Private 13, 16-18, 21-22, 26, 31-37, 39-41, 43, 52, 72, 74-76, 80, 84, 90, 95, 100, 105, 109, 111, 119, 121, 133, 137, 139, 141, 147, 150-152, 155, 157, 182, 186, 201-202, 205-207, 209-210, 213, 216-217, 220, 244-246, 257

Producer 9, 11, 13-16, 18-21, 26, 33, 38, 43-50, 52-54, 56-60, 62-63, 74, 78-79, 91, 93, 98-100, 103, 108-109, 119-127, 129-133, 144-145, 147, 149, 153, 159, 171, 174, 196, 216, 223, 237, 239-243, 245, 252-253, 268

Public 13, 17, 22, 26, 32, 34-35, 40, 43, 61, 72, 94, 110-111, 119-120, 129, 133, 137-139, 141, 145, 149, 157, 182, 186, 209-210, 212-213, 221, 244-246, 257

Regulation 11, 17, 19, 21, 23, 25, 51, 60, 92, 96, 98, 100, 103-105, 107, 111, 121, 132, 148-150, 152-153, 158-159, 166, 188-191, 217, 219, 245-246

Research 9, 12-17, 20, 25, 31-33, 35, 37-38,
40-41, 43-44, 47, 76, 78-79, 82, 85, 93-94,
97, 109-111, 137, 139, 143-144, 157-158, 160,
166-168, 179, 181-182, 186, 201, 203, 211, 213,
216, 218, 222, 244, 255, 267, 270
Services 13, 16, 21, 27, 33-34, 36, 47-50, 55, 57,
59, 73, 76, 79, 83, 85, 93, 126, 130, 147, 163
Sorghum 10, 25, 71-72, 76-84, 96, 245
South Africa 16, 23, 40, 51, 99, 102, 207,
242-243
Standard 12-13, 17-19, 21, 26, 32, 37, 44, 50,
53, 55-60, 73, 77, 82, 84, 91, 99-100, 107, 111,
119-126, 129-133, 137-138, 148, 150, 152, 159,
207, 210, 242-246, 253
Sugar 11, 16, 267
Sustainable 11-12, 15, 20, 24, 26-27, 31-40, 53,
61, 75, 85, 91, 94, 96, 98, 104-105, 107-108,
119-120, 137, 144, 149-151, 153-159, 165, 201,
203, 208-211, 213-216, 218, 225-228, 238,
244, 246-247

Tanzania 16, 20, 22-23, 25, 27, 40, 51, 202-
204, 206, 213, 215-217, 224, 228, 244, 247,
253-254, 256, 261
Theory (theoretical, theories) 9, 12, 19,
24-25, 32-33, 36, 40-41, 45-48, 63, 104,
138-139, 145, 154, 165, 181, 210, 216, 237
Tourism 25, 27, 91, 94-95, 98, 109, 202-208,
213-224, 228, 247
Trust 17-22, 24, 26-27, 34, 47-48, 57, 63, 73-
74, 76, 139, 141-142, 158, 208, 210, 212, 227,
243-244, 271
Upgrading 9, 12, 15, 17-22, 24, 26, 39, 44, 46,
48, 59-61, 63-64, 72, 74-75, 78, 81-85, 126,
129, 138, 142-143, 158-159, 196, 202-203,
205, 208-211, 214-216, 218-228, 235, 237-
247, 252, 271
Value chain passim
Viability 12, 20, 25, 82, 90, 92, 96, 99, 104-
105, 108, 110
Zambia 10, 16, 20-23, 72, 75, 77, 79-81, 83, 85

 EADI– the European Association of Development Research and Training Institutes – is the leading professional network for development and regional studies in Europe (www.eadi.org).

PREVIOUSLY PUBLISHED

Andrew Mold (ed.): *EU Development Policy in a Changing World: Challenges for the 21st Century* (2007)
ISBN 978 90 5356 976 4
Gordon Crawford & Christof Hartmann (eds.): *Decentralisation in Africa: A Pathway out of Poverty and Conflict?* (2008)
ISBN 978 90 5356 934 4
Meine Pieter van Dijk (ed.): *The New Presence of China in Africa* (2009)
ISBN 978 90 8964 136 6
Paul Hoebink (ed.): *European Development Cooperation: In Between the Local and the Global* (2010)
ISBN 978 90 8964 225 7
Eric Rugraff & Michael W. Hansen (eds.): *Multinational Corporations and Local Firms in Emerging Economies* (2011)
ISBN 978 90 8964 294 3